Technology Road Mapping for Quantum Computing and Engineering

Brojo Kishore Mishra
GIET University, India

A volume in the Advances in
Systems Analysis, Software
Engineering, and High Performance
Computing (ASASEHPC) Book Series

Published in the United States of America by
    IGI Global
    Engineering Science Reference (an imprint of IGI Global)
    701 E. Chocolate Avenue
    Hershey PA, USA 17033
    Tel: 717-533-8845
    Fax: 717-533-8661
    E-mail: cust@igi-global.com
    Web site: http://www.igi-global.com

Library of Congress Cataloging-in-Publication Data

Names: Mishra, Brojo Kishore, 1979- editor.
Title: Technology road mapping for quantum computing and engineering /
  Brojo Mishra, editor.
Description: Hershey PA : Engineering Science Reference, [2022] | Includes
  bibliographical references and index. | Summary: "The aim of the book is
  to publish in all the aspects of quantum computing concepts,
  engineering, technologies, operations, and applications from basics to
  future advances"-- Provided by publisher.
Identifiers: LCCN 2021051903 (print) | LCCN 2021051904 (ebook) | ISBN
  9781799891833 (hardcover) | ISBN 9781799891840 (paperback) | ISBN
  9781799891857 (ebook)
Subjects: LCSH: Quantum computing. | Quantum computers. | Computer
  engineering. | Computer programming.
Classification: LCC QA76.889 .T43 2022 (print) | LCC QA76.889 (ebook) |
  DDC 006.3/843--dc23/eng/20211120
LC record available at https://lccn.loc.gov/2021051903
LC ebook record available at https://lccn.loc.gov/2021051904

This book is published in the IGI Global book series Advances in Systems Analysis, Software Engineering, and High Performance Computing (ASASEHPC) (ISSN: 2327-3453; eISSN: 2327-3461)

British Cataloguing in Publication Data
A Cataloguing in Publication record for this book is available from the British Library.

All work contributed to this book is new, previously-unpublished material.
The views expressed in this book are those of the authors, but not necessarily of the publisher.

For electronic access to this publication, please contact: eresources@igi-global.com.

Advances in Systems Analysis, Software Engineering, and High Performance Computing (ASASEHPC) Book Series

Vijayan Sugumaran
Oakland University, USA

ISSN:2327-3453
EISSN:2327-3461

MISSION

The theory and practice of computing applications and distributed systems has emerged as one of the key areas of research driving innovations in business, engineering, and science. The fields of software engineering, systems analysis, and high performance computing offer a wide range of applications and solutions in solving computational problems for any modern organization.

The **Advances in Systems Analysis, Software Engineering, and High Performance Computing (ASASEHPC) Book Series** brings together research in the areas of distributed computing, systems and software engineering, high performance computing, and service science. This collection of publications is useful for academics, researchers, and practitioners seeking the latest practices and knowledge in this field.

COVERAGE

- Distributed Cloud Computing
- Metadata and Semantic Web
- Software Engineering
- Network Management
- Computer Networking
- Enterprise Information Systems
- Virtual Data Systems
- Engineering Environments
- Computer Graphics
- Performance Modelling

IGI Global is currently accepting manuscripts for publication within this series. To submit a proposal for a volume in this series, please contact our Acquisition Editors at Acquisitions@igi-global.com or visit: http://www.igi-global.com/publish/.

Titles in this Series

For a list of additional titles in this series, please visit: *http://www.igi-global.com/book-series/*

Advancing Smarter and More Secure Industrial Applications Using AI, IoT, and Blockchain Technology
Kavita Saini (Galgotias University, India) and Pethuru Raj (Reliance Jio Platforms Ltd., Bangalore, India)
Engineering Science Reference • © 2022 • 309pp • H/C (ISBN: 9781799883678) • US $245.00

Deep Learning Applications for Cyber-Physical Systems
Monica R. Mundada (M.S. Ramaiah Institute of Technology, India) S. Seema (M.S. Ramaiah Institute of Technology, India) Srinivasa K.G. (National Institute of Technical Teachers Training and Research, Chandigarh, India) and M. Shilpa (M.S. Ramaiah Institute of Technology, India)
Engineering Science Reference • © 2022 • 293pp • H/C (ISBN: 9781799881612) • US $245.00

Design, Applications, and Maintenance of Cyber-Physical Systems
Pierluigi Rea (University of Cagliari, Italy) Erika Ottaviano (University of Cassino and Southern Lazio, Italy) José Machado (University of Minho, Portugal) and Katarzyna Antosz (Rzeszow University of Technology, Poland)
Engineering Science Reference • © 2021 • 314pp • H/C (ISBN: 9781799867210) • US $225.00

Methodologies and Applications of Computational Statistics for Machine Intelligence
Debabrata Samanta (Christ University (Deemed), India) Raghavendra Rao Althar (QMS, First American India, Bangalore, India) Sabyasachi Pramanik (Haldia Institute of Technology, India) and Soumi Dutta (Institute of Engineering and Management, Kolkata, India)
Engineering Science Reference • © 2021 • 277pp • H/C (ISBN: 9781799877011) • US $245.00

701 East Chocolate Avenue, Hershey, PA 17033, USA
Tel: 717-533-8845 x100 • Fax: 717-533-8661
E-Mail: cust@igi-global.com • www.igi-global.com

Editorial Advisory Board

Table of Contents

Chapter 10
Tunable Attenuator Based on Hybrid Metal-Graphene Structure on Spoof
Surface Plasmon Polaritons Waveguide

Aymen Hlali, University of Carthage, Tunisia
Hassen Zairi, ENICarthage, University of Carthage, Tunisia

Detailed Table of Contents

    Poornima Nedunchezhian, SRM Valliammai Engineering College, India
    Rajkumar Rajasekaran, Vellore Institute of Technology, India

Quantum computing is a fascinating topic, and the authors attempt to give a detailed explanation about the history of quantum computing, double slit experiment, introduction about quantum computers, quantum super position, quantum entanglement, overview about quantum supremacy, building quantum computing, single bit gates, multi-bit gates, model of quantum computing with applications, and case study. The quantum computing was developed using quantum algorithms and quantum devices. Firstly, the quantum algorithms are developed as mathematical models, and the performance is evaluated through simulations, algebraic algorithms (cryptography, Diffie-Hellman, shor algorithm, for RSA) and amplitude amplification (database searching, pattern matching, etc.). Secondly, the quantum devices are the original physical devices built with optical connections instead of electrical connections. The qubit control uses the microwave for superconducting, laser, quantum dots, and photonics (optical instrument).

Chapter 2

Ankur Biswas, University of Engineering and Management, Kolkata,
India
Amartya Chakraborty, University of Engineering and Management,
Kolkata, India
Stobak Dutta, University of Engineering and Management, Kolkata,
India
Anirban Mitra, Amity University, Kolkata, India
Brojo Kishore Mishra, GIET University, India

Computational capabilities are reaching their limits with the current technology. Quantum computing is the answer to this limitation. It has unraveled new possibilities of solving the unsolvable and computationally hard problems within a feasible time frame. In this chapter, the authors have discussed the basics of quantum computing, which include the need for quantum computers and how it internally works without getting into too much mathematics for an introductory understanding. The authors have also discussed different technologies in which the scientific communities and industries are working to make these computers feasibly work and the different programming techniques and tools available to implement the algorithms in these computers and the testbeds available to common people for testing the feasibilities of their programs.

Chapter 3

R. Nagarajan, Gnanamani College of Technology, India
Kannadhasan S., Cheran College of Engineering, India
Kanagaraj Venusamy, University of Technology and Applied Sciences-
AI Mussanah, Oman

Today, major corporations such as IBM, Google, Microsoft, and Amazon are racing to build cloud quantum computers. They integrate quantum computers with cloud computing to create a system that can be accessible via a network without the need for quantum computing power in a cloud computing environment. The authors describe cloud quantum computing in this chapter and conduct research to compare cloud quantum computing providers across the globe. In this study, the authors look at the various cloud quantum computing options and the outcomes they provide. At the conclusion, each cloud quantum computing service will be compared based on its performance, amplitudes, times, and architecture. The study will primarily focus on IBM and Qutech cloud quantum computing technologies.

Quantum computing exploits quantum-mechanical principles such as entanglement and superposition to offer significant computational advantages over conventional classical computing. Many complex and computationally challenging problems are expected to be solved by quantum computing in a number of fields, such as data science, industrial chemistry, smart energy, finance, secure communications, and many others. In order to understand the current status of quantum computing and identify its challenges, a systematic review of the existing literature will be valuable. An overview of quantum computing literature and its taxonomy is presented in this chapter. Further, the proposed taxonomy aims to identify research gaps by mapping various related studies. There is a detailed analysis of quantum technologies with the most current state of the art. Finally, the chapter presents a highlight of open challenges and future research directions.

Computational technologies drive progress in industry, science, government, and society. While these technologies form the foundation for intelligent systems and enable scientific and business innovation, they are also the limiting factors for progress. Quantum computing promises to overcome these limitations with better and faster solutions for optimization, simulation, and machine learning problems. Quantum computing is broadly applicable to business problems in optimization, machine learning, and simulation, impacting all industries. In the last couple of years, researchers investigated if quantum computing can help to improve classical machine learning algorithms. Therefore, it is instrumental for industry to seek an active role in this emergent ecosystem. In this chapter, the authors present a brief overview on various applications of quantum computing in machine learning.

Chapter 6

The need for IR4 technologies with faster and accurate results for huge health datasets is required. Healthcare has made a lot of advancements with technologies and has certain issues in terms of carbon emission. This in turn sets the patient's life in risk. The study proposes a model for all the healthcare sectors. The study deals with the various quantum neural networks implemented on diabetes retinopathy and COVID-19 images. The quantum computing model outperformed all other machine learning and deep learning models giving more accurate results in less time. The revolution of quantum computing has proven the healthcare in diabetes retinopathy and COVID-19 detection to be faster. It can henceforth be implemented for early warning of the diseases and provide treatment for the patients.

Chapter 7

Quantum technology works with and relies on sub-atomic particles or physics that operates on the quantum level. Quantum computing has become a mature field, having diversified applications in supply chain and logistics, chemistry, economics and financial services, energy and agriculture, medicine and health, etc. In the recent years, companies have started to incorporate quantum software to benefit the research and the practitioner communities. Software engineering and programming practices need to be brought into the domain of quantum computing. Quantum algorithms provide the ability to analyze the data and offer simulations based on the data. A few of the quantum computing programming languages include QISKit, Q#, Cirq, and forest are used to write and run quantum programs. In this chapter, the authors provide an overall picture of the problems and challenges of developing quantum software and up-to-date software engineering processes, methods, techniques, practices, and principles for the development of quantum software to both researchers and practitioners.

Chapter 8

Harsha Vardhan Garine, BML Munjal University, India
Atul Mishra, BML Munjal University, India
Anubhav Agrawal, BML Munjal University, India

The Bloch sphere is a generalisation of the complex number z with $|z|2 = 1$ being represented in the complex plane as a point on the unit circle. The goal of the research is to create a simulation that can be used to visualise a Bloch sphere of a single quantum bit, also known as a Qbit. QISKIT (developed by IBM) is an open-source lab for education in the realm of quantum computing, and is used to test and validate this simulator. This study made use of both quantitative and qualitative methods of investigation.

Chapter 9

Dillip Kumar Pattanayak, GIET University, India
Arun Kumar Padhy, GIET University, India
Lokesh Kumar Prusty, GIET University, India
Ranjan Kumar Bhuyna, Government College, Anugul, India
Samita Pattanayak, Odisha University of Technology and Research,
    Bhubaneswa, India

Quantum computing is based on physical materials. The choice of material is important, and semiconductor materials have become a widely trailed choice in recent years. A lot of initial research into quantum computing only manifested that it could operate at temperatures close to absolute zero. However, because semiconductors are now used in the construct of these systems, it has enabled researchers to utilize quantum computers in room temperature conditions. This is one of the major reasons why quantum computing is close to commercial realization, so the role played by semiconductors is of major importance. It is true that the implementation of semiconductors has been challenging in its own way. Many semiconducting materials can exhibit many quantum degrees of freedom, and this causes the qubits to interact with each and decode quickly. Here the authors try to project a systematic study of different semiconducting materials used for quantum computing.

Chapter 10

Tunable Attenuator Based on Hybrid Metal-Graphene Structure on Spoof
Surface Plasmon Polaritons Waveguide

Aymen Hlali, University of Carthage, Tunisia
Hassen Zairi, ENICarthage, University of Carthage, Tunisia

A novel type of tunable attenuator on spoof surface plasmon polaritons (SSPP)
waveguide based on hybrid metal-graphene structure for terahertz applications is
proposed in this chapter. Two structures are analyzed and designed, where the first
is composed of a graphene sheet at only one cell of the SSPP waveguide and the
second at all cells. By varying the graphene chemical potential via a biased voltage,
the surface conductivity of graphene can be adjusted. Therefore, the attenuation can
also be adjusted. Moreover, an equivalent circuit model is proposed to facilitate
the designs of the proposed attenuator and offer the general understanding of the
attenuation mechanism. Numerical simulation results with the CST simulator and
WCIP method have a good agreement with the theoretical results. The simulated
results show that the attenuator can obtain adjustment range from 6.02 to 14.32 dB
for the first structure and from 1.58 to 30.93 dB for the second, as the chemical
potential rises from 0 to 0.5 eV.

Preface

Quantum computing is radically different from the conventional approach of transforming bit-strings from one set of zeros and ones to another. With quantum computing, everything changes. The physics used to understand bits of information and the devices that manipulate them are vastly different. Quantum engineering is a revolutionary approach to quantum technology.

Technology Road Mapping for Quantum Computing and Engineering explores all the aspects of quantum computing concepts, engineering, technologies, operations, and applications from the basics to future advancements. Covering topics such as machine learning, quantum software technology, and technology road mapping, this book is an excellent resource for data scientists, engineers, students and professors of higher education, computer scientists, researchers, and academicians.

The book is organized into 10 chapters. Chapter 1 explained about the history of quantum computing, double slit experiment, introduction about quantum computers, quantum super position, quantum entanglement, overview about quantum supremacy, building quantum computing, single bit gates, multi-bit gates, model of quantum computing with applications and case study.

In Chapter 2, the authors tried to give the readers an introductory knowledge of the working of quantum computers, their prospects and how the quantum computers are programmed. The readers are introduced to the terms associated with quantum computers, different approaches to creating quantum computers and lastly about quantum programming. This chapter will be very beneficial to get the introductory knowledge on the topic and basic understanding.

In Chapter 3, the authors provided a summary based on the study and findings in many types of cloud quantum computing services and the performance power of quantum computers in a cloud computing environment.

Chapter 4 gives an insight into quantum computing, quantum mechanisms, and details of quantum algorithms. These quantum algorithms have applications in numerous fields, such as security, finance, biomedical, chemical, and economic development. There is a detailed analysis of quantum technologies with the most current state-of-the-art. Finally, the article presents a highlight of open challenges and future research directions.

Chapter 5 focused on the different applications of Quantum Computing within the Machine Learning Environment. And also introduce the basic concepts of quantum computing and describes well-known quantum applications.

In Chapter 6, the authors discussed about the Quantum Computing related to all other machine learning and deep learning models, giving more accurate results in lesser time. Quantum computing improves COVID-19 detection, diagnosis, and treatment. Quantum computer is seen accessible for daily use in medicine and research. QNN and CQNN methods on large datasets, tests and then automatically upload the results to a cloud-based epidemiological and early-warning monitoring.

In Chapter 7, the authors provided an overall picture of the problems and challenges of developing quantum software and up-to-date software engineering processes, methods, techniques, practices, and principles for the development of quantum software to both researchers and practitioners.

In Chapter 8, the authors developed a simulation that can visualise a Bloch sphere of a single quantum bit, also known as a Qbit. QISKIT (developed by IBM) is an open-source lab for education in quantum computing, and it was used to test and validate this simulator. This study made use of both quantitative and qualitative methods of investigation.

In Chapter 9, the authors provided a systematic and well-organized content about different semiconducting materials used in supercomputing since its intersection to till date. Hope it will supplement the necessary requirement of the learners.

In Chapter 10, the authors proposed a novel type of tunable attenuator on spoof surface plasmon polaritons (SSPP) waveguide based on hybrid metal-graphene structure for terahertz applications.

Brojo Kishore Mishra
GIET University, India

Acknowledgment

The editor would like to acknowledge the help of all the people involved in this project and, more specifically, to the authors and reviewers that took part in the review process. Without their support, this book would not have become a reality.

First, the editor would like to thank each one of the authors for their contributions. Our sincere gratitude goes to the chapter's authors who contributed their time and expertise to this book.

Second, the editor wishes to acknowledge the valuable contributions of the reviewers regarding the improvement of quality, coherence, and content presentation of chapters. Most of the authors also served as referees; we highly appreciate their double task.

Finally, the editor wishes to acknowledge the best supports received from the IGI Global publication house, GIET University team, past & present students, well-wishers and my lovely family members.

Brojo Kishore Mishra
GIET University, India

Introduction

In the era of digitalization, quantum computing is an emerging platform with a faster growth rate. The quantum computing platform is a well-proportionate balanced mixture of quantum physics and computing. This intersection of physics and computer science i.e. the utilization of quantum physics in computing is rapidly changing the technology, which is felt today and better realized in day-to-day life. In this book, our focus will be on the basic principle of quantum computing, such as superposition, quantum measurement, entanglement, and their role in the applications. To narrow down the gaps between the popular quantum physics articles and findings, look for the technical aspect in the computing world. This may help to the grass root of the technical education involved persons, students, faculties as well as the researchers, working or interest in this field and platform. We try to start with the domain of quantum physics and mechanics concepts, which is basic of need to understand the environment of quantum computing, characteristics, and its development & utilization in different applications.

The classical computing machine and platform is a discussion started with the concept of the Turing machine. The concept of the Turing machine is associated with intuitive strength and computability with a higher degree of stability (this concept leads to much alternative computing definition) for a longer time in the classical computing platform. In the Church-Turing thesis, if the number-theoretic function $\mathbf{f}$ is computable from an intuitive point of view if $\mathbf{f}$ is Turing-computable, this leads to the reasonable conjecture in computing. This hypothetical statement is supported by the number of studies for alternative computing platforms or machines at their first sight appearance with the more liberal view. It is very much interesting that the Turing machine is non-deterministic (or probabilistic), operates within the limits of the definitions. Whereas for probabilistic, the Turing machine needs to be simulated with a deterministic one.

The mathematical model for the quantum computer is proposed by Feynman, is often referred to as the quantum Turing machine, is a classical Turing machine representation in a quantum computing machine. So we need to understand what is quantum Turing machines and computing processes? Still the quantum Turing machine fails to meet the goal as a solid rigorous "institutional" concept, but it reflects is clearly that, it is strongly inspired by the classical definition of the Turing machine with a referral tape (where the symbol are defined and written) to utilize in computing. These concepts are merely applicable to real physical quantum computers. We should put our focus on the intriguing situations that arise due to the nature of quantum uncertainties. Our concern needs to focus on the moving heads and their behaviors.

At present, we are in the era of digital technology and communication. Here the information is represented is as logic, '1' or '0'. Represent as binary digit or bit. This binary digit is utilized in classical computing terms of voltage level and transmitted & received for communication, these voltage levels are varied as implementation and fabrication technology differ, but it is scalable. So, Quantum computation theories and implementation need to be naturally inspired new ideas in the field of logic, which needs appropriate changes in the quantum-logical investigations for the minimum energy to consider as quantum. There is a long history, where the interaction between logic to quantum logic. In 1936, the famous "The logic of quantum mechanics" published by Birkhoff and von Neumann', initially the logician ignore this proposed suggestion for quantum computing, which is quite a "revolutionary logical idea", of quantum logic: the possible divergence between the concepts of maximal information and logically complete information. The logic state in classical computing physical system represents pieces of information, whereas quantum logic needs to consider the energy level in the packet with a definition of quantum.

Quantum computing is the upcoming platform, which can achieve the digitalization and complexity needed to address in low power highly precision machines. The quantum as duality nature needs to handle properly for the definitions or represent the quantum logic. The fabrication technologies need to address to handle this duality nature, where the more efficient adaptive machine can be achieved, which can be implemented in AI/Machine learning platforms more effectively. Quantum computing as a technology can be revolutionary like quantum mechanics change whole physics and its application in technology. The proper definition of quantum logic and its related gates can be changed over for fabrication technology, as well as the system and application technology. More research work needs to regard the same.

The field of Engineering is rapidly evolving. Quantum Engineering is a new approach to working with quantum technology. Quantum Engineering combines the broad skills of engineering with fundamental physics in a unique way that allows engineers to solve contemporary problems and engineer solutions for the future. Quantum mechanics opens the doors for Quantum Engineers to leverage quantum physics to deliver unprecedented solutions to engineering problems. Or in other words Quantum engineering exploits unique features of quantum physics to generate technological solutions surpassing the capabilities of their classical counterparts.

Quantum technology is transforming in particular the fields of communication, computing and measurement technology.

Information theory has driven the evolution of our society in the past decades in a period known as the Information Age. It studies the quantification, storage, and communication of digital information. In a similar fashion, Quantum Information is an area of research found at the intersection of Mathematics and Physics. It is born from the fundamental principles of Quantum Mechanics, applied to Information Theory. Quantum Information exploits concepts like state superposition, entanglement and wave function collapse to establish new paradigms in information processing, whether it is for computing applications, cryptography, the simulation of quantum entities or the measurement of physical parameters beyond what is achievable using classical methods. Quantum engineering takes the next steps, and applies those concepts to realistic scenarios, developing algorithms, protocols, devices and systems.

A quantum engineer will be trained to use the tools and language from quantum mechanics, electrical and electronic engineering, systems engineering and computer science as well as other physical sciences.

Introduction Over time, rapid and complex developments and competitive markets have resulted in businesses investing in emerging sciences. Such areas may provide many ways to gain more benefits from markets, but if they make wrong choices, they may create significant problems for companies and ultimately the company will be in crisis. The companies need to learn criteria in this matter which are relevant to emerging sciences. One such criteria is a roadmap that can be designed in various aspects such as strategic, capacity, product, technology, and research. Roadmap is a valuable method for defining an organization's path to achieving its goals. For example, in the strategic roadmap, managers will recognize the external environment's opportunities and challenges, and the internal environment's strengths and weaknesses in entering new markets. Based on features of roadmaps, we can discover connections among roadmaps and to develop appropriate roadmaps, the organization needs to understand these connections.

Chapter 1
Introduction and Beginners Guide to Quantum Computing

Poornima Nedunchezhian
SRM Valliammai Engineering College, India

Rajkumar Rajasekaran
iD https://orcid.org/0000-0002-0983-7259
Vellore Institute of Technology, India

ABSTRACT

Quantum computing is a fascinating topic, and the authors attempt to give a detailed explanation about the history of quantum computing, double slit experiment, introduction about quantum computers, quantum super position, quantum entanglement, overview about quantum supremacy, building quantum computing, single bit gates, multi-bit gates, model of quantum computing with applications, and case study. The quantum computing was developed using quantum algorithms and quantum devices. Firstly, the quantum algorithms are developed as mathematical models, and the performance is evaluated through simulations, algebraic algorithms (cryptography, Diffie-Hellman, shor algorithm, for RSA) and amplitude amplification (database searching, pattern matching, etc.). Secondly, the quantum devices are the original physical devices built with optical connections instead of electrical connections. The qubit control uses the microwave for superconducting, laser, quantum dots, and photonics (optical instrument).

DOI: 10.4018/978-1-7998-9183-3.ch001

INTRODUCTION

The quantum computers are similar to classic computers that are built in the year 1950s which has hardware's, algorithms, Operating System with associated complier, high level languages and algorithms. The code is written in low level assembly language. Many companies have invested in the research on quantum computing viz Google, IBM, Amazon, DARPA, Honeywell (Alvarez-Rodriguez et al., 2016) (Hu et al., 2016) etc. The processing speed of the computer depends on the number of transistors that exists in the CPU. It is well-known that the computers process the inputs as binary values either zero or one. The transistors act as a switch and sends the input signals as zero or one. Gordon Moore cofounder of Intel quoted that "the transistor in CPU or the overall processing power doubles every two years". The prediction came true from 1965 to 2013 i.e., the transistor (Vermersch et al., 2016) (Brecht et al., 2016) (Monz et al., 2016) capacity doubled every 18 months. But after 2013th the process started slowing down. So, more transistors needed to be incorporated. To place a transistor in the Integrated Circuits (IC) the size has to reduced and the method is followed till the year 2012. In 2013 the attempt was made to increase the speed by reducing the transistor size to the size of the atom but it led to the problem which is referred to as quantum tunneling. Quantum tunneling is the stage of the transistor that conducts the electron even in OFF state. Hence the concept of quantum computing arose to solve quantum tunneling (Veldhorst et al., 2014). The quantum physics and quantum mechanics concepts are used to develop the quantum computers. The quantum mechanics is the most fascinating concept. It works on the basis of "reality is stranger than fiction".

Quantum supremacy: The processing speed of the quantum computing processor is represented as 2n where n represents the number of electrons. The quantum computer thus calculates $220 = 10,48,576$ operations per time. Google has also developed a quantum computer and claimed they have achieved the quantum supremacy. It generated random numbers one million times in the processing speed of 200 seconds. The Google researchers and engineers are responsible for this huge success. The invented quantum computing chip was named as sycamore. It works with 54 qubits (Albrecht et al., 2016). Each qubit ranges in the size of 0.22 millimeter in width. The main challenge maintains the qubit in proper climatic and vibration less environment else it will be prone to error. So, google placed the sycamore in a very lowest temperature of 15 milli kelvin which is 200 times lesser than the normal temperature.

Also, the sycamore is also protected from the outer vibrations. The Google CEO Sundhar Pichai also addressed that they have achieved the quantum supremacy and assures their achievement will be applied to various fields in the future. The problem which can't be solved by the normal computer is hence proved to be solved by the quantum computer in an optimal time. Then the question "Will quantum computer replace our regular normal computers?" arises. But it is clear that due to the maintenance of the quantum computers it can't replace the normal computers rather shall be used for various other applications. The real-time applications need millions of qubits. Since the maintenance of qubits are more expensive it is suspected to be prone to more errors when replaced instead of classical computers. Hence concluded that the problems that can be solved by classical computers are called as intractable problems and the quantum computers solves them in seconds.

The content is organized as follows: Firstly, section 2 explains the very short introduction about the ideas of building the quantum computer utilizing the functionalities of the quantum gates namely single qubit and multiple qubit gates. Secondly, the section 3 portrays the strength of quantum computers along with its properties. Then section 4 gives the dimensions of quantum computing. Finally the conclusion is in section 5.

1. BUILDING QUANTUM COMPUTER

The quantum information(Grilo & Kerenidis, 2017) (Sarma et al., 2015) is passed to the quantum computer using the quantum circuit which comprises of physically connected wires and quantum gates. Single qubit gates, multiple qubit gates and many other gates are used. As an introduction the above mentioned two gates are explained.

Single qubit gates: The gates are used to process the single qubit information. The classical computers shall process the binary {0,1} but quantum computers handle the input differently due to its superposition. The state shall remain as zero or one and shall interchange the input when needed. The single bit NOT gate is considered for explanation. The linearity is considered for quantum computing rather non-linearity. The paradoxes (Corcoles et al., 2015) like time travel, violations in the law of thermodynamics and faster communication than light are the reason for not acquiring the non-linearity property.

The quantum matrix representation of binary inputs is given as I in Eq. (1) and the representation are given as,

$$I = \begin{pmatrix} 0 & 1 \\ 1 & 0 \end{pmatrix} \tag{1}$$

Multiple qubit gates: The multiple qubits consist of gates comprising of all gates other than NOT gate. The OR, AND, XOR, NAND and NOR gates. the multiple qubit gates comprise of CNOT (Controlled NOT) gate which has two inputs namely control and target qubit. The gate input is represented as two lines. First line gives the control input and the second line gives the target input.

Model of Quantum Computing: There are several models of quantum computing like, quantum Turing Machine, Adiabatic quantum computing and quantum circuits etc. the functioning of quantum computation is based on the Turing Machine model which works based on the Albert Einstein words "If you can't explain to your computer, you don't understand it yourself". The tools like Jupyter Notebooks, IBM quantum experience, Quirk and D-wave Leap (Fowler, 2015) (Lloyd et al., 2016) are used. The quantum computers are built using superconducting loops comprising of microwaves, capacitor and the inductor. The current flows over these superconducting loops. It works faster on the existing semi-conductor circuit. The electron in the atom is utilized to transfer data and is referred as trapped ions by the ionQ company. The quantum dots made of silicon are developed by Intel. Even though the existing semiconductor devices (Childs & van Dam, 2010) (Nagayama et al., 2017) are used the qubit dots have to be maintained in proper temperature and pressure. There are many frameworks and programming languages on which the quantum computer works namely Ocean(D-Wave), Q# (Microsoft), Cirq(Google), Qiskit(IBM) and so on. The quantum circuits (Hill et al., 2015) are designed and simulated. The quantum circuits are designed using qubits(data), operations (quantum gates) and the associated results (measurements).

Applications: Hence, the quantum computer has more scope in various fields and also challenges the cyber security domain. The quantum computing is believed to solve complex problems like whether prediction, financial stock predictions and various other applications in Artificial Intelligence (AI).

Case study: Mercedes Benz is in the next stage of development and they focus on the future. The plan is to develop a carbon free car in the planet. So, the batteries (Lithium Ion) are simulated to see its working. So, it collaborated with the IBM quantum computing (Bacon & van Dam, 2010) technology to develop the efficient batteries to automate the driving process and to develop the more efficient electric cars by 2039.

In short, the difference between the classic and quantum computing are the classical computers ha automated design, and it has the structured computer architecture with optimized compiler. It uses high-level programming languages with its associated software (Hucul et al., 2014). The quantum computers follow the qubit design with the quantum control. The performance improvement of quantum computers depends upon its error correcting system. The low-level assembly language is used for the quantum computing applications.

2. STRENGTH OF QUANTUM COMPUTERS

From the previous section the strength of the quantum computer is concluded.

- *Solves intractable problems:* The complex problems are believed to be solved by quantum computers. Problems like factoring prime numbers (Orsucci et al., 2016), modeling the working of battery, whether prediction and so on are believed to be solved by quantum computers.
- *Strong theoretical argument:* The complex problems (Riste et al., 2015) shall be modelled theoretically using the mathematical notations. The intractable problem shall be thus either physically modeled or shall be derived using theorems to derive the theoretical solution.
- *Time and space complexity:* The time and space complexity (Farhi & Neven, 2018) of the classical and quantum computers are different. The complexity for classical computers to solve a problem is unrelated to the complexity of quantum computer.

2.1 Properties of Qubits

- *Quantum superposition:* Quantum physics explains the behavior of electron in the quantum world using two properties namely, quantum superposition and quantum entanglement. All atom has protons and electrons (Farhi et al., 2017)(Kashefi & Pappa, 2017)(Biamonte et al., 2017). The electrons move in the atoms and is movements are termed as spin. The normal computers use bits to transfer or store its data. A bit can either store zero or one at a time but the quantum computer uses the qubits to store the data. Spin up is equivalent to one and spin down (Salmilehto et al., 2017) i.e., equal to zero. The advantage of the ability of qubit to store either zero, one, or both zero and one at a time. Hence the quantum bits are more efficient comparative to normal bit representation. The quantum position is a stage of the electron to store one, zero or both zero or one. The classic example is explained using spinning the coin. While the coin spins and hence remains in both the stages head and tail respectively but finally, it settles in either head or tail. Similarly, the qubit can remain in a stage of the combination stage but finally will settle to a state. The qubit resembles the spin of electron.
- *Quantum Entanglement:* The second property of quantum entanglement states the connection between two electrons irrespective of the distance which was commented as "spooky action at a distance" by Einstein.
- *Double slit experiment:* The double slit experiment focuses on the behaviour of the atoms. The nature of light is a great confusion and Newton believed

it travels as particles later it was identified to be traveled as waves. Then the photonics were identified where the light is travelled as discrete packets which is termed as photons. Similarly, the electrons believed to be travelled as particles later they identified it to be as waves using electron diffraction experiment. The confusion was solved after the discovery of quantum mechanics. Then it was concluded light either move as waves or particles (Pfeiffer et al., 2016)(Van Meter & Devitt, 2016)(Bravyi et al., 2017). They move in their own nature.

The quantum computers are designed considering the above explained properties super position and entanglement and thus the unbelievable processing speed is achieved using qubits. For example, to crack the password of the computer the normal processor checks the password (Ofek et al., 2016) (Lloyd & Weedbrook, 2018) one-by-one as trial-and-error method and thus the processing speed (Somaschiet, 2016) (Wigley et al., 2016) becomes low in traditional computers. Whereas, the quantum computers use its superposition property and checks all possible passwords at-a-time and hence the processing speed is much higher. Thus, the quantum computers can check all possible solutions to the given problem at-a-time.

3. DIMENSIONS OF QUANTUM COMPUTING

The quantum computing will be greatest challenge to various fields and dimensions and are detailed below.

- Quantum randomness: The random numbers generated by quantum computers are unable to break whereas the classical computers random number pattern (Dehollain, 2016) (Oszmaniec et al., 2016) (Bremner et al., 2016) will undoubtably be predicted by the quantum computers.
- Cryptography: The emergence of quantum computer is the biggest challenge to the existing cryptographic techniques (Lamata, 2017)(Altaisky et al., 2016) available in classical computers. The main challenge is to develop more resistant cryptographic methodologies to quantum computing techniques.
- Information sharing break through: The information shared using quantum bits are more secure and hence can be used for applications like sharing secret key for cryptography and for other confidential applications like banking, military and so on.
- Optimization: The optimization of the Nondeterministic Polynomial problem is preceded by applying the given condition one after the another by the classical computer to identify the more optimal solution. The quantum

computers out-performs the situation by applying all possible constraints at-a-time to find all possible solutions from which the optimal solution shall be filtered easily.

- Error correction: The quantum computing error correction is complex. The noisy gates and the cost of maintaining the qubits are more in number. With the trapped ions the noise is thousand times higher than the trapped ions. The error correction rate (Brown et al., 2016) using superconducting circuits in quantum computer world is only one percent. Hence the super conducting computers are advisable over the trapped ions.
- Quantum annealing: The quantum annealing (Fujii, 2015) is also known as adiabatic computation method. It helps to find the optimal solution for the problems with more than one solution using quantum tunneling, superposition and entanglement.
- Quantum tunneling: quantum physics explains that the electron has both wave and particle like properties. The wave like movement of the electron in the atom is termed as tunneling in quantum computing.

4. CONCLUSION

The extradentary power of quantum computers are achieved using the quantum properties like super position and entanglement. But practically the real-time applications that uses the quantum computers is unbelievable to replace the classical computers due to its high-cost maintenance. Also, the scientists have developed the error correcting procedures. The content explained focus on providing knowledge to the beginners of quantum computing. Simple theoretical explanation is provided for ease of understanding. The explanation about the advantages, challenges and properties of quantum computers are explained.

REFERENCES

Albrecht, S. M., Higginbotham, A. P., Madsen, M., Kuemmeth, F., Jespersen, T. S., Nygard, J., Krogstrup, P., & Marcus, C. M. (2016). Exponential protection of zero modes in Majorana islands. *Nature*, *531*(7593), 206–209. doi:10.1038/nature17162 PMID:26961654

Altaisky, M. V., Zolnikova, N. N., Kaputkina, N. E., Krylov, V. A., Lozovik, Y. E., & Dattani, N. S. (2016). Towards a feasible implementation of quantum neural networks using quantum dots. *Applied Physics Letters*, *108*(10), 103108. doi:10.1063/1.4943622

Alvarez-Rodriguez, U., Sanz, M., Lamata, L., & Solano, E. (2016). Artificial life in quantum technologies. *Scientific Reports*, *6*(1), 20956. doi:10.1038rep20956 PMID:26853918

Bacon, D., & van Dam, W. (2010). Recent progress in quantum algorithms. *Communications of the ACM*, *53*(2), 84–93. doi:10.1145/1646353.1646375

Biamonte, J., Wittek, P., Pancotti, N., Rebentrost, P., Wiebe, N., & Lloyd, S. (2017). Quantum machine learning. *Nature*, *549*(7671), 195–202. doi:10.1038/nature23474 PMID:28905917

Bravyi, S., Gosset, D., & Koenig, R. (2017). *Quantum advantage with shallow circuits*. arXiv:1704.00690.

Brecht, T., Pfaff, W., Wang, C., Chu, Y., Frunzio, L., Devoret, M. H., & Schoelkopf, R. J. (2016). Multilayer microwave integrated quantum circuits for scalable quantum computing. *NPJ Quantum Information*, *2*(2), 16002. doi:10.1038/npjqi.2016.2

Bremner, M. J., Montanaro, A., & Shepherd, D. J. (2016). Average-case complexity versus approximate simulation of commuting quantum computations. *Physical Review Letters*, *080501*(117). doi:10.1103/PhysRevLett.117.080501 PMID:27588839

Brown, K. R., Kim, J., & Monroe, C. (2016). *Co-designing a scalable quantum computer with trapped atomic ions*. arXiv:1602.02840.

Childs, A. M., & van Dam, W. (2010). Quantum algorithms for algebraic problems. *Reviews of Modern Physics*, *82*(1), 1–52. doi:10.1103/RevModPhys.82.1

Corcoles, A. D., Magesan, E., Srinivasan, S. J., Cross, A. W., Steffen, M., Gambetta, J. M., & Chow, J. M. (2015). Demonstration of a quantum error detection code using a square lattice of four superconducting qubits. *Nature Communications*, *6*(6), 6979. doi:10.1038/ncomms7979 PMID:25923200

Dehollain, J.P. (2016). Bell'states inequality violation with spins in silicon. *Nat. Nano, 11*(3), 242–246.

Farhi, E., Goldstone, J., Gutmann, S., & Neven, H. (2017). *Quantum algorithms for fixed qubit architectures*. arXiv:1703.06199v1.

Farhi, E., & Neven, H. (2018). *Classification with quantum neural networks on near term processors*. arXiv:1802.06002v1.

Fowler, A.G. (2015). Minimum weight perfect matching of fault-tolerant topological quantum error correction in average o(1) parallel time. *Quant. Inf. Comp., 15*.

Fujii, K. (2015). *Quantum Computation with Topological Codes*. From Qubits to Topological Fault-Tolerance. doi:10.1007/978-981-287-996-7

Grilo, A. B., & Kerenidis, I. (2017). *Learning with errors is easy with quantum samples*. arXiv:1702.08255.

Hill, C. D., Peretz, E., Hile, S. J., House, M. G., Fuechsle, M., Rogge, S., Simmons, M. Y., & Hollenberg, L. C. L. (2015). A surface code quantum computer in silicon. *Science Advances*, *1*(9), e1500707. doi:10.1126ciadv.1500707 PMID:26601310

Hu, X. M., Hu, M.-J., Chen, J.-S., Liu, B.-H., Huang, Y.-F., Li, C.-F., Guo, G.-C., & Zhang, Y.-S. (2016). Experimental creation of superposition of unknown photonic quantum states. *Physical Review. A*, *94*(3), 033844. doi:10.1103/PhysRevA.94.033844

Hucul, D., Inlek, I. V., Vittorini, G., Crocker, C., Debnath, S., Clark, S. M., & Monroe, C. (2014). Modular entanglement of atomic qubits using photons and phonons. *Nature Physics*, *11*(1), 37–42. doi:10.1038/nphys3150

Kashefi, E., & Pappa, A. (2017). *Multiparty delegated quantum computing*. arXiv: 1606.09200.

Lamata, L. (2017). Basic protocols in quantum reinforcement learning with superconducting circuits. *Scientific Reports*, *7*(1), 16. doi:10.103841598-017-01711-6 PMID:28487535

Lloyd, S., Garnerone, S., & Zanardi, P. (2016). Quantum algorithms for topological and geometric analysis of data. *Nature Commun.*, (7). arXiv:1408.3106

Lloyd, S., & Weedbrook, C. (2018). Quantum generative adversarial learning. *Physical Review Letters*, *121*(4), 040502. doi:10.1103/PhysRevLett.121.040502 PMID:30095952

Monz, T., Nigg, D., Martinez, E. A., Brandl, M. F., Schindler, P., Rines, R., Wang, S. X., Chuang, I. L., & Blatt, R. (2016). Realization of a scalable shor algorithm. *Science*, *351*(6277), 1068–1070. doi:10.1126cience.aad9480 PMID:26941315

Nagayama, S., Fowler, A. G., Horsman, D., Devitt, S. J., & Van Meter, R. (2017). Surface code error correction on a defective lattice. *New Journal of Physics*, *19*(2), 023050. doi:10.1088/1367-2630/aa5918

Ofek, N., Petrenko, A., Heeres, R., Reinhold, P., Leghtas, Z., Vlastakis, B., Liu, Y., Frunzio, L., Girvin, S. M., Jiang, L., Mirrahimi, M., Devoret, M. H., & Schoelkopf, R. J. (2016). Extending the lifetime of a quantum bit with error correction in superconducting circuits. *Nature*, *536*(7617), 441–445. doi:10.1038/nature18949 PMID:27437573

Orsucci, D., Tiersch, M., & Briegel, H. J. (2016). Estimation of coherent error sources from stabilizer measurements. *Phys.*, *93*(4), 042303. doi:10.1103/PhysRevA.93.042303

Oszmaniec, M., Grudka, A., Horodecki, M., & Wojcik, A. (2016). Creating a superposition of unknown quantum states. *Physical Review Letters*, *116*(11), 110403. doi:10.1103/PhysRevLett.116.110403 PMID:27035290

Pfeiffer, P., Egusquiza, I. L., Di Ventra, M., Sanz, M., & Solano, E. (2016). Quantum memristors. *Scientific Reports*, *6*(6), 29507. doi:10.1038rep29507 PMID:27381511

Riste, D., Poletto, S., Huang, M.-Z., Bruno, A., Vesterinen, V., Saira, O.-P., & DiCarlo, L. (2015). Detecting bit-flip errors in a logical qubit using stabilizer measurements. *Nature Communications*, *6*(6), 6983. doi:10.1038/ncomms7983 PMID:25923318

Salmilehto, J., Deppe, F., Ventra, M., & Di. (2017). Quantum memristors with superconducting circuits. *Scientific Reports*, *7*(1), 42044. doi:10.1038rep42044 PMID:28195193

Sarma, S. D., Freedman, M., & Nayak, C. (2015). Majorana zero modes and topological quantum computation. *NPJ Quantum Information*, *1*(1), 15001. doi:10.1038/npjqi.2015.1

Somaschiet, N. (2016). Near-optimal single-photon sources in the solid state. *Nature Photon.*, *10*(5), 340–345.

Van Meter, R., & Devitt, S. J. (2016). Local and distributed quantum computation. *IEEE Comput.*, *49*(9), 31–42. arXiv:1605.06951v1.

Veldhorst, M., Hwang, J. C. C., Yang, C. H., Leenstra, A. W., de Ronde, B., Dehollain, J. P., Muhonen, J. T., Hudson, F. E., Itoh, K. M., Morello, A., & Dzurak, A. S. (2014). An addressable quantum dot qubit with fault-tolerant control fidelity. *Nature Nanotechnology*, *9*(9), 981–985. doi:10.1038/nnano.2014.216 PMID:25305743

Vermersch, B., Guimond, P. O., Pichler, H., & Zoller, P. (2016). *Quantum state transfer via noisy photonic and phononic waveguides.* arXiv:1611.10240.

Wigley, P. B., Everitt, P. J., van den Hengel, A., Bastian, J. W., Sooriyabandara, M. A., McDonald, G. D., Hardman, K. S., Quinlivan, C. D., Manju, P., Kuhn, C. C. N., Petersen, I. R., Luiten, A. N., Hope, J. J., Robins, N. P., & Hush, M. R. (2016). Fast machine-learning online optimization of ultra-cold atom experiments. *Scientific Reports*, *6*(6), 258. doi:10.1038rep25890 PMID:27180805

Chapter 2
An Introductory Study to Quantum Programming

Ankur Biswas
University of Engineering and Management, Kolkata, India

Amartya Chakraborty
University of Engineering and Management, Kolkata, India

Stobak Dutta
University of Engineering and Management, Kolkata, India

Anirban Mitra
iD https://orcid.org/0000-0002-6639-4407
Amity University, Kolkata, India

Brojo Kishore Mishra
iD https://orcid.org/0000-0002-7836-052X
GIET University, India

ABSTRACT

Computational capabilities are reaching their limits with the current technology. Quantum computing is the answer to this limitation. It has unraveled new possibilities of solving the unsolvable and computationally hard problems within a feasible time frame. In this chapter, the authors have discussed the basics of quantum computing, which include the need for quantum computers and how it internally works without getting into too much mathematics for an introductory understanding. The authors have also discussed different technologies in which the scientific communities and industries are working to make these computers feasibly work and the different programming techniques and tools available to implement the algorithms in these computers and the testbeds available to common people for testing the feasibilities of their programs.

DOI: 10.4018/978-1-7998-9183-3.ch002

INTRODUCTION

The curious mind of human beings and the quest to solve those problems is what makes us different from the other species of the planet. From the beginning of humanity, we are exploring different queries arising in our minds and trying to solve the problems in the fastest way possible. Most of the time we find a way out to reach the solution to these queries but many times it is not possible to get the result due to its sheer complexity and technological constraints in the current classical computational environment. Many problems are so complex that the most powerful supercomputers available today, cannot solve them within a feasible amount of time. Moreover, we are reaching the boundaries of computational capabilities with the current technology which enforces us to quickly shift to a new technology that will be the epitome of the new computational era.

The answer to the above came through a much older concept of physics, quantum mechanics, and the computers made of this principle is known as quantum computers. It is not a way to find a faster computational capability in the existing framework but a completely new technology where the particle and wave nature of a matter and their entanglement at the subatomic level is used to reach a new level of computational capabilities. The quantum computers are needed to be maintained in a very restricted environment which may include keeping the quantum computer chip in near absolute zero temperature or establishing a tabletop size computing setup. They are not built to replace the existing classical computers but to solve some specific extremely complex and computationally hard problems along with them. In fact, there is nothing such as stand-alone quantum computers. They work alongside of the classical computers. With the advancement of technologies, we might also be able to see a quantum computer in our palmtop but currently, it seems to be a faraway thought. In this introductory chapter, we have tried to unravel the basic concepts of quantum computers and their working in a very lucid manner and above all, what are the different programming techniques available right now to reach the solutions of the unsolvable.

FROM CLASSICAL COMPUTERS TO QUANTUM COMPUTERS

Whenever we are talking about computers, the basic understanding of computation is based on the concept of the electrical signals passed through the computer system poising high and low voltage signals which are interpreted as 1 and 0 respectively. This whole concept of computing is based on the classical understanding of information in the form of these values known as bits. The classical bits are the energy states that are used to communicate with the computer system and the same is stored in some media in the form of magnetic charge or optical information which is translated to the electrical signals for any kind of computation.

As stated by Gordon E. Moor, the number of transistors in a chip will double every eighteen months which later he proposed to be in 2 years. This is known as Moor's Law and it is pretty much working fine but it is now reaching its practical limitations with the advancement of technology. At the moment the MOSFET scaling has come down to 5nm in 2020 (Shalf, 2020) and it is expected that the scaling will further reduce by 3nm by 2022 and 2nm by 2024. In such a scenario, the transistor will be harnessed by 4-5 atoms. The whole concept of transistors is to create a barrier in electron flow by some means of impurities. If it keeps on scaling in the same manner, by 2030, we will be talking about transistors with the distance between *source* and *drain* of a transistor to the scale of a single atom which is the ultimate level of scaling. Essentially, transistors contain two conductors which are highly conducting silicon made by adding enough impurities (such as phosphorus) termed as source and drain which is separated by non-conducting silicon atoms. The source and drains are covered by a layer of insulator above which a semiconducting GATE exist which is connected by an electrode. The barrier between the source and drain do not allow the flow of these electrons between them but once the GATE is positively charged enough, the electrons accumulate under the insulator as the electrons are negatively charged and get attracted by the positive flux created eventually creating a conducting channel between the source and drain. The MOSFET scaling we are talking about is this distance between the source and drain. Even if the technology allows us to bring this distance to 1 or 2 atoms between this source and destination, it will not be possible to confine the flow of electrons as at this level, due to the quantum behaviour of an atom, the electrons may flow through them based on the concept of quantum tunnelling and as we require some kind of barrier to stop the flow of these electrons and the distance will not be large enough to do so. This limitation is forcing scientists to look forward to completely new technology for computation.

The answer comes through Quantum Computing as at the atomic level the behaviour of elements completely changes and the realm of the quantum behaviour of atom begins. Quantum computing is not a faster or superior supercomputer but a completely new breed of computers that is quite different from the current understanding of the existing computers (*further referred to as classical computers in this chapter*) currently have. The basics of computation which is standing on the concepts of bits change to a completely different way of implementation which is based on Qubits.

UNDERSTANDING THE QUBITS

The classical states of computation may either be "0" or "1" which is known as bits. Qubits or Quantum bits are the fundamental building blocks of quantum computers which consist of two levels labelled zero |0> and one |1> described by the Dirac bracket notation. In order to fully describe qubits, we need two complex numbers that are because qubits are represented by two-dimensional vector space over the complex number C to the power of two. Classical computers are performing calculations by manipulating bits. Classical bits can be only in one state at a time 0 or 1. In comparison to quantum computers, that scenario represents the biggest limitation and obstacle for solving the most complex problem considering time and computational power since Alan Turing set up the foundations of computer science as we know today back in the 1930s with his prototype of the computational machine called the Turing Machine. Quantum computers do not have that kind of limitations as they operate on qubits. The reason why qubits are much more powerful than classical bits is that they can exist in two states at the same time. Let us consider a spinning coin on a table. At any moment, the coin is in both heads or tails state or a superposition of these two states. We can find the final state only when the coin stops rotating which may be either head or tail. The quantum bits may also be compared with the same. A quantum bit at any moment can be in 0 state or 1 state or a superposition of these two states.

A quantum state bit q can be any complex linear combination $q = \alpha |0 + \beta|1$, where $\alpha, \beta \in \mathbb{C}$ and α, β are not both zero. The coefficients α and β are called *amplitudes* of the quantum state.

If we consider two classical bits, then they may carry any of the two information, 00,01,10,11 but when we are considering two quantum bits, they may simultaneously remain in all 4 logical states. When we consider n quantum bits, the number of logical states grows exponentially to 2^n. All the qubits maintain privacy in the sense that neither cloning of qubits is possible, i.e., quantum information cannot be copied by any other person or device who have created the information but has no way around it. Nor deleting of information is possible, or flipping of unknown qubits would be allowed.

Quantum Entanglement

The quantum entanglement comes into play when there is more than one particle is participating in the computation. When the quantum particles are in an entangled state, they are linked in the strongest possible way even if they are far apart from each other. Quantum entanglement is another weirdest feature of the quantum world with allows us to do amazing tasks which are otherwise impossible. Let's again take the example of spinning coins. Suppose we are having two spinning coins at quite a distance apart that is spinning completely independently. Now one of the coins stops rotating and faces the head. When the second coin stops, it will always come out to be tails irrespective of how many times you are doing this experiment. Thus, the state of physically apart coins depends upon each other though they are not connected in any way. This is an example of entanglement. In the case of quantum entanglement, the same characteristic may be generated between different quantum particles and once they are entangled, an invisible link is generated among them irrespective of how far apart they are. The entanglement among these quantum particles gives rises to the enormous number of possibilities of states for quantum communication.

DIFFERENT APPROACHES TO CREATE QUANTUM COMPUTERS

After understanding the QUBITS, we should understand that quantum computation creates and computational advantage if we want to solve a certain mathematical problem. Just, for example, Quantum computers can in solving the Schrodinger equation for complicated molecules. The properties of a material may be explored without synthetically producing it. These quantum computers can also be used to solve certain logistic problems to optimize financial systems. Thus there is real potential for applications of quantum computers. But it should be taken into account that quantum computing doesn't help for all types of calculations. They are special-purpose machines that cannot operate all by themselves. The quantum parts have to be controlled and read out by conventional computers. It may be compared with wormholes in space travel. They might not bring you everywhere you want to go but where ever it takes, you reach there very fast. The most amazing capability of quantum computers also makes it so challenging. To use quantum computers, we have to maintain the entanglement between the qubits long enough to actually do the calculations. And quantum effects are extremely sensitive to even the smallest disturbances. To be reliable, quantum computers need to operate with several copies of the information, along with an error correction protocol. To perform these error corrections, we require more qubits and that number is quite high. The exact number of qubits required to perform a specific calculation depends upon the type of problem we are trying to solve, the algorithm used and the quality of the qubits. As stated by (Preskill, 2018) in his paper that noise resilient quantum circuits are quite effective in stimulating quantum computing in a classical computing environment but we are way beyond the requirement of proper error-free implementation in real life. Currently, D-Wave's Advantage quantum computer is having 5000+ qubits that use quantum annealing. There are different types of qubits that have their own advantages and disadvantages which are stated below:

Superconducting GATE model Quantum Computing: Superconducting qubits are the most widely used and most advanced type of qubits. They are basically small currents on a chip. The two-state qubits can be physically realized either by the distribution of the charge or by the flux of the current. One of the major advantages of superconducting qubits is that they can be produced by the same techniques that the electronics industries used for the last 5 decades. These qubits are basically microchips but they have to be cooled to extremely low temperatures of about 10-20 milliKelvin. The need for these low temperatures is to make the circuits superconducting, else these keeping them in the two-qubit states wouldn't have been possible. The problem with these superconducting qubits is that, though the chips are maintained in these extremely low temperatures, the quantum effect in superconducting qubits disappear extremely fast. This disappearance of quantum effects is measured in the decoherence time, which is a few 10s of microseconds for these superconducting qubits. This technology is used by Google, IBM and a number of smaller companies such as Rigetti. In 2019, Google demonstrated for the first time, "quantum supremacy" means they performed a task that a conventional computer could not have done in a reasonable time. The processor used in it had 53 qubits. Although the claim of supremacy by Google was later debated by IBM stating that the actual calculation could have been done by conventional supercomputers within a reasonable time. Currently, IBM's quantum computer has got 65 of these superconducting qubits and are in the research and production phase of a quantum computer with more than 1000 qubits by 2023. IBM's smaller quantum computers, the ones with 5 and 16 qubits are free to access in the cloud as of date. The biggest problem of these superconducting qubits is cooling. Beyond few thousand, it'll become difficult to put all the qubits into one cooling system and hence it becomes more challenging.

Photonic Quantum Computing: In photonic quantum computing, the qubits are properties related to photons. That may be the presence of the photon itself or the uncertainty in a particular state of the photon. This approach is pursued example by the company Xanadu in Toronto. It is also the approach that was used a few months ago by a group of Chinese researchers, which demonstrated quantum supremacy for photonic quantum computing. The biggest advantage of using photon is that they can be operated at the room temperature, and the quantum effect last much longer than the superconducting qubits, typically some milliseconds but it can go up to some hours in ideal cases. This makes photonic quantum computers much cheaper and easier to handle. The biggest disadvantage is that the system becomes very large very quickly due to the laser guides and optical components. For example, the photonic system of the Chinese group covers a whole tabletop, whereas superconducting circuits are just tiny chips. The Company PsiQuantum however claims they have solved the problem and have found an approach to photonic quantum computing that can be scaled up to a million qubits. Though there is not enough ground to verify that as they have not shared any information about their approach.

Ion Traps: In ion traps, the qubits are atoms that are missing some electrons and therefore have a net positive charge. We can then trap these ions in electromagnetic fields, and use lasers to move them around and entangle them. Such ion traps are comparable in the size to the qubit chips. They also need to be cooled but not quite as much, "only" to temperatures of the few Kelvins. The biggest play in trapped ion quantum computing is Honeywell, but the star-up IonQ use the same approach. The advantages of trapped ion computing are longer coherence times than superconducting qubits – up to few minutes. The other advantage is that trapped ions can interact with more neighbours than superconducting qubits. But ion traps also have disadvantages. Notably, they are slower to react than superconducting qubits, and it is more difficult to put many traps onto a single chip. However, they've kept up with superconducting qubits well. Honeywell claims to have the best quantum computer in the world by quantum volume. Quantum volume is a metric originally introduced by IBM, that combines many different factors like errors, crosstalk and connectivity. Honeywell reports a quantum volume of 128, and they are also moving to the cloud very soon. IonQ's latest model contains 32 trapped ions sitting in a chain. They also have a roadmap according to which they expect quantum supremacy by 2025 and to be able to solve interesting problems by 2028.

Superconducting Quantum Annealing: D-wave is so far the only company that sells commercially available quantum computers and they also use superconducting qubits. Their 2020 advantage model have more than 5000 qubits. However, the D-wave computers can't be compared to the approaches pursued by Google and IBM because D-wave uses a completely different computation strategy as they use quantum annealing. D-wave computers can be used for solving certain optimization and probabilistic sampling problems that are defined by the design of the machine, whereas the technology developed by Google and IBM is good to create a programmable computer that can be applied to all kinds of different problems. The optimization problems can be solved through Quantum annealing by finding the minimum energy state of something whereas in the case of probabilistic sampling problem, instead of focusing on trying to find the minimum energy state, what they have tried to do is a sample from any low energy state and try and characterize the shape of the energy landscape. This is useful for applications like machine learning where we try to build a probabilistic representation of the world and these samples give us information about what our model looks like now and we can use these models over time. Both superconducting qubits and quantum annealing are interesting, but completely different approaches.

Topological Quantum Computing: Topological quantum computing is the wild card. There isn't currently any workable machine that uses this technique. But the idea is great: In topological quantum computers, information will be stored in conserved properties of "quasi-particles", which are collective motions of particles. The great thing about this is that this information would be very robust to decoherence. According to Microsoft "the upside is enormous and there is practically no downside." In 2018, their director of quantum computing business development told the BBC Microsoft would have a commercially available quantum computer within five years, however, Microsoft had a bed setback when they had to retract a paper that demonstrated the existence of the quasi-particles they hoped to use.

Semi-Conducting Qubits: They are very similar to the superconducting qubits, but here the qubits are either the spin or charge of a single electron. The advantage is that the temperature doesn't need to be quite as low. Instead of 10mK, one "only" has to reach a few Kelvin. This approach is presently pursued by researchers at TU Delft in the Netherlands, supported by Intel.

Nitrogen-Vacancy System: In the nitrogen-vacancy system, the qubits are places in the structures of a carbon crystal where a carbon atom is replaced by a nitrogen atom. The great advantage of this is that they are small and can be operated at room temperature. This approach is pursued by the Hanson lab at Qutech. Some people at MIT and a startup in Australia called Quantum Brilliance.

So far there hasn't been any demonstration of the last two approaches but they seem to be promising.

Quantum Programming

Quantum computers are specifically built to cater for some specific type of highly complex and computationally enormous problem in magnitude in an extremely efficient manner. The problem-solving using qubits might not be as fast as in classical computers but the number of steps to reach the solution is reduced drastically and parallelism may be incorporated and hence the solutions to unsolvable problems may be achieved. The algorithms for quantum programming are generally made in the form of pseudo-codes. Semantically there are two models of quantum computation viz. quantum networks which is more relevant in the design implementation of gates and quantum Turing machines that are more appropriate in complexity analysis. As discussed by (Feynman, 2018), reversible computers complete calculations with almost zero loss. We require to use new types of logic gates that are reversible in nature and we can reconstruct the input from the output we are getting. For instance, if we consider NOT gates, it is a reversible gate as two NOT operations will produce the original input value. To implement the reversible computation, the Controlled

NOT gate or CNOT gate is used to have control and implementation of entangled states of a qubit. It not only helps in controlling the flow of quantum particles over the channels but also conserves the energy during any computation as described by (Hey, 1999). The logic gates need to be designed in such a manner that the reverse calculation may be possible. To make this possible, a controlled-NOT (CN) gate may be used as two CNs may be placed back-to-back to reverse the operation. Quantum programming is mainly done at the chip level by applying different gates and controlling the flow of quantum particles.

The programming language design may be classified based on imperative languages, functional languages and λ-calculi and other language paradigms and the semantics that are used may be application of linear logic, categorical and domain-theoretic technique or some other semantic techniques and also the way they are compiled.

While talking about imperative languages, the initial formal quantum programming language was imperative pseudocode which was better suited on a quantum random-access machine (QRAM). Later on, QCL came out as a real quantum programming language where the syntaxes are primarily taken from C. Later on another imperative language qGCL was invented which was based on a guarded-command language. It is emphasized to derive quantum algorithms.

To talk about functional languages and λ-calculi, two initial approaches exist. A probabilistic λ -calculus (λ^p -calculus) that allows functions to return randomized results and the second one is a quantum λ -calculus (λ^q-calculus) where there may be destructive interference as the distributions are combined. Another first-order functional programming language known as QML was developed where the data and control both may be quantum.

In (Bettelli, 2003), the researchers have stated the requirement of quantum languages to have the ability to implement pseudo-classical operators, i.e., transformations like $U_f : |x\rangle|y\rangle \oplus f(x) >$ where $f : \mathbb{Z}_{2^n} \to \mathbb{Z}_{2^m}$ is a classical function and n and m are the size of registers. In their proposed language, they have set high-level primitive programming on a QRAM machine. This was implemented using the description of the algorithms in their circuit model and was working on implementing it using the C++ programming language. They have implemented it into the controlled circuits by recognizing the elementary gates which are $\{H, R_k, C_{R_k}\}_{k \in N}$ and implementing them to depth bounded by global constants. The qubit addresses are managed and algorithms are implemented to the design circuits.

The quantum algorithms are implemented using different types of gates and they need to be programmed and the very basic programming language used to do so is QASM (Khammassi et al., 2018) which first appeared in 2005 by MIT. Many different dialects of QASM either as quantum circuit representation or as input has been defined. One such variation is cQASM which supports around 24 Quantum Gates that includes notably CNOT Gate, Hadamard Gate, Identity Gate, Swap Gate, CR & CRK controlled phase shift gates which can handle arbitrary angle and $\pi / 2^k$ phase shifts respectively, T dagger and Toffoli gates etc. It also supports eight different state preparation and measurements. It is essentially a way forward to hardware-agnostic language that may be used to achieve large-scale quantum computation. The research group of (Cross et al., 2017) has proposed Open QASM which has elements of C and assembly languages. For trapped ion quantum computer testbed, as introduced by (Landahl et al., 2020), QSCOUT (Quantum Scientific Computing Open User Testbed) and Jaqal language is developed by Sandia Nonnational Laboratories. The QSCOUT is an assembly-level language whereas Jaqal is a programming language to realize the quantum gate creation in a language similar to C/C++.

Currently, the two major open-source programming platforms available are Cirq and Qiskit. Both the programming languages use universal gate-based quantum computing and both of them are python based. Due to this similarity, the basics and syntax of both languages is pretty similar. The primary difference between the two languages is access to quantum computing hardware. Currently, Google does not provide any quantum computing hardware but the IBM does. IBM provides 5 and 15 qubit quantum computing hardware to work around and test the logic. Qiskit also provides an IBM composer which is based on drag and drop of the universal gates for up to 7 qubits which is quite helpful for those beginners who are not very comfortable with programming languages. For any higher entanglement, Qiskit python-based coding is required. This huge advantage that if someone is not very familiar with coding, then also they may implement their logic is making Qiskit quite popular. As there are limitations to hardware, it is better to use simulators. The simulators are actually running on classical computers but it tries to mimic the real quantum hardware by implementing the properties of a qubit in an ideal condition and showing the enormous capabilities of calculations by exponentially scaling up the classical hardware to make it comparable to the number of qubits used. Moreover, when we use the real hardware, a considerable amount of noise, mainly due to hardware limitations, occurs which restricts the output to reach its perfectness. Through simulators, we get better outputs and the limitations of qubits can also be overcome. Presently proper working simulators of Qiskit provides 32 qubits whereas that of Cirq provides 30 qubits. However, the biggest advantage of using Cirq is the use of TensorFlow Quantum. TensorFlow Quantum focuses on quantum data and hybrid quantum models. The TensorFlow Quantum combines these quantum computing algorithms from Cirq and matches them with TensorFlow repository. Qiskit has a package called AQUA (which stands for Algorithms) for Quantum Applications where prebuilt algorithms that we can use without having to deal with at the gate level. Using the Qiskit we may get the quantum advantage but even if we may find a way to work on properly entangled algorithmic implementation of a hard problem to find the quantum supremacy, we won't be able to run it as the required number of qubits are not available to us to solve our problem. If we can successfully run a quantum program in a quantum computer then we say that we have made quantum advancement and if we can find a way of running a computationally hard problem which is not possible for any current superconductor to run within a considerable time of single lifetime or less but a quantum computer can solve the problem in a feasible amount of time, we say that we have reached quantum supremacy.

CONCLUSION

In this chapter, we have discussed the basic concepts of quantum computing as without knowing the basics of such computing, quantum programming will not be possible as it is not an advancement of the existing technology but a completely new technology. The fundamental understanding of quantum computation is very different from that of a classical counterpart. One must know the difference between to two before getting into programming. Here we have also discussed the different techniques through which the scientific community and the industries are working to realize the quantum advancement and reach quantum supremacy and some of the programming techniques and tools available in public to implement their algorithms and pros and cons of these working environments along with the testbeds available to check the outcomes. It is to be noted that quantum computers are not a replacement of the current classical computers but are a supplement to them to solve some computationally unsolvable problems within a feasible time. It is the answer to the physical limitations of miniaturization of the transistor size at the atomic level as here we talk about the subatomic properties and controlling them. At last, we would like to say that the coming era of computational marvel has already arrived and soon many solutions to the unsolvable may be achieved. To be a part of the revolutionary change, it is very necessary to learn about the programming techniques and controlling capabilities of the quantum bits and working around with the quantum entanglement to reach the pinnacle of quantum advancement and further to quantum supremacy.

REFERENCES

Bettelli, S., Calarco, T., & Serafini, L. (2003). Toward an architecture for quantum programming. *The European Physical Journal D-Atomic, Molecular, Optical and Plasma Physics*, 25(2), 181–200.

Cross, A. W., Bishop, L. S., Smolin, J. A., & Gambetta, J. M. (2017). *Open quantum assembly language*. arXiv preprint arXiv:1707.03429.

Feynman, R. P., Hey, T., & Allen, R. W. (2018). *Feynman lectures on computation*. CRC Press. doi:10.1201/9780429500442

Hey, T. (1999). Quantum computing: An introduction. *Computing & Control Engineering Journal*, 10(3), 105–112. doi:10.1049/cce:19990303

Khammassi, N., Guerreschi, G. G., Ashraf, I., Hogaboam, J. W., Almudever, C. G., & Bertels, K. (2018). *cqasm v1. 0: Towards a common quantum assembly language*. arXiv preprint arXiv:1805.09607.

Landahl, A. J., Lobser, D. S., Morrison, B. C., Rudinger, K. M., Russo, A. E., Van Der Wall, J. W., & Maunz, P. (2020). Jaqal, the quantum assembly language for QSCOUT. arXiv preprint arXiv:2003.09382. doi:10.2172/1606475

Preskill, J. (2018). Quantum computing in the NISQ era and beyond. *Quantum*, 2, 79. doi:10.22331/q-2018-08-06-79

Shalf, J. (2020). The future of computing beyond Moore's Law. *Philosophical Transactions - Royal Society. Mathematical, Physical, and Engineering Sciences*, 378(2166), 20190061. doi:10.1098/rsta.2019.0061 PMID:31955683

KEY TERMS AND DEFINITIONS

Ion Trap: In ion traps, the qubits are atoms that are missing some electrons and therefore have a net positive charge. We can then trap these ions in electromagnetic fields, and use lasers to move them around and entangle them. Such ion traps are comparable in the size to the qubit chips. They also need to be cooled but not quite as much, "only" to temperatures of the few Kelvins.

Nitrogen-Vacancy System: In the nitrogen-vacancy system, the qubits are placed in the structures of a carbon crystal where a carbon atom is replaced by a nitrogen atom.

Photonic Gate: In photonic quantum computing, the qubits are properties related to photons. That may be the presence of the photon itself or the uncertainty in a particular state of the photon.

Quantum Annealing: Quantum annealing is the process of finding the minimum energy state of something where instead of focusing on trying to find the minimum energy state, a sample from any low energy state is taken and try and characterize the shape of the energy landscape. This is useful for applications like machine learning where we try to build a probabilistic representation of the world and these samples give us information about what the model looks like now and these models can be used over time.

Quantum Entanglement: Quantum entanglement comes into play when there is more than one particle is participating in the computation. When the quantum particles are in an entangled state, they are linked in the strongest possible way even if they are far apart from each other. once they are entangled, an invisible link is generated among them irrespective of how far apart they are. The entanglement among these quantum particles gives rise to the enormous number of possibilities of states for quantum communication.

Semiconducting Qubits: Semiconducting qubits are very similar to superconducting qubits, but here the qubits are either the spin or charge of a single electron.

Superconducting Gate: Superconducting qubits are the most widely used and most advanced type of qubits. They are basically small currents on a chip. The two-state qubits can be physically realized either by the distribution of the charge or by the flux of the current.

Topological Quantum Computing: In topological quantum computers, information will be stored in conserved properties of "quasi-particles," which are collective motions of particles. The great thing about this is that this information would be very robust to decoherence.

Chapter 3
Recent Developments in Quantum Computing and Their Challenges

R. Nagarajan
Gnanamani College of Technology, India

Kannadhasan S.
(iD) https://orcid.org/0000-0001-6443-9993
Cheran College of Engineering, India

Kanagaraj Venusamy
(iD) https://orcid.org/0000-0001-9479-8073
University of Technology and Applied Sciences-Al Mussanah, Oman

ABSTRACT

Today, major corporations such as IBM, Google, Microsoft, and Amazon are racing to build cloud quantum computers. They integrate quantum computers with cloud computing to create a system that can be accessible via a network without the need for quantum computing power in a cloud computing environment. The authors describe cloud quantum computing in this chapter and conduct research to compare cloud quantum computing providers across the globe. In this study, the authors look at the various cloud quantum computing options and the outcomes they provide. At the conclusion, each cloud quantum computing service will be compared based on its performance, amplitudes, times, and architecture. The study will primarily focus on IBM and Qutech cloud quantum computing technologies.

DOI: 10.4018/978-1-7998-9183-3.ch003

INTRODUCTION

In this study, we'll look at the various cloud quantum computing options and the outcomes they provide. At the conclusion, each cloud quantum computing service will be compared based on its performance, amplitudes, times, and architecture. The study will primarily focus on IBM and Qutech cloud quantum computing technologies. The reason we chose IBM's cloud quantum computing is because they have created a cloud-based quantum computing platform that anybody can access, making it simple for us to examine and evaluate its performance. IBM, on the other hand, has been working on quantum computers for more than a decade and is said to have developed one of the strongest, if not the strongest quantum computer, with 53 qubits. Qutech, on the other hand, not only offers cloud-based quantum computing platforms, but also a variety of hardware chips with which we may attempt to run our algorithm on their Spin-2 or Starmon-5 quantum processors (Simsao, 2018; Gyongyosi, 2019). The remainder of this paper will be organised as follows: The fundamental concepts underpinning Cloud quantum computing, such as superposition and entanglement, will be explained in the Methodology section. The definition and comparison of cloud quantum computing services will be presented in the research section. In the discussion section, the results of the tests and comparisons will be discussed in general. Finally, in the conclusion section, I will provide a summary based on the study and findings in the hopes of providing some clarity and understanding into the many types of cloud quantum computing services and the performance power of quantum computers in a cloud computing environment (Karalekas, 2020).

We will describe cloud quantum computing in this article, as well as conduct research to compare cloud quantum computing providers across the globe. In this study, we'll look at the various cloud quantum computing options and the outcomes they provide. At the conclusion, each cloud quantum computing service will be compared based on its performance, amplitudes, times, and architecture. The study will primarily focus on IBM and Qutech cloud quantum computing technologies. The reason we chose IBM's cloud quantum computing is because they have created a cloud-based quantum computing platform that anybody can access, making it simple for us to examine and evaluate its performance. IBM, on the other hand, has been working on quantum computers for more than a decade and is said to have developed one of the strongest, if not the strongest quantum computer, with 53 qubits. Qutech, on the other hand, not only offers cloud-based quantum computing platforms, but also a variety of hardware chips with which we may attempt to run our algorithm on their Spin-2 or Starmon-5 quantum processors. The remainder of this paper will be organised as follows: The fundamental concepts underpinning Cloud quantum computing, such as superposition and entanglement, will be explained in the

Methodology section. The definition and comparison of cloud quantum computing services will be presented in the research section. In the discussion section, the results of the tests and comparisons will be discussed in general. Finally, in the conclusion section, I will provide a summary based on the performed study and results in the hopes of providing some clarity and insight into the various types of cloud quantum computing service performances.

The continuing quantum computing revolution, which began a decade ago, is shaking the current age. Quantum computers in the form of superconductor chips, such as the IBM Quantum Experience computers, are accessible as a free Cloud service enabling anybody to do complicated computations with very high precision in extremely short time frames, or to mimic quantum systems phenomena. Quantum computing is here to stay, and it has already started to alter our approaches to physics, engineering, mathematics, and chemistry, allowing us to tackle critical issues that traditional computers will never be able to handle. Within a decade, quantum computers are expected to have an effect on fundamental human activities, and perhaps everyday life, all across the globe (Jordan, 2018; Asher, 1995). It is thus critical that we begin to think about how to integrate quantum computing knowledge, both foundations and technology, into our undergraduate physics, electronics, computer science, physics engineering, and material science curriculum. Quantum computing is a difficult and intriguing topic that our science and technology undergraduate students may now study.

What are the applications of quantum computers? After all, powerful traditional computers, such as Turing's machine, have been developed in the past thirty years that are capable of crunching complicated numerical issues or solving complex computational problems in tens of hours. Furthermore, today's laptop computers are thousands of times quicker than the huge mainframe computers of the 1950s and 1970s. However, there are certain critical issues that no current conventional computer, constructed with highly integrated micro-electronics circuits composed of doped semi-conductors, would ever be able to address. In a traditional computer, each bit may take just two values, typically represented by 0 and 1, which are then ingeniously exploited to encode and process data utilising a large number of them (e.g. megabits). As will be described, qubits in a quantum computer may assume not two but a really huge number of basic quantum states, and when correctly built and programmed, a small number of qubits can conduct many calculations at the same time! i.e. enormous parallelism, which enables us to create quantum computing algorithms that operate at very high speeds or tackle extremely difficult problems with unprecedented precision (Ying, 2010; Elebent, 2020).

QUANTUM COMPUTING

Even if a highly fast conventional computer is utilised, searching for a specific item in a big and unsorted database, such as finding a certain phone number in a city's enormous telephone directory, may take a very long time. It's a challenge similar to looking for a needle in a haystack, but we'd be looking for a specific needle (the phone number) among a huge pile of needles of various shapes (the massive data in the directory). Using a quantum computer and his now-famous Grover search method, the time it takes to answer these issues may be significantly reduced. (Another problem that we could eventually address using a quantum computer is linked to our food security.) It entails understanding the Nitrogenase molecule's complicated quantum electronic structure as well as its chemical characteristics. Nitrogenase is a bacterial enzyme that converts nitrogen (N2) to ammonia (NH3), which is used to make fertilisers. The current industrial method for converting N2 to NH3 necessitates high temperatures and uses 2% of world energy output! Instead, specialised bacteria utilize Nitrogenase to accomplish the same thing in nature at normal temperature and pressure! with very little energy expenditure. Let us remember that nitrogen fixation is needed for the production of important macromolecules in plants, such as aminoacids, which are consumed by animals and humans. We now know that only a computer built with quantum objects (e.g., electrons, photons) can unravel the chemical bonds of extremely complex molecules like Nitrogenase, allowing us to better understand their chemical interactions and, as a result, produce fertilisers more efficiently using quantum control. Such molecular physics knowledge will lead to the discovery of new medications to treat diseases like cancer, as well as a better understanding of the intricate molecule interactions that are the secrets to life's genesis.

The quantum bit, or qubit for short, is the most basic concept in quantum computing. While a conventional bit may have the value 0 or 1 at any given moment, the value of a qubit $|x$ is any combination of these two values: $|x=|0+|1$ (we write $|x$ instead of x for the latter to differentiate bits from qubits). One source of quantum computing's power is the so-called superposition. A measurement is used to ascertain the real value of a qubit. The probability that the classical value "0" or "1" will occur after the qubit is measured are 2 and 2. Because one of the outcomes will be "0" or "1," the probability add up to 1: $2+2=1$. Qubits are integrated into quantum registers in the same way that bits are combined into registers in a conventional computer. A n-qubit quantum register $|r$ has a value that is a superposition of the 2n values $|0...0, |0...01$, and up to $|1...1$. A quantum register manipulation therefore changes these 2n values at the same time: quantum parallelism is another source of quantum computing's strength. The Internet of Things (IoT) is one of the most significant technologies that is totally hidden from our view, but it is woven into the fabric of everyday life. This is becoming a well-known idea in many organisations, as well as in daily life for the average person. The necessity for big companies to track their manufacturing chain, which they are immersed in, is driving the development of the Internet of Things (IoT). When it initially came into usage in the 1990s, the Internet of Things (IoT) was a significant change in the IT industry. But now, whether it's a home network or a corporate network, Internet of Things (IoT) may be found in the medical sector, education sector, businesses, and everywhere else where a vast network of embedded devices is required. To put it another way, the Internet of Things (IoT) is a network of linked computing devices, mechanical and digital equipment, or items that can exchange data without needing human-to-human or computer-to-human contact. The Internet of Things is mostly used to automate or minimise human involvement. The objects or things (sensors and actuators) in an IoT network collaborate to solve a problem that needs more precision, frequent computing, and less human involvement. Because there may be thousands of nodes in the network, they must have certain common criteria because there is a little probability that they will be placed in the arena and monitored or physically cared for on a regular basis. Data security, surveillance, direct internet access, and other problems arise as a consequence of this. The network may be built and connected using Quantum Computing technologies to alleviate these problems.

Quantum computing is the use of quantum characteristics such as entanglement and superposition to solve problems. Conjugate Coding was invented by a research physicist called Stephen J. Wiesner in 1960, and later in 1973, when a Soviet and Russian mathematician named Alexander Holevo published a paper demonstrating that n number of qubits may store more information than n number of conventional bits. Due to the lack of progress in quantum systems at the time, and some disagreement among physicists, it was thought that it was impossible to build a system that could manage quantum particles in such a way that it could perform any sort of computing on them. However, development continues, and the first functional 5-qubit Nuclear Magnetic Resonance (NMR) computer was put to the test in 2000 at the Technical University of Munich. About 15 years later, big computer behemoths such as Google, IBM, and Microsoft enter the race for Quantum Supremacy. In 2017, IBM released their first Quantum Computer (IBM Q) prototype for public use, which can be accessed via the cloud. The pace of research is such that, in 10 years or less, everyone will have a tiny quantum gadget in their pockets, similar to smartphones. But, for the time being, the work is still in process, and it may take up to 10 or even 20 years before it reaches the hands of the average person. Theoretically, assuming quantum systems' design and communication protocol (i.e. entanglement) stay unchanged, they may be incorporated into IoT networks using the suggested architecture to make them safe and extremely fast in comparison to what we have currently. It will not be feasible to replace every node in an IoT network with a quantum device because it will create too much overhead and managing this much entanglement would be too chaotic and complex. In an IoT network with ten quantum devices, each device must be able to interact with the others, and to do so, each device must contain qubits that are entangled with other devices. Because only two qubits are entangled at a moment, each device must have 2n-1 qubits, where n is 10 in this instance, thus each device must have 19 qubits to communicate with each other. Qubits are not the same as the traditional bits used in today's technologies. Noise (changes in temperature, pressure, or any other external phenomena) may cause qubits to lose their entanglement and superposition. Furthermore, the quantum system necessitates a highly isolated and cold environment; yet, since quantum devices may be as tiny as a bottle cap and thousands in number, isolation is not feasible. To address this problem, the suggested design would use a quantum server as a gateway, which can be readily deployed by just replacing the router.

Computers minimize human labour while simultaneously focusing on improving performance in order to advance technology. To boost computer performance, a variety of methods have been developed. Reduce the size of the transistors utilised in the systems is one such method. The usage of quantum computers is another important strategy. When used to factor huge numbers, it proved to be extremely successful. It was discovered that it could decode codes in 20 minutes, while traditional computers required billions of years. This provided excellent incentive for concentrating on this subject. A quantum computer may have three states for a quantum bit, or qubit: 0, 1, and 0 or 1. The cohesive state is the final state. This allows you to execute an operation on two different values at the same time. This, however, raises the issue of decoherence. Using quantum computers to do the calculation gets challenging. A quantum computer should have five features: a scalable system, an initializable state, a lengthy decoherence period, a universal set of quantum gates, and great measurement efficiency. The architecture of quantum computers is a new field of study. Quantum arithmetic, error control, and cluster-state computing all have an impact on it. The quantum algorithms would not be as efficient without it. The algorithms employed should be based on quantum parallelism to fully exploit the capabilities of a quantum computer.

CHALLENGES IN QUANTUM COMPUTING

Even if today's computers have enormous processing capacity, there are endless issues that need to be addressed or that may take years to solve. There is a fast rise of data with the quick increase in people. Traditional computers are adequate for the time being, but will suffer in the future as scientific demand grows rapidly. As a result, a Quantum Computer is required. "Quantum computers will revolutionise in the same manner that the light bulb revolutionised when it replaced candles." Bulbs and candles both operate the same way but have distinct physical appearances. Quantum computers will not have the same physicality as conventional computers, but they will do the same tasks more efficiently.

Quantum Circuits are built on quantum bits, also known as Qubits, which are analogous to bits in conventional computers. Qubits may be either a 1 or a 0 Quantum state, or a superposition of both (1 and 0). When studying qubits, the outcome is always a 0 or a 1. Quantum logic gates, which are similar to conventional logic gates, are used to manipulate qubits for computation. Since 1950, the number of atoms required to represent a bit of memory has been steadily reducing. Gordon Moore's discovery in 1965 set the groundwork for what became known as "Moore's Law," which states that computer processing power doubles every eighteen months. According to a paper published in the journal Nature, recent quantum computing research has resulted in two 53 qubit processors, one from IBM and one from Google. The paper claims that a normal supercomputer would take 10,000 years to perform the same task that a Quantum Computer performs in 2.5 days. The concept of superposition, which is a sufficiently realistic natural occurrence, is used in quantum computing to execute data operations. Transistors are used to support traditional and digital computers. Quantum computers, on the other hand, are based on theoretical principles. Qubits are used in quantum computers, while binary digits (1 or 0) are used in conventional computers. The qubit is often in superpositions of states, meaning that it may take any value between 0 and 1. The universal quantum computer, which is a theoretical model of such computers, is known as a quantum computer. Theoretically, quantum computers are comparable to non-deterministic and probabilistic algorithms. Because a classical computer performs worse than a quantum computer, it is wise to use the conventional machine for the bulk of computation. We'll transform a traditional computer into a quantum computer using a reasonable quantum circuit and a kind of interface between conventional and quantum logic.

These are bricks that will integrate quantum computing's form. It will provide an overview of qubits, gates, and circuits. Quantum computers operate on qubits, which may be in a state of superposition, which is an additional feature, and are the same as bits used by conventional or machine computers. In comparison to a classical computer, a quantum register with two qubits can concurrently store four numbers in superposition, while a conventional register with two bits can only store two numbers, and a 300 qubit register can contain more numbers than the entire number of atoms in the universe. This eventually results in the storing of limitless data at the moment of calculation, but we are unable to access it. The problem arises when reading an output that is in an extremely superposition state, including many distinct values. When the superposition state collapses, we are left with just one value. This excites us, but it may also provide us with a computational advantage.

Quantum computers seem to have a major effect on the commercial world. Glover's database search method and Shor's integer factoring algorithm are two of the most well-known quantum algorithms. Both quantum algorithms are known to substantially outperform conventional computer methods and may be used to break encryption systems (such as AES, RSA, and ECC) that are widely used on the Internet (e.g., online shopping sites.) Governments have been boosting financing for quantum computing research and development for a variety of reasons, including progress of computer technology and national security. However, following D-wave, a Canadian firm, revealed a commercial annealer-based annealer.

The process of changing the states of a physical system to solve a problem is known as computation. Quantum computing stores and transfers digital information using a tiny item (e.g., electron, photon, or ion) as the medium. Two orthogonal states of a tiny item may be used to encode one-bit information (i.e., zero or one). A quantum bit is a quantum two-state system with two states (or qubit). A quantum computer solves a problem by placing qubits in starting states and then modifying the states to get the desired output. Because such tiny particles do not obey the laws of conventional physics, quantum mechanics is utilised to explain the states in order to build such a quantum circuit. Many new fields of science and technology study and development have opened up since the advent of quantum physics. Quantum Computing and Communication is one such area, where there is a chamber sealed that was previously just a fantasy in the realm of computing and communication. This article provides a short overview of what is currently taking on in the area of information processing systems, with a focus on Big Data Analytics. We have quantum computation and communication in this article. With the ever-increasing demands for processing speed and compactness, traditional computers are unable to keep up with these few requirements. Because classical computers are based on classical physics, their growth has reached its pinnacle. As a result of these limitations, quantum mechanics has emerged as a game changer in the race of computing.

Quantum theory is one of the most influential ideas of the twentieth century, influencing the path of scientific development. It has offered a new line of scientific thinking, anticipated previously unthinkable scenarios, and impacted a variety of contemporary technological fields. There are many methods to represent scientific rules in general and physics laws in particular. Information, like physical laws of nature, may be represented in a variety of ways. Because information may be represented in a variety of ways while maintaining its fundamental essence, it is possible to manipulate data automatically. "There is no information without physical representation," says one who uses a physical system to communicate information. Said words are transmitted by air pressure fluctuations: "There is no information without physical representation." Information is an apparent contender for fundamentally essential roles in physics, such as contact, energy, momentum, and other abstractors, since it is indifferent to how it is represented and may be easily transferred from one form to another.

Big Data is a phrase that refers to data that exceeds the storage and processing capabilities of traditional computers, and extracting insight from enormous amounts of data is a huge problem. Quantum Computing saves the day by reviewing the literature on Big Data Analytics using Quantum Computing for Machine Learning and the present state of the art. The goal of this study is to conduct a survey in the fascinating area of quantum computing. The article starts with a summary of quantum mechanics' history. From a physics standpoint, major components of quantum computing such as quantum superposition, quantum tunnelling, and qubits are discussed next. In addition, different quantum physics techniques and applications are investigated. Bits are used to encode information in traditional computers. Each bit may be either a 1 or a 0. This 1 and 0 serve as on and off switches for computer operations. Quantum computers are made up of qubits, which work on the basis of two quantum physics principles: superposition and entanglement. Using these two concepts, qubits may serve as additional high-degree-of-complexity switches, allowing quantum computers to tackle challenging problems that are now unsolvable by conventional computers. A metal on a silicon chip produces superconducting when it is placed in such a manner that it becomes superconducting when cooled to a low enough temperature. Without any electrical resistance, all electrons may flow freely and take on distinct quantum states. Refrigerators are used to chill them down, and they utilise dilution refrigerators with a temperature of 10-15 milikelvins. The temperature is 0.051 kelvin lower than that of outer space. Microwave cables link the quantum chip to the signals, which are sent to the chip, which processes them and outputs the results.

Imagine an electron in a magnetic field as a qubit. A spin-up state is when the electron's spin is aligned with the field, whereas a spin-down state is when the electron's spin is opposing the field. Using a pulse of energy, such as from a laser - let's say 1 unit of laser energy - we can change the electron's spin from one state to another. But what if we just utilise half a unit of laser energy, thereby isolating the particle from all other influences? The particle subsequently enters a superposition of states, in which the qubits may act as if they were in both states at the same time, according to quantum law. Each qubit may be in both a 0 and a 1 superposition. As a result, the maximum number of calculations a quantum computer can do is 2n, where n is the number of qubits in use. A quantum computer with 500 qubits has the ability to do 2500 computations in a single step. This is a huge quantity - 2500 is an infinite number of atoms more than the known cosmos has. This is real parallel processing: even today's so-called parallel processors can only perform one thing at a time: there are only two or more of them working on it. Quantum entanglement will be used to interact between these particles.

When European Union members declared their plan to spend $13 million in the research and development of a secure communications system based on quantum cryptography, it made headlines. The SECOQC (Secure Communication based on Quantum Cryptography) system will act as a strategic counter to the Echelon intelligence collection system utilised by the US, Australia, the United Kingdom, Canada, and New Zealand. In addition, a few quantum information processing companies, such as MagiQ Technologies and ID Quantique, are developing quantum cryptography solutions to meet the needs of businesses, governments, and other institutions where preventing unauthorised information disclosure has become a critical success factor in maintaining a competitive advantage over competitors. While current cryptosystems are claimed to be extremely successful, or "INTRACTABLE," why is so much money being spent on the development of a new cryptosystem - quantum cryptography? Public key cryptography is used to exchange keys rather than to encrypt large quantities of data since it requires complicated computations that are rather sluggish. To distribute symmetric keys across distant participants, widely established methods like as the RSA and Diffie-Hellman key negotiation techniques are often employed. Many institutions choose a hybrid method to take advantage of the speed of a shared key system and the security of a public key system for the first exchange of the symmetric key since asymmetric encryption is considerably slower than symmetric encryption. As a result, this method takes use of a symmetric key system's speed and performance while utilising the scalability of a public key infrastructure. Public key cryptosystems like RSA and Diffie-Hellman, on the other hand, are not dependent on actual mathematical proofs. Rather, years of public examination of the basic process of factoring big numbers into their primes, which is believed to be "intractable," has led to the conclusion that these methods are fairly safe. To put it another way, by the time the encryption method could be overcome, the data being secured would have lost all of its value. As a result, the strength of these algorithms is predicated on the fact that, given today's computer processing capacity, there is no known mathematical procedure for rapidly factoring extremely big integers. While today's public key cryptosystems may be "good enough" to offer a reasonable degree of confidentiality, they are vulnerable to a number of dangers. For example, advances in computer processing, like as quantum computing, may be able to overcome systems like RSA in a timely manner, rendering public key cryptosystems obsolete. For example, although the DES method, which uses a 56-bit key, was previously believed to be safe, it is no longer deemed such since technological advances have made it easy to defeat. The fact that powerful computers could break DES in a matter of hours sparked the creation of the Advanced Encryption Standard. As a result, one area of concern is that public key cryptography may be susceptible to future advances in computer processing capability.

Second, it's unclear if a theory that can factor big numbers into their primes in a timely way will be created in the future or is currently accessible. There is currently no evidence that such a factoring theorem cannot be developed. As a consequence, public key systems are susceptible to the unknown existence of such a theorem in the future, which would have a major impact on the algorithm's mathematical intractability. This ambiguity poses a threat to national security and intellectual property, both of which need absolute protection. To summarise, contemporary encryption is susceptible to both technical advancements in computer power and mathematical development that allows one-way operations like factoring big numbers to be rapidly reversed. If a factoring theorem were to be made public, or if computing became powerful enough to defeat public cryptography, businesses, governments, militaries, and other affected institutions would be forced to spend significant resources investigating the risk of damage and potentially deploying a new and expensive cryptography system quickly. Quantum cryptography, rather than relying on the difficulty of factoring big numbers, is based on the basic and unchangeable laws of quantum physics. In reality, quantum cryptography is based on two pillars of quantum physics from the twentieth century: the Heisenberg Uncertainty Principle and the Photon Polarization Principle. It is impossible to measure the quantum state of any system without disrupting it, according to the Heisenberg Uncertainty principle. As a result, the polarisation of a photon or light particle can only be determined at the time of measurement. In a quantum cryptography-based cryptosystem, this concept is essential for resisting eavesdropper efforts. The photon polarisation principle, on the other hand, explains how light photons may be polarised in particular directions. Furthermore, a photon filter with the appropriate polarisation can only detect polarised photons; otherwise, the photon is destroyed. Quantum encryption is an appealing alternative for guaranteeing data privacy and thwarting eavesdroppers because of photons' "one-way-ness" and the Heisenberg Uncertainty principle.

CONCLUSION

In 1984, Charles H. Bennet and Gilles Brassard created the idea of quantum cryptography as part of a physics and information research. According to Bennet and Brassad, an encryption key may be generated based on the number of photons received and how they were received. Their view is supported by the fact that light may exhibit particle-like properties in addition to light waves. These photons may be polarised in a variety of ways, which can be used to represent bits that include both ones and zeros. These bits may be used to create one-time pads and assist PKI systems by securely transmitting keys. The basis of quantum cryptography is the encoding of bits using polarised photons, which is also the fundamental concept of quantum key distribution. While the strength of contemporary digital encryption is based on the computational complexity of factoring big numbers, quantum cryptography is entirely based on physical laws and is unaffected by current computer systems' processing capacity. Because the laws of physics will always hold true, quantum cryptography solves the uncertainty problem that plagues current cryptography; it is no longer necessary to make assumptions about malicious attackers' computing power or the development of a theorem in order to solve the large integer Factorization problem quickly.

REFERENCES

Asher, P. (1995). *Quantum Theory: Concepts and Methods*. Kluwer Academic Publishers.

Gyongyosi, L., Bacsardi, L., & Imre, S. (2019). A survey on quantum key distribution. *Infocommunications J*, *11*(2), 14–21. doi:10.36244/ICJ.2019.2.2

Jordan, S. (n.d.). *Quantum Algorithm Zoo Archived 2018-04-29 at the Wayback Machine*. Academic Press.

Karalekas, P. J., Tezak, N. A., Peterson, E. C., Ryan, C. A., Da Silva, M. P., & Smith, R. S. (2020). A quantum-classical cloud platform optimized for variational hybrid algorithms. *Quantum Science and Technology*, *5*(2), 24003. doi:10.1088/2058-9565/ab7559

Kiyani, F., & Copuroglu, F. (2018). Quantum Computers vs Computers Computing. *Int Res J ComputSci*, *5*, 2014–2018.

Ying, M. (2010). Quantum computation, quantum theory and AI. *Artificial Intelligence*, *174*(2), 162–176. doi:10.1016/j.artint.2009.11.009

Ying, M. (2010). Quantum computation, quantum theory and AI. *Artificial Intelligence*, *174*(2), 162–176. doi:10.1016/j.artint.2009.11.009

Chapter 4
A Taxonomy of Quantum Computing Algorithms:
Advancements and Anticipations

Lopamudra Hota
National Institute of Technology, Rourkela, India

Prasant Kumar Dash
C. V. Raman Global University, India

ABSTRACT

Quantum computing exploits quantum-mechanical principles such as entanglement and superposition to offer significant computational advantages over conventional classical computing. Many complex and computationally challenging problems are expected to be solved by quantum computing in a number of fields, such as data science, industrial chemistry, smart energy, finance, secure communications, and many others. In order to understand the current status of quantum computing and identify its challenges, a systematic review of the existing literature will be valuable. An overview of quantum computing literature and its taxonomy is presented in this chapter. Further, the proposed taxonomy aims to identify research gaps by mapping various related studies. There is a detailed analysis of quantum technologies with the most current state of the art. Finally, the chapter presents a highlight of open challenges and future research directions.

DOI: 10.4018/978-1-7998-9183-3.ch004

1. INTRODUCTION

Quantum Computing will rescript the definition of impossible, making a world of all possibilities. To begin with we will go back to a popular example of Schrödinger's cat of Quantum Mechanics that demonstrates the paradox of superposition. A cat is left in room with assumption that no one is watching. A hammer is present connected to pulley above a green coloured poison. If the cat tamper with the pulley, it falls on the glass tube containing poison and the cat will die, otherwise, it is alive. So, an observer, is in a superposition of state that whether the cat is dead or alive. The probability of being alive and dead is half. Similarly, if we take an un-biased coin toss it to make a decision, it ends up with a head or a tail. But, if it is a quantum-based coin, it will spin and spin and never come back to make a decision, once it takes a decision, the problem becomes classical and not quantum mechanics based. Why Quantum? The universe can be thought of a quantum computer, with a massive amount of quantum computation going on regular basis. Quantum Computing is one of the most hyped topics in today's world due to the capability to compute task in real-time and used in numerous fields like Machine Learning, Artificial Intelligence, Big Data, Neural Networks, etc. The beginning of this concept had already originated in 1980 by the pioneering proposal of Benioff and Feynman, who proposed the idea that systems using quantum concept rather than classical ones are capable of dealing with more complex problems (Benioff, 1980).

Quantum Turing Machine was proposed and universal models were developed based on quantum mechanics (Deutsch, 1985) and proved. The computational capabilities of classical computers are enhanced by quantum models, showing advantage over classical algorithms to solve complex problems. Factorization of large prime numbers is considered as one of the NP-Hard problem. A quantum algorithm for solving this was proposed by Shor in 1994 (Shor, 1994). He proved that only in polynomial time, the RSA encryption used in factorization problem can be deciphered by using quantum mechanism. Further, Groover research mechanism for finding data from an un-ordered database by use of quantum searching. He implemented quantum parallelism, processing all data at the same time thereby reducing complexity and time consumption. By these and many more quantum algorithms have attracted researchers in the area of algorithm design.

Since ten researchers and scientist have study various aspects of quantum algorithms and its applications and further have experimented and designed many efficient algorithms in various fields. For this they have implemented and brought forth the concept of qubits which are quantum bits for computation in quantum environment. A conventional classical digital computing has the information stored in bits taking definite binary values as '0' and '1'. In contrast, Quantum computers, has the capability of accessing large Hilbert space i.e computational space, where there are n number of bits called qubits. These are in 2n number of outcomes at a given time called superposition state, this overcomes large space problem. Although these qubits are more reliable for computation than classical bits but are prone to environmental noise. Physicist John Preskill proposed the concept of Noisy Intermediate Scale Quantum (NISQ) technology for upcoming generation quantum systems which will be resistant to external noise factor (Preskill, 2018). The major challenge faced by qubits are decoherence, thereby degrading the mechanism of information processing capabilities. This paved a path for the future research in quantum computing arena, by minimizing the noise effect without comprising on information processing by various quantum algorithms. Next, major problem arises for connectivity of qubits with inter and inter qubits connectivity and couplings for a better quantum device functionality. Another, major challenge is to achieve real-time applications and problem not traceable by classical computing, which has been started by many companies like Google long back (Ball, 2016) and also is adapted globally for development.

Some of the proposed intelligent algorithms of quantum computing includes Quantum Clustering Algorithms, Quantum Evolutionary Algorithms, Quantum Neural Network, Quantum Particle Swarm Optimization Algorithms, Quantum Wavelet Transform, Quantum Machine Learning based Algorithms. These algorithms are being implemented and tested in real quantum systems to compete with the traditional computational intelligent algorithms. The quantum algorithms can be basically classified as Optimization algorithms and Learning algorithms. Some of which will be discuss later in this chapter.

1.1 Structure of Quantum Mechanism

Some of the base principles of quantum mechanics includes quantum interference, quantum entanglement and superposition. Quantum mechanisms and technologies are still in incubation phase gradually increasing its domain. The figure 1 below depicts building blocks of a quantum-based system consisting of central processing units, gates, circuitry, memory, error detection and correction. Quantum states performs quantum operations; quantum error correction and detection can locate and correct errors during ongoing operation. The array of quantum states, inputs to form a stable system constitutes quantum memory.

A. Quantum Algorithms

Quantum algorithms come a long way from simulation of quantum physics to quantum computers. These have high computing power and can process large volumes of data. Daniel Simon was to propose quantum algorithm that was first of its type providing high evaluation than that of classical algorithms (Ball, 2016). We have classified these algorithms as Quantum Optimization, Quantum Learning and Quantum Clustering.

B. Quantum Optimization

These are algorithms proposed for computing optimization problem with accuracy and speed due to the functionality of parallel execution. Quantum optimization provides a global search strategy with quantum based intelligent algorithms and processing capabilities. Here, we have briefly noted down some of the quantum optimization algorithms along with future challenges and research scope.

2. QUANTUM EVOLUTIONARY ALGORITHM (QEA)

The QEA is a robust and efficient quantum computing algorithm based on evolutionary algorithms. The fist quantum evolutionary proposal started with implementation of genetic algorithm on quantum computing scenario (Narayanan & Moore, 1996). A QEA algorithm must have the functionality of global search space with faster convergence and high population density. These can easily be implemented with other algorithms too.

Quantum-based evolutionary algorithms simulated quantum bits, superposition, measurements, gates for classical computers with its standardized framework. In general, this line of work intends to benefit from a richer quantum representation. These quantum-bits are simulated which permits linear superposition of different states, handled by quantum gates (Zhang, 2011)(Krylov & Lukac, 2019). In 1996, Narayanan demonstrated the principles of quantum mechanics for evolutionary methods (Narayanan & Moore, 1996) to solve Travelling Salesman Problem (TPS); by qubits fixed-point interference operator. Then after, this methodology was in used for quantum algorithms to tackle Np-hard problems with high feasibility and reliability.

Contrast to traditional evolutionary algorithms, QEA is implemented on quantum bit, for superposition of quantum chromosome involving multiple states. The size of population is small and can handle diversity, making it suitable for parallel computation and searching with high efficiency. QEA was further extended to Genetic Quantum Algorithm (GQA).

Figure 1. Structure of Quantum Mechanism

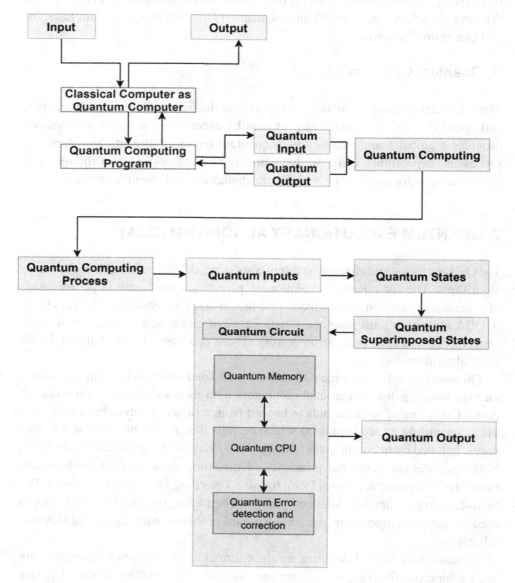

3. REAL-CODED QUANTUM-INSPIRED EVOLUTIONARY ALGORITHM

(RQIEA) is an enhanced version of QEA algorithm. This algorithm used real-values function for quantum optimization as, proposed in (da Cruz et al., 2007) which was further simplified in, which use real coded form rather than binary-coded form as that of the later. The RQIEA deal with two different populations, i.e. it maintains a differentiation between population of quantum chromosomes and observed population containing real-valued vector solutions. Here, Q(t) have N quantum individuals q_i, i = 1, 2, . . ., N, with each individual having G genes. Each gene is represented g_{ij} = (ρ_{ij}, σ_{ij}) where, j = 1, 2, . . ., G. The mean and width of a squared pulse are denoted as ρ_{ij} and σ_{ij}, respectively. Each gene depicts an interval in the search space. The flow of RQIEA algorithm is described in figure 2.

Figure 2. Flow of RQIEA

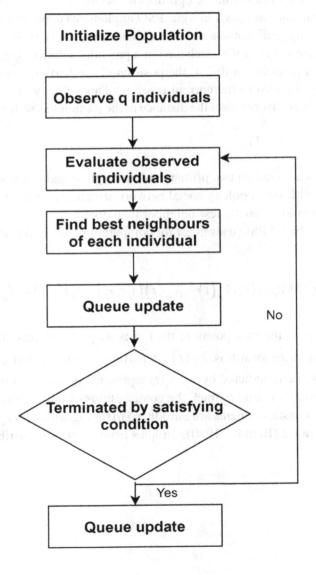

4. QUANTUM INSPIRED PARTICLE SWARM OPTIMIZATION

It is part of Quantum Swarm Algorithm with merging of QEA and Particle Swarm Optimization technique (Alfares & Esat, 2006). It uses different Q-bit denotation termed quantum angle which are updated by improved PSO method. The proposed mechanism was implemented for traveling salesman problem (TSP) as well as for 0-1 knapsack problem.

The Swarm Intelligence Algorithms are inspiration of swarm or colonies formed by social organisms. They iterate with neighboring individuals and environment for communication. PSO is a stochastic optimization technique with social behavior of various organisms such as flies, birds etc. PSO implements population-based search mechanism with hyperdimensional search space cumulatively called swarm. Here, the particle set are swarm with peach having a potential solution. Let, $x_i(t)$ denotes the position of a particle i at time t, the position of the particle i is changed by a velocity term $v_i(t)$ added to the current position. This velocity vector depicts the optimization process. It considers the distance of the particles as well as the velocity.

$$x_i(t + 1) = x_i(t) + v_i(t + 1)$$

Initial PSO was based on two primary solutions gbest and lbest; where gbest is the global best with star topology social network structure and lbest was the local best with ring topology having less neighbor than gbest.

The quantum based PSO uses gbest for computation, where particle velocity is computed as:

$$V_{ij}(t+1) = V_{ij}(t) + c_1 r_1 j(t)[Y_{ij}(t) - X_{ij}(t)] + c_2 r_2 j(t)[\hat{Y}_j(t) - X_{ij}(t)]$$

If particle i is in the best position, then yi is its personal best. Therefore, the optimal position in the swarm is $\hat{Y}_j(t)$. A particle i in dimension j, j = 1......,∞, at time t has a velocity indicted by V_{ij}. $X_{ij}(t)$ represents the position of particle i in dimension j at time t; c_1 and c_2 track the contributions of the cognitive and social components. Stochastic elements are introduced to the algorithm by $r_1 j(t)$ and $r_2 j(t)$. They are in the range (Benioff, 1980), samples from a uniform distribution.

5. SOME OF THE OTHER ALGORITHMS

5.1 Quantum learning algorithms

Intelligent Optimization has been growing its pace with Quantum computing. Then researchers came up with the idea of quantum implementation with learning algorithm taking into account advantage of quantum computing for learning algorithms. Quantum Neural Network (QNN) is one of its mostly used algorithms.

A. Quantum Neural Network (QNN)

QNN is a supervised learning technique, developed as feed-forward networks. The QNN takes input from one layer of qubits and passes further. The qubits layer computes information and forwards the results to the next output layer, leading to final layer of output. The layers are not necessarily having same qubits numbers in every layers. The layers are trained for modelling as in Artificial Neural Networks. For neuron simulation a threshold logic unit, M-P neuron model is proposed (Wang et al., 2007). The fist idea for quantum neural network was proposed in 1995 by Subash Kak and Ron Chrisleyln. For synapses simulation, Hebb proposed a model which is a building model for learning neural network model (McCulloch & Pitts, 1943). According to researchers it was found that QNN had better performance than traditional Neural Networks and thereafter, new QNN models were developed. It is estimated that a single quantum neuron performs XOR functions that is not achieved by classical neuron. QNN has been growing is application rapidly, and for training the model various training algorithms are proposed.

A complex version of the learning algorithm is one of the areas of focus. (Nitta, 1993) demonstrates the back-propagation algorithm using a complex numbered version, and (Nitta, 1994) discusses the characteristics of the learning rule. Using quantum conjugate gradients, a back-propagation network is built in (Zhang et al., 2010). Conjugate gradient algorithms are preferred over steepest gradient algorithms to accelerate convergence. The complex-valued version of (Chen et al., 2005) also proposes a backpropagation algorithm by including an error component in the conventional error function. The algorithm outlined in (Li et al., 2006) is designed to deal with the local minima problem. Moreover, (Zhang et al., 2016) places a greater emphasis on training QNN connection weights and thresholds using an improved PSO. The multi-layer QNN is trained supervised, instead of using back-propagation, by applying a real-coded genetic algorithm in (Takahashi et al., 2014).

B. Quantum Clustering Algorithms

It is data clustering algorithm using conceptual and mathematical tools for quantum computations. The clusters are formed by maximum density data points. It is mostly implemented for data mining and used in data analysis and knowledge discovery process. It is also used in fields like computer vision, pattern recognition and information retrieval. Cluster analysis is done to segregate objects to various categories based on its similarities. The clustering algorithms are categorized as density-based, partition-based, grid-based and hierarchy-based (Rosenblatt, 1958). Further, it can be classified based on Evolutionary inspired quantum mechanics and quantum optimization. Evolutionary mechanism is used to find the optimum solution to update clustering center and minimize the dependency on the previous center. In (Xu & Wunsch, 2005), authors used gradient descent to solve potential energy computation and estimation of clustering center and in (Xie & Beni, 1991) authors took clustering on physical basis. Appropriate cluster centers can be computed by Schrodinger equation and gradient descent mechanism.

In quantum optimization-based clustering optimizes the clustering for better results. For better performance similarity of data is computed for clustering by the formula below;

$$P\left(C^*\right) = MIN_{c \in \Omega} P\left(C\right)$$

where $_\Omega$ is set of clustering results, C is dataset division and P is computed criterion function for checking the data similarity. To minimize the value of P, the function is optimized using quantum optimization algorithm. Compared to traditional clustering, the function P is not much difference. The implementation of quantum optimization in quantum clustering makes the difference, representing the results as qubits, thereby increasing the probability of global optimum. The flow of generalized clustering mechanism in quantum is depicted in figure 3.

Clustering techniques such as fuzzy C-means clustering and K-means quantum clustering are among their basic types. In (Horn & Gottlieb, 2001), the fuzzy C-Hadrian method and quadratic clustering methods are merged, and network structure is presented at several levels. A fuzzy C-Means soft clustering algorithm is combined with random fuzzy membership input in (Sun & Hao, 2009) to enable the segmentation of remote-sensed multi-band images. Furthermore, a quantum local potential function network, which utilizes waves and potential functions to inherit the outstanding features of QC, is discussed in (Zhong et al., 2010). (Lu & Zhao, 2010) avoids the sinking of the updated cluster centers into areas of obstacles by introducing the detour distance in QPSO, as well as a particle escaping principle. The algorithm used in (Zhang et al., 2012) updates the number of cluster centroids in a dynamic manner in order to reduce particle accumulation near boundary conditions and find optimal conditions in a variety of dimensions in order to overcome the problem of predefined cluster numbers in PSO. Using quantum entanglement-based discrete PSO, the clustering of complex networks can be achieved using reference (Li et al., 2017). QPSO and K-medioids used together allows (Teng-Fei & Xue-Ping, 2010) to further simplify the procedure of separating clusters by using QPSO and K-medioids. The QPSO clustering algorithm is paired with fuzzy C-means clustering in (Sengupta et al., 2018). Soft clustering of FCM assists with partitioning and reducing stagnation in local optima by using membership probabilities, whereas global search of QPSO helps avoid stagnation. Generally, clustering criteria selection is a hotspot. Gradient descent is used as the clustering technique inspired by quantum mechanics to determine the clustering center. Taking advantage of quantum mechanics, this method fully utilizes the information contained in data by making use of particle distribution in quantum space.

Figure 3. Flow of Quantum Clustering

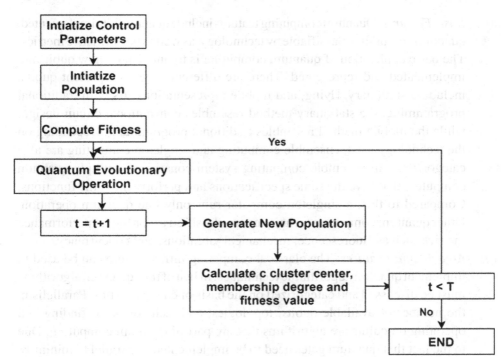

6. TAXONOMY OF QUANTUM

The following sections describe the different types of quantum computing technologies and their operating methods in detail. A quantum computing taxonomy comprises the following elements: a) Basic Features, b) Algorithmic Features, c) Gate Time Features, and d) Other characteristics. Figure 4 illustrates a diagrammatic depiction of quantum computing's taxonomy (Gill et al., 2020). The following subsections have brief descriptions of each of the elements in quantum computing taxonomy.

Figure 4. Quantum Taxonomy (Gill et al., 2020)

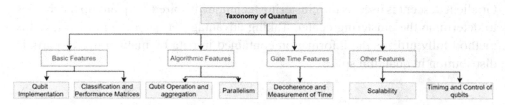

a) *Basic Features:* Quantum computing features include quantum bits implemented, quantum computing classifiable by technology, as well as performance metrics. The basic application of quantum computing is to understand how qubits are implemented and represented. There are different ways to represent qubits, including stationary, flying, and mobile representations. As with traditional programming, the stationary method resembles conventional circuit design, while the mobile method resembles traditional programming. Depending on the technology used, ensemble computing and singleton computing are also categorized. An ensemble computing system consists of multiple quantum computers that have the same specifications and perform the same functions. Compared to this, a singleton computer runs only one quantum operation. Other quantum computing techniques are classified according to performance metrics such as fluorescence, mechanical vibrations, and concurrency.

b) *Algorithmic Features*: The classical computing infrastructure can be used to implement quantum algorithmic techniques. In lieu of this, quantum algorithms must be discussed and categorized on the basis of characteristics. Parallelism, the number of available qubits, topologies, and techniques for finding and operating on qubits are algorithms that are part of quantum computing. Due to the fact that quantum gates need to be implemented in parallel to minimize or prevent qubit decoherence, parallelism is a crucial feature. In addition to the aggregate number of available qubits, the quantum computer can also be scalable and reliable. Quantum computers can be thought of as having multiple topologies in terms of arranging different physical devices. An optimized architecture ensures the smooth flow of data and information between the different physical units of the system. It is logically very complex to address each qubit individually. In terms of the quantum computer physical implementation, this feature enables us to examine qubit states more precisely.

c) *Gate Time Features*: Quantum computing technologies can also be classified according to their gate and time characteristics, which include decoherence times and measurement times. Qubits can be held in a particular state up to the decoherence time. Nowadays, quantum computing researchers are investigating the decoherence time. The measurement time (time required to precisely measure the qubit state) is another essential characteristic of classification.

d) *Other Characteristics:* Further classification of quantum computing technologies takes into account few other aspects of quantum computing such as scalability or control of gate levels of qubits. Qubits can scale up to larger numbers based on all the above-mentioned features. To prevent constant representation of a single ion or photon, it is recommended to use multiple qubits. As qubit states change continuously over time, it is essential that gates be timed accurately. In order to place multiple qubits in their relative phases simultaneously, their arrival times should be precisely adjusted.

7. OPEN RESEARCH CHALLENGES AND FUTURE DIRECTIONS

Quantum computation is still a challenging problem because experimental quantum error correction does not exist. Since quantum states are delicate, quantum error correction cannot be performed. Bits must be operated at very low temperatures, and fabrication should be extremely precise. Verification is also difficult due to the challenge of measuring the quantum state in its entirety accurately. Comparing classical computing to modern computing, there is a significant risk of errors. In order for quantum architectures to function as intended, an effective error correction mechanism is needed. To verify precise fabrication constraints, quantum communication architecture will need to be redesigned. In order to reduce the occurrence of error, qubit placement must be avoided, which is very difficult after fabrication due to tight tolerances. To achieve sustainable quantum computation, recursive error correction is required. Automated detection and correction of errors can be achieved in the future using AI and machine learning techniques to provide valuable and reliable services. Nevertheless, the AI/ML techniques require more training.

Supercomputers consume a great deal of energy to solve different problems, so energy management is a major challenge in the field. The performance of quantum computers should be superior to that of supercomputers. A quantum computer, on the other hand, uses less energy to conduct extensive calculations, thereby reducing emissions. The quantum computer has the property of enabling identification of optimal solutions for complex problems while using a less amount of energy, unlike the classic computer, which employs binary bits (0s or 1s). Quantum processors consume less energy because they are designed to operate at low temperatures, and they are superconducting without any resistance, which means that they don't generate any heat. The hybrid applications fall into two categories: high- and low-energy. The quantum part is executed using quantum computing, and the classical part is executed using the cloud. In order to curb energy consumption and costs dramatically, hybrid computing must be implemented to solve these problems. Before hybrid computing can be used to solve today's most challenging business problems, more research must be conducted. In order to improve computational speed, reliability, and security using quantum computing, which is energy-intensive, cooling devices can be used to control the temperature. It might be possible to satisfy the energy demand of quantum computers by utilizing renewable energy.

When powerful quantum computers become widely available in the future, unconditionally secure quantum cloud computing can be a major ingredient in various real-life applications. In a cloud, a few powerful quantum-computers could significantly improve the client's productivity. A quantum link would be needed for the client to transfer their job and associated qubits to the quantum cloud. There have been efforts in this direction to demonstrate blind quantum computing where inputs, delegations, computations, and outputs are unknown to the quantum servers. However, such advances have been constrained because quantum clusters are universal and powerful. Secure quantum computations that can be verified cryptographically, quantum cloud computing, and quantum cryptography primitives that are error-free for cloud computing, as well as quantum techniques for access control. As a result, quantum cloud computing needs to be studied in-depth in order to be secure and efficient on a large scale. To support the quantum computing community, cloud-based environments would be an efficient way to store, compute, and distribute data. Typically, network latency and bandwidth can be a barrier to the execution of small tasks in these systems, but edge or fog computing can solve these problems. Moreover, a blockchain-based service can provide a secure and reliable means of communication.

8. CONCLUSION

A structured review of quantum computing literature is presented in this chapter. A taxonomy of quantum computing is presented along with open challenges, and promising future directions. To date, a single quantum computing technique lacks the ability to combine all the performance attributes. The most suitable quantum computing method for building a quantum computer that can perform concurrent operations is one that can incorporate all of the necessary classified features with quantum I/O. Using the proposed taxonomy framework, the best strategy that can be applied to classical computing infrastructure can be compared against existing quantum computing methods. A topic of research in the field of quantum computing is the scaling of quantum bits and the trade-off between speed and decoherence time.

Further, the current industrial quantum computers are not yet capable of replacing classical supercomputers on account of scaling problems with the number of qubits that can be operationally realized. There is still uncertainty about when quantum computers will start replacing classical counterparts in complex tasks, even though the next decade is poised to be thrilling for industrial quantum computers. While quantum computing will become a reality in the future, digital supercomputers will endure. The key design challenge is to make the quantum algorithm run efficiently. It requires a large number of physical qubits, which require tight and continuous connections between the classical platform and quantum chip, creating a huge control overhead. Due to quantum error correction, which is still an open problem, fault-tolerant and reliable quantum computations are challenging to achieve. Considering the fragile nature of quantum states, bits must be operated at extremely low temperatures, and fabrication should be precise. Energy management is an important area of research in quantum computing. The use of hybrid computing is needed to drastically reduce energy consumption and costs by combining quantum and classical computing. To solve today's toughest business problems, hybrid computing needs more work before it can be implemented practically. The design of quantum simulators can take advantage of the entanglement and superposition properties of quantum computing while taking into account complex quantum experiments. AI-based robotics deal with a variety of problems utilizing graph search to find new information, but complexity grows as more data is amassed. Quantum algorithms will benefit a variety of fields, including security, finance, biomedical, chemical, and economic development.

REFERENCES

Alfares, F. S., & Esat, I. I. (2006, November). Real-coded quantum inspired evolution algorithm applied to engineering optimization problems. In *Second International Symposium on Leveraging Applications of Formal Methods, Verification and Validation (isola 2006)* (pp. 169-176). IEEE. 10.1109/ISoLA.2006.12

Ball, P. (2016). Google moves closer to a universal quantum computer. *NATNews*. Advance online publication. doi:10.1038/nature.2016.20032

Benioff, P. (1980). The computer as a physical system: A microscopic quantum mechanical Hamiltonian model of computers as represented by Turing machines. *Journal of Statistical Physics, 22*(5), 563–591. doi:10.1007/BF01011339

Chen, X., Tang, Z., & Li, S. (2005). An modified error function for the complex-value backpropagation. *Neural Information Processing-Letters and Reviews, 8*(1).

da Cruz, A. A., Vellasco, M. M. B. R., & Pacheco, M. A. C. (2007). Quantum-inspired evolutionary algorithm for numerical optimization. In *Hybrid evolutionary algorithms* (pp. 19–37). Springer. doi:10.1007/978-3-540-73297-6_2

Deutsch, D. (1985). Quantum theory, the Church–Turing principle and the universal quantum computer. *Proceedings of the Royal Society of London. A. Mathematical and Physical Sciences, 400*(1818), 97-117.

Gill, S. S., Kumar, A., Singh, H., Singh, M., Kaur, K., Usman, M., & Buyya, R. (2020). *Quantum computing: A taxonomy, systematic review and future directions.* arXiv preprint arXiv:2010.15559.

Horn, D., & Gottlieb, A. (2001). Algorithm for data clustering in pattern recognition problems based on quantum mechanics. *Physical Review Letters, 88*(1), 018702. doi:10.1103/PhysRevLett.88.018702 PMID:11800996

Krylov, G., & Lukac, M. (2019, April). Quantum encoded quantum evolutionary algorithm for the design of quantum circuits. In *Proceedings of the 16th ACM International Conference on Computing Frontiers* (pp. 220-225). 10.1145/3310273.3322826

Li, L., Jiao, L., Zhao, J., Shang, R., & Gong, M. (2017). Quantum-behaved discrete multi-objective particle swarm optimization for complex network clustering. *Pattern Recognition, 63*, 1–14. doi:10.1016/j.patcog.2016.09.013

Li, S., Okada, T., Chen, X., & Tang, Z. (2006, May). An individual adaptive gain parameter backpropagation algorithm for complex-valued neural networks. In *International Symposium on Neural Networks* (pp. 551-557). Springer. 10.1007/11759966_82

Lu, P., & Zhao, A. X. (2010, December). Fuzzy clustering with obstructed distance based on quantum-behaved particle swarm optimization. In *2010 Second WRI Global Congress on Intelligent Systems* (Vol. 1, pp. 302-305). IEEE. 10.1109/GCIS.2010.57

McCulloch, W. S., & Pitts, W. (1943). A logical calculus of the ideas immanent in nervous activity. *The Bulletin of Mathematical Biophysics*, *5*(4), 115–133. doi:10.1007/BF02478259

Narayanan, A., & Moore, M. (1996, May). Quantum-inspired genetic algorithms. In *Proceedings of IEEE international conference on evolutionary computation* (pp. 61-66). IEEE. 10.1109/ICEC.1996.542334

Nitta, T. (1993, October). A back-propagation algorithm for complex numbered neural networks. In *Proceedings of 1993 International Conference on Neural Networks (IJCNN-93-Nagoya, Japan)* (Vol. 2, pp. 1649-1652). IEEE. 10.1109/IJCNN.1993.716968

Nitta, T. (1994, June). Structure of learning in the complex numbered back-propagation network. In *Proceedings of 1994 IEEE International Conference on Neural Networks (ICNN'94)* (Vol. 1, pp. 269-274). IEEE. 10.1109/ICNN.1994.374173

Preskill, J. (2018). Quantum Computing in the NISQ era and beyond. *Quantum, 2*, 79. arXiv preprint arXiv:1801.00862.

Rosenblatt, F. (1958). The perceptron: A probabilistic model for information storage and organization in the brain. *Psychological Review*, *65*(6), 386–408. doi:10.1037/h0042519 PMID:13602029

Sengupta, S., Basak, S., & Peters, R. A. (2018, January). Data clustering using a hybrid of fuzzy c-means and quantum-behaved particle swarm optimization. In *2018 IEEE 8th Annual Computing and Communication Workshop and Conference (CCWC)* (pp. 137-142). IEEE. 10.1109/CCWC.2018.8301693

Shor, P. W. (1994, November). Algorithms for quantum computation: discrete logarithms and factoring. In *Proceedings 35th annual symposium on foundations of computer science* (pp. 124-134). IEEE. 10.1109/SFCS.1994.365700

Sun, J., & Hao, S. N. (2009, January). Research of fuzzy neural network model based on quantum clustering. In *2009 Second International Workshop on Knowledge Discovery and Data Mining* (pp. 133-136). IEEE. 10.1109/WKDD.2009.193

Takahashi, Kurokawa, & Hashimoto. (2014). *Multi-layer Quantum Neural Network Controller Trained by Real-Coded Genetic Algorithm*. Elsevier.

Teng-Fei, Y., & Xue-Ping, Z. (2010, September). Spatial clustering algorithm with obstacles constraints by quantum particle swarm optimization and K-Medoids. In *2010 Second International Conference on Computational Intelligence and Natural Computing* (Vol. 2, pp. 105-108). IEEE. 10.1109/CINC.2010.5643776

Wang, Y., Feng, X. Y., Huang, Y. X., Pu, D. B., Zhou, W. G., Liang, Y. C., & Zhou, C. G. (2007). A novel quantum swarm evolutionary algorithm and its applications. *Neurocomputing*, *70*(4-6), 633–640. doi:10.1016/j.neucom.2006.10.001

Xie, X. L., & Beni, G. (1991). A validity measure for fuzzy clustering. *IEEE Transactions on Pattern Analysis and Machine Intelligence*, *13*(8), 841–847. doi:10.1109/34.85677

Xu, R., & Wunsch, D. II. (2005). Survey of clustering algorithms. *IEEE Transactions on Neural Networks*, *16*(3), 645–678. doi:10.1109/TNN.2005.845141 PMID:15940994

Zhang, G. (2011). Quantum-inspired evolutionary algorithms: A survey and empirical study. *Journal of Heuristics*, *17*(3), 303–351. doi:10.100710732-010-9136-0

Zhang, L., Lu, Y., & Liu, J. (2010, August). Deep web interfaces classification using QCGBP network. In *2010 5th International Conference on Computer Science & Education* (pp. 457-461). IEEE. 10.1109/ICCSE.2010.5593580

Zhang, L., Zhang, L., Yang, G. Z., & Zhang, M. (2012). A quantum particle swarm optimization clustering algorithm using variable dimensions searching. *Journal of Chinese Computer Systems*, *33*(4), 804–808.

Zhang, Q., Lai, X., & Liu, G. (2016, August). Emotion recognition of GSR based on an improved quantum neural network. In *2016 8th International Conference on Intelligent Human-Machine Systems and Cybernetics (IHMSC)* (Vol. 1, pp. 488-492). IEEE. 10.1109/IHMSC.2016.66

Zhong, Q., Yao, M., & Jiang, W. (2010, April). Quantum fuzzy particle swarm optimization algorithm for image clustering. In *2010 International Conference on Image Analysis and Signal Processing* (pp. 276-279). IEEE. 10.1109/IASP.2010.5476115

KEY TERMS AND DEFINITIONS

Evolutionary Algorithm: The evolutionary algorithm (EA) emulates the behavior of living organisms by using mechanisms inspired by nature to solve problems. Both evolutionary computing and bio-inspired computing incorporate EA. Evolutionary algorithms are modeled after Darwin's concepts.

Noisy Intermediate Scale Quantum: A noisy intermediate-scale quantum (NISQ) processor contains 50 to a few hundred qubits, but are neither sufficiently advanced nor large enough to profit sustainably from quantum supremacy. This term describes the current state of the art in quantum processor fabrication. The term 'noisy' refers to quantum processors that are very sensitive to their environment and may lose their quantum state due to quantum decoherence. During the era of NISQ, quantum processors are not advanced enough to continuously use quantum error correction.

Quantum Clustering: Quantum Clustering refers to a class of algorithms that use concepts and mathematical tools from quantum mechanics to cluster data. Clusters are defined by higher densities of data points, and QC belongs to the family of density-based clustering algorithms.

Quantum Computing: A quantum computing system is a computer technology based on quantum theory (which explains how energy and matter behave at atomic and subatomic levels). Modern computers can only encode information in bits that have a value of 1 or 0, which limits their capabilities. Qubits, on the other hand, are an essential part of quantum computing. It takes advantage of the unique property of subatomic particles, which allows them to exist in more than one state at once (i.e., as a 1 and a 0).

Quantum Machine Learning: Quantum machine learning is the integration of quantum algorithms into machine learning programs. Quantum algorithms can be used to analyze quantum states instead of analyzing classical data. Furthermore, quantum algorithms can be used to analyze quantum states instead of classical data. These routines can be more complex in nature and executed more quickly on a quantum computer.

Quantum Mechanics: Fundamental to physics, quantum mechanics describes the physical properties of matter on an atomic level and at a subatomic scale. Among its many applications are quantum chemistry, quantum field theory, quantum technology, and quantum information science.

Quantum Neural Network: The quantum neural network is a computational neural network that is based on quantum mechanics. Machine learning algorithms and quantum neural networks (QNN) combine concepts from quantum computing and artificial neural networks. In the past decade, the term has been applied to describe a variety of ideas, ranging from quantum computers that emulate the exact functions of neural nets to general trainable quantum circuits that bear little resemblance to the multilayer structure of perceptron.

Quantum Optimization: A quantum optimization algorithm is used to solve a problem of optimization. From a set of possible solutions, mathematical optimization aims to find the most optimal solution. Most optimization problems are presented as minimization problems, where one attempts to minimize an error which is a function of the solution: the optimal solution has the smallest error. There are many optimization techniques used in fields like mechanics, economics, and engineering, and as the complexity and amount of data involved rise, it becomes increasingly important to find more efficient solutions to optimization problems. There is a possibility that quantum computing may allow problems which are beyond the capabilities of classical computers to be resolved, or may suggest a significant speedup over the fastest known classical algorithm.

APPENDIX

Google's breakthrough in quantum computation has increased interest in the field. Some of the other use-cases of quantum computing include: Optimization, Research, Cryptography, Industry applications with significant impact in healthcare, business and science. The first quantum computing platforms are being offered by Google, IBM, and Microsoft. In addition, many other companies aim to lead the way in their areas of specialization using quantum computing. With the help of quantum simulations, Bosch, for example, is developing new energy storage and functional materials. Optimization problems exist in every industry and in every business function, and some of them are too complicated to solve with traditional computers. These problems can be solved using quantum computers by using the following techniques: ● An optimization heuristic called quantum annealing is expected to be superior to classical computers in certain optimization problems. It is far simpler and cheaper to construct specialized quantum annealers than a universal quantum computer for quantum annealing. However, it has yet to be demonstrated definitively that such computers are superior to classical computers. Using classical computing, cheaper digital annealers simulate quantum annealers.

● The universal quantum computer is capable of addressing a wide range of computational problems. Their commercial availability will take longer, however, as more research is needed to increase their reliability.

Here are a few optimization problems from various industries where firms are relying on quantum computing instead of sub-optimal heuristics:

● Transportation:
  ○ Using quantum computing for the design of autonomous vehicles is one way Volkswagen and Google are collaborating to optimize large autonomous fleets.
● Energy:
  ○ The Dubai Electricity and Water Authority (DEWA) has been working with Microsoft to optimize energy efficiency using quantum computing since 2020.
  ○ The U.S. Department of Energy (DOE) has established two labs dedicated to the integration of quantum computing into grid optimization.
  ○ For precise weather forecasting, IBM employs quantum computing, which is currently used by almost all consumer tech giants such as Apple, Amazon, Google, and Facebook.

- Finance:
  - Predicting financial markets by using automated trading.
  - In 2020, Banks will be using quantum computing for risk classification in a pilot program.
  - In 2021, quantum computing is being tested against any other benchmarking method for near-term investments in their portfolio management benchmarking pilot.
  - In 2022, PayPal will partner with IBM to use quantum computing for fraud detection.
- Insurance:
  - For data intensive tasks such as identifying health anomalies, Anthem plans to use IBM's quantum computing solution for the valuation of instruments and premiums in complex cases.
- Logistics:
  - In a research study, DWave, a QC company, partnered with Toyota for traffic prediction and optimization using QC. The study showed that QC produces better results than existing tools.
  - Supply chain and inventory optimization: QC applications have yet to be established as a solution for supply chain optimization, but big companies such as Coca Cola Japan have begun large-scale pilot programs.
- Pharmaceutical:
  - Using quantum computing for molecular comparison in drug development.
  - The adoption of personalized medicine that takes into account genomics.
- Technology
  - Machine learning: Quantum computers have the potential of accelerating machine learning processes drastically

Chapter 5
A Review on Applications of Quantum Computing in Machine Learning

Subrata Paul
Maulana Abul Kalam Azad University of Technology, India

Anirban Mitra
(iD) https://orcid.org/0000-0002-6639-4407
ASET, Amity University, Kolkata, India

ABSTRACT

Computational technologies drive progress in industry, science, government, and society. While these technologies form the foundation for intelligent systems and enable scientific and business innovation, they are also the limiting factors for progress. Quantum computing promises to overcome these limitations with better and faster solutions for optimization, simulation, and machine learning problems. Quantum computing is broadly applicable to business problems in optimization, machine learning, and simulation, impacting all industries. In the last couple of years, researchers investigated if quantum computing can help to improve classical machine learning algorithms. Therefore, it is instrumental for industry to seek an active role in this emergent ecosystem. In this chapter, the authors present a brief overview on various applications of quantum computing in machine learning.

DOI: 10.4018/978-1-7998-9183-3.ch005

1. INTRODUCTION

The proliferation of personal computers and the emergence of the Internet have fueled the need for more and more computing power. The trend for decades has been packing more computing power into smaller spaces. People are turning to different ways of computing, such as quantum computing, to find ways to cut energy use. It is believed that quantum computers will harness the power of atoms and molecules to perform memory and processing tasks. Quantum computers could be exponentially faster at running artificial-intelligence programs and handling complex simulations and scheduling problems.

Quantum computing is the study of information processing tasks using quantum mechanical principles. It combines ideas from classical information theory, computer science, and quantum physics. It is commonly believed that QC holds the key to true artificial intelligence.

One of the significant advantages of quantum computation is the ability of massively parallel computation. By using a quantum superposition state, $2n$ inputs can be stored in n qubits simultaneously. Since universal quantum gates allow us to design an arbitrary quantum circuit, the n qubits can be used as the input for a quantum circuit, which performs an arbitrary computation. For example, four classical values {0, 1, 2, and 3} can be stored in two qubits simultaneously, which can be written as the state (6). For example, a circuit can be designed to compute $(x)=x+5$. It seems that four computations can be performed with only one step by placing the qubits in the superposition states in the circuit. However, the output state is a superposition state of four possible output values {5, 6, 7, and 8}. The result of the measurement on the output qubits is one of the four possible outputs. In short, when a classical logic is implemented as a quantum circuit, the output qubits are the superposition of $2n$ outputs for $2n$ inputs.

The interest in using quantum computers to compute artificial intelligent algorithms has increased exponentially with the many successful implementations of AI showing that quantum computers can be relied for calculations.

Quantum machine learning is the integration of quantum algorithms within machine learning programs (Schuld et al., 2014; Wittek, 2014; Biamonte et al., 2017). The most common use of the term refers to machine learning algorithms for the analysis of classical data executed on a quantum computer, i.e. quantum-enhanced machine learning. While machine learning algorithms are used to compute immense quantities of data, quantum machine learning utilizes qubits and quantum operations or specialized quantum systems to improve computational speed and data storage done by algorithms in a program (Perdomo-Ortiz et al., 2018). This includes hybrid methods that involve both classical and quantum processing, where computationally difficult subroutines are outsourced to a quantum device. Beyond quantum computing, the term "quantum machine learning" is also associated with classical machine learning methods applied to data generated from quantum experiments (i.e. machine learning of quantum systems), such as learning the phase transitions of a quantum system or creating new quantum experiments (Wiebe et al., 2014). Quantum machine learning also extends to a branch of research that explores methodological and structural similarities between certain physical systems and learning systems, in particular neural networks (Huembeli et al., 2018).

The chapter is organized as follows. In section 2, the authors have presented a brief literature review on the existing papers which are present in this area. In the subsequent section 3, authors have discussed on a few basic concepts related to the quantum computing. Further in section 4, a discussion has been made on the approaches taken to enhance the application of machine learning through quantum computing. In section 5, authors have illustrated the different machine learning applications in quantum computing. Finally a conclusion to the paper is drawn in section 6.

2. LITERATURE REVIEW

Quite a few studies have been made by the researchers around the world regarding the study of quantum computing. Some of the works have been discussed by the authors in the present section. (Lloyd et al., 2013) in their paper provided supervised and unsupervised quantum machine learning algorithms for cluster assignment and cluster finding. Quantum machine learning can take time logarithmic in both the number of vectors and their dimension, an exponential speed-up over classical algorithms. (Schuld et al., 2014) Researchers investigated if quantum computing can help to improve classical machine learning algorithms. Ideas range from running computationally costly algorithms or their subroutines efficiently on a quantum computer to the translation of stochastic methods into the language of quantum theory. This contribution gives a systematic overview of the emerging field of quantum machine learning. It presents the approaches as well as technical details in an accessible way, and discusses the potential of a future theory of quantum learning.

(Cai et al., 2015) reported their first experimental entanglement-based classification of 2, 4 and 8-dimensional vectors to different clusters using a small-scale photonic quantum computer, which are then used to implement supervised and unsupervised machine learning. The results demonstrate the working principle of using quantum computers to manipulate and classify high-dimensional vectors, the core mathematical routine in machine learning. The method can in principle be scaled to larger number of qubits, and may provide a new route to accelerate machine learning.

(Powell et al., 2015) summarizes the perspectives into an outlook on the opportunities for quantum computing to impact problems relevant to the DOE's mission as well as the additional research required to bring quantum computing to the point where it can have such impact.

(Kopczyk, 2018) has given an overview of selected quantum machine learning algorithms; however there is also a method of scores extraction for quantum PCA algorithm proposed as well as a new cost function in feed-forward quantum neural networks is introduced. The text is divided into four parts: the first part explains the basic quantum theory, and then quantum computation and quantum computer architecture are explained in section two. The third part presents quantum algorithms which will be used as subroutines in quantum machine learning algorithms. Finally, the fourth section describes quantum machine learning algorithms with the use of knowledge accumulated in previous parts.

(Fastovets et al., 2019) shown basic ideas of quantum machine learning where they have presented several new methods that combine classical machine learning algorithms and quantum computing methods. A demonstration has been made on the multiclass tree tensor network algorithm, and its approbation on IBM quantum processor. Also, an introduction has been made on the neural networks approach to quantum tomography problem. Our tomography method allows us in the prediction of quantum state excluding noise influence. Such classical-quantum approach can be applied in various experiments to reveal latent dependence between input data and output measurement results.

(Abdelgaber and Nikolopoulos, 2020) This paper will review the basic building blocks of quantum computing and discuss the main applications in artificial intelligence that can be addressed more efficiently using the quantum computers of today. Artificial intelligence and quantum computing have many features in common. Quantum computing can provide artificial intelligence and machine learning algorithms with speed of training and computational power in less price. Artificial intelligence on the other hand can provide quantum computers with the necessary error correction algorithms. Some of the algorithms in AI that have been successfully implemented on a quantum computer, that has been presented are both unsupervised learning algorithms (clustering and Principal component analysis) and also supervised learning classification, such as support vector machines.

(Kanamori and Seong-Moo, 2020) This paper introduces the basic concepts of quantum computing and describes well-known quantum applications for non-physicists. The current status of the developments in quantum computing is also presented.

(Jiang et al. 2021) has carried out a case study to demonstrate an end-to-end implementation. On the neural network side, multilayer perceptron has been employed to complete image classification tasks using the standard and widely used MNIST dataset. On the quantum computing side, a target has been made on IBM Quantum processors, which can be programmed and simulated by using IBM Qiskit. This work targets the acceleration of the inference phase of a trained neural network on the quantum processor. Along with the case study, a demonstration has been made on the typical procedure for mapping neural networks to quantum circuits.

(Bova et al., 2021) In this article, a discussion is made on the solutions that some companies are already building using quantum hardware. Framing these as examples of combinatorics problems, illustrations are made on their application in four industry verticals: cyber security, materials and pharmaceuticals, banking and finance, and advanced manufacturing. While quantum computers are not yet available at the scale needed to solve all of these combinatorics problems, identification has been made on three types of near-term opportunities resulting from advances in quantum computing: quantum-safe encryption, material and drug discovery, and quantum-inspired algorithms.

3. SOME BASIC CONCEPTS

3.1 Quantum computers

Quantum computers (QC) are different from binary digital electronic computers based on transistors. A major difference between classical and quantum computing lies in the way they encode data. While digital computer requires that the data be encoded into binary digits (0 or 1), quantum computers uses quantum bits, which can be in superpositions of states (Schuld et al., 2014). In other words, instead of storing information in bits as conventional digital computers do, quantum computers use quantum bits, or qubits, to encode information. Qubits are the basic units of quantum information. In addition to ones and zeros, qubits have a third state called "superposition" that allows them to represent a one or a zero at the same time. Figure 1 shows the comparison between the bit and qubit (Vizzotto, 2013). The computing power of a QC grows exponentially with the number of qubits it uses.

The behavior of a quantum computer is governed by the basic principles of quantum mechanics. Some physicists claim that quantum mechanics is the most complete and accurate description of our world (Nagy and Aki, 2006). A QC exploits the laws of quantum mechanics such as entanglement and superposition, which make it possible for QC to perform jobs such as factoring large semiprimes. Entanglement is the property of a QC whereby action on one part of the system affects another part. Using the principle of superposition allows a large amount of information to be stored. Quantum computers have the potential to perform certain calculations significantly faster than any digital computers. QC consists of a quantum processor which operates at a very low temperature (a few tens of mK) and an electronic controller which reads out and controls the quantum processors [5].

The smallest unit of information in a quantum computer is called a qubit, by analogy with the classical bit. A classical system of n bits is at any time in one of 2^n states. Quantum mechanics tells us, however, that a thought must be given on quantum system of n qubits as having a distinct probability of "being in" (that is, "being found in upon measurement") each of the 2^n classical states at any given time. A quantum mechanical system of n qubits can be modeled as a vector of 2^n complex numbers, one probability amplitude for each of the 2^n classical states. The probability of finding the system in a particular state is calculated as the square of the modulus of the corresponding amplitude.

3.2 State Representation and Notation

A representation has been made on the state of an n-qubit system as a unit vector of 2^n complex numbers $[\alpha_0; \alpha_1; \alpha_2; :::: ; \alpha_{2^n-1}]$. Each of these numbers can be viewed as paired with one of the system's classical states. The classical states are called the "computational basis vectors" of the system and are labled by n-bit strings, represented as $|b_{n-1}b_{n-2} \ldots b_j \ldots b_0>$ where each b_j is either 0 or 1^{-1}. The state labels can be abbreviated using the binary number formed by concatenating the bits; that is, $|k>$ can be written in place of $|b_{n-1}b_{n-2}\ldots b_j\ldots b_0>$ where $k = b_0 + 2b_1 + 4b_2 + ::: + 2^{n-1}b_{n-1}$.

3.3 Quantum gates

The primitive operations supported by a quantum computer are called quantum logic gates, by analogy with traditional digital logic gates. Several small sets of quantum logic gates are universal for quantum computation in almost the same sense that NAND is universal for classical computation; one can implement any quantum algorithm with at most polynomial slowdown using only primitive gates from one of these sets (Barenco et al., 1995).

A description has been made on the representation of quantum gates as matrices that operate on a quantum system via matrix multiplication with the vector of amplitudes. Gates representing physically possible dynamics (time-evolution) of a closed (or isolated) quantum system must be unitary—that is, each gate U must satisfy $U^+U = UU^+ = 1$, where U^+ is the Hermitean adjoint of U on a single qubit. In a one-qubit system (which if represented with two amplitudes, one for $|0>$ and one for $|1>$) the quantum NOT operation simply swaps the values of the two amplitudes. That is, a single qubit system in the state $\alpha_0|0> + \alpha_1|1>$ will be transformed by quantum NOT into $\alpha_1|0> + \alpha_0|1>$. Quantum NOT can be represented in matrix form as $\begin{bmatrix} 01 \\ 10 \end{bmatrix}$ and its operation on a one qubit system $\alpha_0|0> + \alpha_1|1>$, represented as

a column vector $\begin{bmatrix} \alpha_0 \\ \alpha_1 \end{bmatrix}$, can be shown $\begin{bmatrix} 01 \\ 10 \end{bmatrix}\begin{bmatrix} \alpha_0 \\ \alpha_1 \end{bmatrix} = \begin{bmatrix} \alpha_1 \\ \alpha_0 \end{bmatrix}$

Another interesting one-qubit gate is the SQUARE ROOT OF NOT (SRN) gate:

$$\begin{bmatrix} \dfrac{1}{\sqrt{2}} & -\dfrac{1}{\sqrt{2}} \\ \dfrac{1}{\sqrt{2}} & \dfrac{1}{\sqrt{2}} \end{bmatrix}$$

A single application of SRN will in effect randomize the state of a qubit that was previously in a "pure" state of 0 or 1. That is, it will transform a situation in which there is a probability of 1 for reading the state as "0" (or a situation in which there is a probability of 1 for reading the state as "1") into one in which there is a probability of 1/2 for reading the state as "0" and a probability of 1/2 for reading the state as "1".

Another useful quantum gate is controlled NOT (or CNOT), which takes two qubit indices as arguments; that will call these arguments control and target. CNOT is an identity operation for basis vectors with 0 in the control position, but it acts like quantum NOT applied to the target position for basis vectors with 1 in the control position. For the case of a two-qubit system, with qubit 1 as the control and qubit 0 as the target. CNOT flips the state with respect to its target qubit wherever its control qubit is 1. By making the condition on this flipping more complex, using more controlling qubits, analogous gates can be established for any classical boolean function.

3.4 Quantum machine learning

Quantum machine learning is a term used to cover 4 types of scenarios:

i.   Quantum-inspired classical algorithms on classical data: such as tensor network and de-quantized recommendation systems algorithms.

ii.   Classical algorithms are applied to quantum data: such as neural network-based quantum States and optimizing pulse sequences.

iii. Quantum algorithms are applied to classical data: such as quantum optimization algorithms and quantum classification of classical data.

iv. Quantum algorithms are applied to quantum data: such as quantum signal processing and quantum hardware modeling (Metwalli, 2020).

4. APPROACHES TO ENHANCE MACHINE LEARNING THROUGH QUANTUM COMPUTING

There are different theories on the ways quantum computing might enhance machine learning. Here are the top 3 arguments:

4.1. If Quantum Computers have Speedups in Linear Algebra Subroutines, it can Speed up Machine Learning

Linear algebra is the core of machine learning. In particular, a group of linear algebra applications called BLAS (Basic Linear Algebra Subroutines) is the fundamentals of all machine learning algorithms. These subroutines include matrix multiplication, Fourier transforms, and solving linear systems.

All these subroutines do obtain exponential speedups when ran on a quantum computer. However, when addressing these speedups, what is not mentioned is, to obtain these speedups, it is necessary in having a quantum memory the holds quantum data and communicates with a quantum processor. Then, only the exponential speedups can be reached.

Currently, our systems are not pure quantum; our data is classical and is stored in a classical memory. This data is then communicated to a quantum processor. The communication between classical memory and the quantum processor is why an exponential speedup can't be reached. Based on the memory and the nature of the linear algebra application used, some sort of speedup over the pure classical approaches is achieved.

4.2. Quantum Parallelism can Help Train Models Faster

One of the main power sources of quantum computers is their ability to perform quantum superposition. This enables us to work on various quantum states at the same time. So, the argument here is, if a model can be trained in a state of superposition of all possible training sets, then maybe the training process will be faster and more efficient.

Efficient here can mean one of two things:

i. Exponentially fewer data needed to train the model -> which researchers have found is inaccurate. However, some linear speedups may be possible in some cases.

ii. Train models faster -> this claim follows the speedup resulted from quantizing any classical algorithm following Grover's algorithm. The result is speedups up to quadratic at best and not exponential.

If I tried running a classical machine learning algorithm on quantum computing, the best I can aim up for is quadratic speedups. If I need more speedups, then the algorithm needs to change as well.

4.3. Quantum Computers can Model Highly Correlated Distributions in a Way Classical Computers can't.

This is true, 100%. However, while it is correct, recent research results proved that this is insufficient for any quantum advantage. Moreover, it showed that some classical models could outperform quantum ones, even on datasets generated quantumly (Metwalli, 2020).

5. APPLICATIONS OF QUANTUM COMPUTERS IN MACHINE LEARNING

5.1 Quantum Computers as AI Accelerators

The limits of what machines can learn have always been defined by the computer hardware which is used for running our algorithms—for example, the success of modern-day deep learning with neural networks is enabled by parallel GPU clusters.

Quantum machine learning extends the pool of hardware for machine learning by an entirely new type of computing device—the quantum computer. Information processing with quantum computers relies on substantially different laws of physics known as *quantum theory*.

5.2 Machine Learning on Near-Term Quantum Devices

Some research focuses on ideal, universal quantum computers ("fault-tolerant QPUs") which are still years away. But there is rapidly-growing interest in quantum machine learning on near-term quantum devices. It might be understood that these devices as special-purpose hardware like Application-Specific Integrated Circuits

(ASICs) and Field-Programmable Gate Arrays (FPGAs), which are more limited in their functionality ("What is Quantum Machine Learning? — PennyLane", 2021).

5.3 Using Quantum Computers like Neural Networks

In the modern viewpoint, quantum computers can be used and trained like neural networks. Systematical adaptation is possible on the physical control parameters, such as electromagnetic field strength or a laser pulse frequency, to solve a problem.

For example, a trained circuit can be used to classify the content of images, by encoding the image into the physical state of the device and taking measurements.

5.4 The Bigger Picture: Differentiable Programming

But the story is bigger than just using quantum computers to tackle machine learning problems. Quantum circuits are *differentiable*, and a quantum computer itself can compute the change in control parameters needed to become better at a given task.

Differentiable programming is the very basis of deep learning, implemented in software libraries such as TensorFlow and PyTorch. Differentiable programming is more than deep learning: it is a programming paradigm where the algorithms are not hand-coded, but learned.

Similarly, the idea of training quantum computers is larger than quantum machine learning. Trainable quantum circuits can be leveraged in other fields like quantum chemistry or quantum optimization. It can help in a variety of applications such as the design of quantum algorithms, the discovery of quantum error correction schemes, and the understanding of physical systems.

5.5 PennyLane for Quantum Differentiable Programming

PennyLane is an open-source software framework built around the concept of quantum differentiable programming. It seamlessly integrates classical machine learning libraries with quantum simulators and hardware, giving users the power to train quantum circuits ("What is Quantum Machine Learning? — PennyLane", 2021).

5.6 Quantum machine learning

Research in recent years has shown that the true potency of quantum computing lies in setting up a pipeline composed of both classical and quantum segments. Consider a scientific application where it is necessary to calculate the ground state of a particle. This problem is often important in studying chemical reactions and equilibria. The ground state would be defined as a state where the particle is at its lowest energy level, and therefore, at its most stable state. Traditionally, obtaining the ground state requires calculating the smallest eigenvalue from the eigenvectors of the states of a particle, which are represented by a matrix known as the *Hamiltonian*. For small systems, classical computers will not break a sweat during the solution, but this simple task grows exponentially for larger systems that have numerous particles and soon overwhelms available computational resources.

Table 1. Overview of methods in machine learning and approaches from a quantum information perspective

Machine Learning Methods	Quantum Approach
k-nearest neighbor	Efficient calculation of classical distances on a quantum computer
Support vector machines	
k-means clustering	
Neural networks	First exploration of quantum models
Decision trees	
Bayesian theory	Reformulation in the language of open quantum systems
Hidden Markov models	

However, this increase in the search space becomes tractable if a hybrid, quantum machine learning algorithm is used. The Variational-Quantum-Eigensolver (VQE) uses both classical and quantum algorithms to estimate the lowest eigenvalue of a Hamiltonian. Simply put, its quantum part, known as the *ansatz*, intelligently searches the space of all possible states of a particle. The classical part tunes the ansatz' parameters with gradient descent to help it approach the optimal answer. This combination has shown that the quantum computer can be especially helpful in particle simulation tasks of this kind.

Various other algorithms under the umbrella of quantum machine learning have been formulated in the past few years as well. The best-known quantum algorithm for the traditional *k-means* clustering optimizes the Lloyd classical distance calculation subroutine (Rebollo-Monedero & Girod, 2009) between the vectors to reduce the classical $O(NkM)$ computational complexity exponentially down to $O(Mklog(N))$, where k is the number of clusters, M is the count of the training examples, and N is the feature count (Biamonte & Wittek, 2017, 195-202).

5.6.1 Quantum Versions of k-nearest Neighbor Methods

A very popular and simple standard textbook method for pattern classification is the k-nearest neighbor algorithm. Given a training set T of feature vectors with their respective classification as well as an unclassified input vector $\vec{x}$, the idea is to choose the class c^x for the new input that appears most often amongst its k nearest neighbors. This is based on the assumption that 'close' feature vectors encode similar examples, which is true for many applications. Common distance measures are thereby the inner product, the Euclidian or the Hamming distance. Choosing k is not always easy and can influence the result significantly. If k is chosen too big, there is a loss of the locality information and end up in a simple majority vote over the entire training set, while a very small k leads to noise-biased results. A variation of the algorithm suggests not to run it on the training set, but to calculate the means or centroid $1/N_c \sum_p \vec{v}^p$ of all N_c vectors belonging to one class c beforehand, and to select the class of the nearest centroid (nearest-centroid algorithm). Another variation weights the influence of the neighbors by distance, gaining an independence of the parameter k (the weighted nearest neighbors algorithm (Hechen bichler, and Schliep, 2004)). Methods such as k-nearest neighbors are obviously based on a distance metric to evaluate the similarity of two feature vectors. Efforts to translate this algorithm into a quantum version therefore focus on the efficient evaluation of a classical distance through a quantum algorithm.

(Wiebe et al., 2014) also use a swap test in order to calculate the inner product of two vectors, which is another distance measure between feature vectors. However, they use an alternative representation of classical information through quantum states. Given n-dimensional classical vectors $\vec{a}$, $\vec{b}$ with entries $a_j = |a_j| e^{i\alpha_j}, b_j = |b_j| e^{i\beta_j}, j = 1, ..., n$ as well as an upper bound r_{max} for the entries of the training vectors in T and an upper bound for the number of zeros in a vector d (the sparsity), the idea is to write the parameters into amplitudes of the quantum

states $$|A\rangle = \frac{1}{\sqrt{d}} \sum_j |j\rangle (\sqrt{1 - \frac{|a_j|^2}{r_{max}^2}} e^{-i\alpha_j} |0\rangle + \frac{a_j}{r_{max}} |1\rangle) |1\rangle \quad \text{and}$$

$$|B\rangle = \frac{1}{\sqrt{d}} \sum_j |j\rangle |1\rangle (\sqrt{1 - \frac{|b_j|^2}{r_{max}^2}} e^{-i\beta_j} |0\rangle + \frac{b_j}{r_{max}} |1\rangle)$$

and perform a swap test on $|A\rangle$ and $|B\rangle$. According to Eq. (2), the probability of measuring the swap-test ancilla in the ground state is then $P(|0\rangle_{anc}) = \frac{1}{2} + \frac{1}{2} |\frac{1}{dr_{max}^2} \sum_i a_i b_i|^2$ and the inner product of $\vec{a}, \vec{b}$ can consequently be evaluated $|\sum_i a_i b_i|^2 = d^2 r_{max}^4 (2P(|0\rangle_{anc}) - 1)$, which is altogether independent of the dimension n of the vector. The authors in fact claim a quadratic speed-up compared to classical algorithms (Schuld et al., 2014).

5.6.2 Quantum Computing for Support Vector Machines

A support vector machine is used for linear discrimination, which is a subcategory of pattern classification. The task in linear discrimination problems is to find a hyperplane that is the best discrimination between two class regions and serves as a decision boundary for future classification tasks. In a trivial example of one-dimensional data and only two classes, it is necessary to query of whether, point x lies exactly between the members of class 1 and 2, so that all values left of x belong to one class and all values right of x to the other. In higher dimensions, the boundary is given by a hyperplane. It seems like a severe restriction that methods of linear discrimination require the problem to be linearly separable, which means that there is a hyperplane that divides the data points so that all vectors of either class are on one side of the hyperplane. It is thus crucial for support vector machines to find a method of evaluating an inner product efficiently. This is where quantum computing comes into play.

   (Rebentrost et al., 2014) claim that in general, the evaluation of an inner product can be done faster on a quantum computer. Given the quantum state $|X\rangle = 1/\sqrt{N_X} \sum_{i=1}^{2^n} |\vec{x_i}||i\rangle |x^i\rangle$, with $N_X = \sum_{i=1}^{2^n} |\vec{x^i}|^2$ are a 2^n-dimensional basis of the training vector space T, so that every training vector $|v^p\rangle$ can be represented as a superposition $|v^p\rangle = \sum \alpha_i |x^i\rangle$. Similar to the same authors' distance measurement, the quantum evaluation of a classical inner product relies on the fact that the quantum states are normalized as

$$\langle x^i | x^j \rangle = \frac{\vec{x_i}.\vec{x_j}}{|\vec{x_i}||\vec{x_j}|}$$

   The kernel matrix of the inner products of the basis of vectors, K with $(K)_{i:j} = \vec{x_i}.\vec{x_j}$, can then be calculated by taking the partial trace of the corresponding density matrix $|X\rangle\langle X|$ over the states

$$|x^i\rangle,$$

$$tr_x[|X\rangle\langle X|] = \frac{1}{N_x} \sum_{i,j=1}^{2^n} \langle x^i | x^j \rangle |\vec{x_i}\|\vec{x_j}\| |i\rangle\langle j| = \frac{\hat{K}}{tr[K]}.$$

(Rebentrost et al., 2014) propose that the inner product evaluation can not only be used for the kernel matrix but also when a pattern has to be classified, which invokes the evaluation of the inner product between the above parameter vector $\vec{w}$ and the new input (Schuld et al., 2014).

5.6.3 Quantum Algorithms for Clustering

Clustering describes the task of dividing a set of unclassified feature vectors into k subsets or clusters. It is the most prominent problem in unsupervised learning, which does not use training sets or `prior examples' for generalization, but rather extracts information on structural characteristics of a data set. Clustering is usually based on a distance measure such as the squared Euclidean distance $((\vec{a} - \vec{b})^2$ with $\vec{a}$; $\vec{b}$ $\in R^N$).

The standard textbook example for clustering is the k-means algorithm, in which alternately each feature vector or datapoint is assigned to its closest current centroid vector to form a cluster for each centroid, and the centroid vectors get calculated from the clusters of the previous step.

(Lloyd et al., 2013) present an unsupervised quantum learning algorithm for k-means clustering that is based on adiabatic quantum computing. Adiabatic quantum computing is an alternative to the above introduced method of implementing unitary gates, and tries to continuously adjust the quantum system's parameters in an adiabatic process in order to transfer a ground state which is easy to prepare into a ground state which encodes the result of the computation. Although not in focus here, quantum adiabatic computing seems to be an interesting candidate for quantum machine learning methods (Pudenz and Lidar, 2013). This is why there is a requirement in sketching the idea of how to use adiabatic quantum computing for k-means clustering.

In (Lloyd et al., 2013), the goal of each clustering step is to have an output quantum superposition $|X\rangle = \frac{1}{\sqrt{N_c}} \sum_{c, p \in c} |c\rangle |\vec{v^p}\rangle$, where as usual $\{|v^p\rangle\}_{p=1,...,N}$ is the set of N feature vectors or data points expressed as quantum states, and $|c\rangle$ is the cluster the subset $\{|v^j\rangle\}_{j=1,...,N_c}$ is assigned to after the clustering step. The authors essentially propose to adiabatically transform an initial Hamiltonian $H_0 = 1 - \frac{1}{k} \sum_{c,c'} |c\rangle\langle c'|$, into a Hamiltonian

$$H_1 = \sum_{c',j} |\overrightarrow{v^p} - \overrightarrow{v^c}|^2 |c'\rangle\langle c'| \otimes |j\rangle\langle j|$$

encoding the distance between vector $\overrightarrow{v^p}$ to the centroid of the closest cluster, v^c . They give a more refined version and also mention that the adiabatic method can be applied to solve the optimization problem of finding good initial or `seed' centroid vectors (Schuld et al., 2014).

5.6.4 Searching for a Quantum Neural Network Model

Researchers have also investigated the power of quantum computers in running neural networks. While a robust formulation of a neural network is still a fair way away in the quantum realm (Schuld & Sinayskiy, 2014), academics have produced varying methods to represent classical neural networks with quantum circuits. One example comes from researchers hailing from ETH Zurich and IBM Q, who compared the dimensionality, optimizability, and trainability of classical neural networks and quantum neural networks (Abbas et al., 2020).

Abbas et.al used the dimensionality of a model to compare the power of different neural networks. Their results showed that a quantum neural network combined with a *'good'* feature map (to encode the data) had higher effective dimensionality than a classical neural network. Moreover, unlike classical neural networks, which sometimes suffer from slow trainability due to highly degenerate Fisher information matrices, the quantum neural network above offered a more descriptive Fisher information matrix with more uniform, non-zero eigenvalues.

5.6.5 Toward a Quantum Decision Tree

Decision trees are classifiers that are probably the most intuitive for humans. Depending on the answer to a question on the features, one follows ascertain branch leading to the next question until the final class is found. More precisely, a mathematical tree is an undirected graph in which any two nodes are connected by exactly one edge.

Decision trees in particular have one starting node, the `root' (a node with outgoing but no incoming edges), and several end points or `leaves' (nodes with incoming but no outgoing edges). Each node except from the leaves contains a decision function which decides which branch an input vector follows to the next layer, or in other words, which partition on a set of data is makes. The leaves then represent the final classification.

Decision trees, as all classifiers in machine learning, are constructed using a training data set of feature vectors. The art of decision tree design lies in the selection of the decision function in each node. The most popular method is to find the function that splits the given dataset into the `most-organized' sub-datasets.

(Lu and Braunstein, 2014) propose a quantum version of the decision tree. Their classifying process follows the classical algorithm with the only difference that quantum feature is used which states $\left|v\right\rangle^P = \left|v_1^p,....,v_n^p\right\rangle$ encoding n features into the states of a quantum system. At each node of the tree, the set of training quantum states is divided into subsets by a measurement (or as the authors call it, estimating attribute v_i; $i = 1;....; n$). Lu and Brainstein do not give a clear account of how the division of the set at each node takes place and remain enigmatic in this essential part of the classifying algorithm. They contribute the interesting idea of using the von Neumann entropy to design the graph partition. Although the first step has been made, the potential of a quantum decision tree is still to be established (Schuld et al., 2014).

5.6.6 Quantum State Classification with Bayesian Methods

Stochastic methods such as Bayesian decision theory play an important role in the discipline of machine learning. It can also be used for pattern classification. The idea is to analyze existing information (represented by the above training data set T) in order to calculate the probability that a new input is of a certain class.

Opposed to above efforts to improve machine learning algorithms through quantum computing, Bayesian methods can be used for an important task in quantum information called quantum state classification. This problem stems from quantum information theory itself, and the goal is to use machine learning based on Bayesian theory in order to discriminate between two quantum states produced by an unknown or partly unknown source. This is again a classification problem, since it is necessary in learning the discrimination function between two classes c_1; c_2. The two (unknown) quantum states are represented by density matrices ρ, σ. The basic idea is to use a positive operator-valued measurement (POVM) with binary outcome corresponding to the two classes as a Bayesian classifier, in other words, to learn (or calculate) the measurement on our quantum states that is able to discriminate them (Guta and Kotlowski, 2010). (Guta and Kotlowski, 2010) found an optimal qubit classification strategy while (Sasaki et al., 2001) are concerned with the related template matching problem8 by solving an optimization problem for the measurement operator. (Sentis et al., 2012) give a variation in which the training data can be stored as classical information. The proposals are so far of theoretical nature and await experimental verification of the usefulness of this scheme (Schuld et al., 2014).

5.6.7 Discussion

The power of quantum computers to manipulate large numbers of high-dimensional vectors makes them natural systems for performing vector-based machine learning tasks. Operations that involve taking vector dot products, overlaps, norms, etc., in N-dimensional vector spaces that take time O(N) in the classical machine learning algorithms, take time O(log N) in the quantum version. These abilities, combined with the quantum linear systems algorithm (Harrow et al., 2009) represent a powerful suite of tools for manipulating large amounts of data. Once the data has been processed in a quantum form, as in the adiabatic quantum algorithm for search engine ranking (Garnerone et al., 2012), then measurements can be made on the processed data to reveal aspects of the data that can take exponentially longer to reveal by classical algorithms Here, a presentation is made on the quantum algorithm for assigning a vector to clusters of M vectors that takes time O (log MN), an exponential speed-up in both M (quantum big data) and N. This algorithm is used as a subroutine for the standard k-means algorithm to provide an exponential speed-up for unsupervised learning (quantum Lloyd's algorithm) via the adiabatic algorithm.

Currently, the rate of generation of electronic data generated per year is estimated to be on the order of 1018 bits. This entire data set could be represented by a quantum state using 60 bits, and the clustering analysis could be performed using a few hundred operations. Even if the number of bits to be analyzed were to expand to the entire information content of the universe within the particle horizon, O (1090 ≈ 2300) bits, in principle the data representation and analysis would be well within the capacity of a relatively small quantum computer.

The generic nature of the quantum speed-ups for dealing with large numbers of high dimensional vectors suggests that a wide variety of machine learning algorithms may be susceptible to exponential speed-up on a quantum computer. Quantum machine learning also provides advantages in terms of privacy: the data base itself is of size O(MN), but the owner of the data base supplies only O (log MN) quantum bits to the user who is performing the quantum machine learning algorithm. In addition to supplying an exponential speedup over classical machine learning algorithms, quantum machine learning methods for analyzing large data sets ('big quantum data') supply significant advantages in terms of privacy for the owners of that data (Lloyd et al., 2013).

5.7 NP-Hard Problems, Searching, and Monte Carlo Simulations

Quantum computers also excel at optimization problems. Optimization problems utilize a particular solution heuristic to find the best-possible solution out of a cohort of valid solutions. To understand how optimization might operate in a quantum computing context, researchers have devised quantum algorithms for some NP-hard problems. One example of this is a quantum algorithm for the *Traveling-Salesman-Problem (TSP)*, which provides a quadratic speedup over the classical brute force method for a large number of cities (Srinivasan et al., 2018).

Other algorithms that exploit a quantum computer's parallelism have highlighted promising results too. *Grover's algorithm* is currently the fastest quantum algorithm to search through an unsorted database with N entries. On a classical computer, this task would require time proportional to N, but the quantum counterpart demonstrates a square-root speedup and gets the job done in $O(sqrt(N))$ instead. Similarly, quantum computers can perform Fourier transforms over N data points, invert sparse $N*N$ matrices, and find their eigenvalues and eigenvectors in time proportional to a polynomial in $log (N)$. For these tasks, optimal classical algorithms known would take time proportional to $N \, log_{[0]}(N)$, that is, the quantum computer exhibits an exponential speed up in such cases as well (Biamonte & Wittek, 2017, 195-202).

The finance industry is also priming itself for potential use cases of quantum computers. The task of analyzing stock markets and their associated metrics can be turned into an optimization problem. Considering this, the immediate practical usage of quantum computers could potentially take root in the finance domain. A study by a Spanish Bank, BBVA, which came out in July this year, found that quantum computers could boost credit-scoring, spot arbitrage opportunities, and accelerate Monte Carlo simulations (The Economist, 2020). Likewise, the head of a research unit at JPMorgan Chase & Co., Marco Pistoia, hopes that quantum computers could potentially boost profits by speeding up asset pricing, digging up better-performing portfolios, and improving existing ML algorithms. Even the head of quantum research at Goldman Sachs, William Zeng, made a bold claim that quantum computers could "revolutionize" the banking and finance industries (The Economist, 2020).

5.8 Entangled future

Quantum computers reveal a promising novel approach to computing and problem-solving. Exponential speedups and polynomial-time solutions to intractable problems are natural consequences of the quantum mechanical properties of qubits. These results in a model of computation that is closer to the one abstractly modeled by a *quantum Turing machine*.

Shifting gears back to our original discussion of Turing machines, a quantum Turing machine is the generalization or *quantization* of the classical Turing machine, where the head and tape are superposed. Formally, the states of a machine are quantum states in *Hilbert space*. The tape of a quantum Turing machine is an infinite 'unilateral tape' which represents the superposed bits. In this context, a quantum computation is a unitary transformation whose result is determined by quantum measurement, which will reduce the 'unilateral tape' in coherent superposition to a classical bilateral tape with separable orthogonal eigen states (Moschovakis, 2003).

Coupling this model of computation with enabling hardware, the demonstration of quantum supremacy by Google is what many people in the research community believe to be a violation of the extended Church-Turing thesis, which asserts that such a model of computation should be *efficiently* modeled by a traditional Turing machine. In fact, (Bernstein & Vazirani, 1993) showed that quantum Turing machines are inherently different from traditional Turing machines and can solve certain problems that would require *super polynomial* time on their classical counterparts.

Tangible applications in chemistry, finance and optimization problems provide avenues for utilizing quantum computers in real-world settings too. Furthermore, the impressive trainability and dimensionality of quantum neural networks provide exciting new avenues for research in the use of quantum computers for machine learning and deep learning.

Aware of their potency, tech firms like IBM, Intel, Zapata, Amazon, and Honeywell are all investing heavily in developing commercial applications for quantum computers. High-level languages, frameworks, and libraries for programming on quantum computers like Q#, Qiskit, TensorFlow Quantum, and Cirq are steadily gaining traction too. These frameworks and their tutorials have eased the barrier to entry for quantum development and if the growing popularity is anything to go by, it can expected in viewing a bunch of exciting new developments in quantum computing in this decade.

Despite these developments, there is requirement of critically contemplating the current state of quantum computers. The concerns posed by a qubit's penchant for decoherence coupled with its exorbitant cryogenic requirements present significant limitations for our existing hardware. Thus, whether quantum computers can truly reign supreme for practical applications might not be the correct question to ask at this point in time. The more pressing inquiry is whether the impracticalities of the NISQ era can be overcome.

6. CONCLUSION

This introduction into quantum machine learning gave an overview of existing ideas and approaches to quantum machine learning. Throughout this chapter a focus has been made on the various approaches available in the implications of quantum computing in machine learning. The chapter starts with a brief introduction and is followed by the literature survey on the existing papers in this area. Focus has been made in the subsequent section on the approaches on machine learning where suitably quantum computing can be applied.

REFERENCES

Abbas, A., Sutter, D., Zoufal, C., & Lucchi, A. (2020). The power of quantum neural networks. arXiv. https://arxiv.org/abs/2011.00027

Abdelgaber, N., & Nikolopoulos, C. (2020). Overview on Quantum Computing and its Applications in Artificial Intelligence. *2020 IEEE Third International Conference on Artificial Intelligence and Knowledge Engineering (AIKE)*, 198-199. 10.1109/AIKE48582.2020.00038

Ather, F. (2021). *Knocking on Turing's door: Quantum Computing and Machine Learning*. The Gradient.

Barenco, A., Bennett, C. H., Cleve, R., DiVincenzo, D. P., Margolus, N., Shor, P., Sleator, T., Smolin, J. A., & Weinfurter, H. (1995). Elementary gates for quantum computation. *Physical Review A*, *52*(5), 3457–3467. doi:10.1103/PhysRevA.52.3457 PMID:9912645

Bernstein, E., & Vazirani, U. (1993, June). *Quantum complexity theory*. ACM Digital Library. https://dl.acm.org/doi/10.1145/167088.167097

Biamonte, J., Wittek, P., Pancotti, N., Rebentrost, P., Wiebe, N., & Lloyd, S. (2017). Quantum machine learning. *Nature*, *549*(7671), 195–202. doi:10.1038/nature23474 PMID:28905917

Bova, F., Goldfarb, A., & Melko, R. G. (2021). Commercial applications of quantum computing. *EPJ Quantum Technology*, *8*(1), 2. doi:10.1140/epjqt40507-021-00091-1 PMID:33569545

Cai, X., Wu, D., Su, Z., Chen, M., Wang, X., Li, L., Liu, N., Lu, C., & Pan, J. (2015). Entanglement-based machine learning on a quantum computer. *Physical Review Letters, 114*(11), 110504.

Fastovets, D. V., Bogdanov, Y. I., Bantysh, B. I., & Lukichev, V. F. (2019). Machine learning methods in quantum computing theory. In *International Conference on Micro-and Nano-Electronics 2018* (Vol. 11022). International Society for Optics and Photonics. 10.1117/12.2522427

Garnerone, S., Zanardi, P., & Lidar, D. A. (2012). Adiabatic Quantum Algorithm for Search Engine Ranking. *Physical Review Letters, 108*(23), 230506. doi:10.1103/PhysRevLett.108.230506 PMID:23003933

Guta, M., & Kotlowski, W. (2010). Quantum learning: Asymptotically optimal classification of qubit states. *New Journal of Physics, 12*(12), 123032. doi:10.1088/1367-2630/12/12/123032

Harrow, A. W., Hassidim, A., & Lloyd, S. (2009). Quantum Algorithm for Linear Systems of Equations. *Physical Review Letters, 15*(15), 150502. doi:10.1103/PhysRevLett.103.150502 PMID:19905613

Hechenbichler, K., & Schliep, K. (2004). *Weighted k-nearest-neighbor techniques and ordinal classification.* Academic Press.

Huembeli, P., Dauphin, A., & Wittek, P. (2018). Identifying Quantum Phase Transitions with Adversarial Neural Networks. *Physical Review. B, 97*(13), 134109. doi:10.1103/PhysRevB.97.134109

Jiang, W., Xiong, J., & Shi, Y. (2021). When Machine Learning Meets Quantum Computers: A Case Study: (Invited Paper). In *26th Asia and South Pacific Design Automation Conference (ASPDAC '21).* ACM. 10.1145/3394885.3431629

Kanamori, Y., & Yoo, S-M. (2020). Quantum Computing: Principles and Applications. *Journal of International Technology and Information Management, 29*(2). Available at: https://scholarworks.lib.csusb.edu/jitim/vol29/iss2/3

Kopczyk, D. (2018). *Quantum machine learning for data scientists.* Quantum Physics.

Lloyd, S., Mohseni, M., & Rebentrost, P. (2013). *Quantum algorithms for supervised and unsupervised machine learning.* arXiv preprint arXiv:1307.0411.

Lowdin, P. (1998). *Linear Algebra for Quantum Theory.* John Wiley and Sons, Inc.

Lu, S., & Braunstein, S. L. (2014). Quantum decision tree classifier. *Quantum Information Processing, 13*(3), 757-770.

Metwalli, S. (2020). *How May Quantum Computing Benefit Machine Learning?* Medium. Retrieved 21 December 2020, from https://towardsdatascience.com/how-may-quantum-computing-benefit-machine-learning-c96de0bef0d4

Nagy, M., & Aki, S. G. (2006). Quantum computation and quantum information. *International Journal of Parallel Emergent and Distributed Systems, 21*(1), 1–59. doi:10.1080/17445760500355678

Patra, B. (2017). Cryo-CMOS circuits and systems for quantum computing applications. *IEEE Journal of Solid-State Circuits*, 1–13.

Perdomo-Ortiz, A., Benedetti, M., Realpe-Gómez, J., & Biswas, R. (2018). Opportunities and challenges for quantum-assisted machine learning in near-term quantum computers. *Quantum Science and Technology*, *3*(3), 030502. doi:10.1088/2058-9565/aab859

Powell, P. (2015). *ASCR Report on Quantum Computing for Science*. doi:10.13140/RG.2.1.3656.5200

Pudenz, K. L., & Lidar, D. A. (2013). Quantum adiabatic machine learning. *Quantum Information Processing*, *12*(5), 2027–2070. doi:10.100711128-012-0506-4

Rebentrost, P., Mohseni, M., & Lloyd, S. (2014). Quantum support vector machine for big data classification. *Physical Review Letters*, *113*(13), 130503. doi:10.1103/PhysRevLett.113.130503 PMID:25302877

Rebollo-Monedero, D., & Girod, B. (2009). *Lloyd Algorithm*. Science Direct. https://www.sciencedirect.com/topics/computer-science/lloyd-algorithm

Schuld, M., Sinayskiy, I., & Petruccione, F. (2014). An introduction to quantum machine learning. *Contemporary Physics*, *56*(2), 172–185. doi:10.1080/00107514.2014.964942

Schuld, M., & Sinayskiy, I. (2014, October 15). *An introduction to quantum machine learning*. Taylor Francis Online. https://www.tandfonline.com/doi/abs/10.1080/00107514.2014.964942

Sentis, G., Calsamiglia, J., Munoz-Tapia, R., & Bagan, E. (2012). Quantum learning without quantum memory. *Scientific Reports*, *2*(708), 1–8. PMID:23050092

Spector, L., Barnum, H., & Bernstein, H. J. (1999). Quantum Computing Applications of Genetic Programming. In L. Spector, U.-M. O'Reilly, W. Langdon, & P. Angeline (Eds.), *Advances in Genetic Programming* (Vol. 3, pp. 135–160). MIT Press. doi:10.7551/mitpress/1110.003.0010

Srinivasan, K., Satyajit, S., & Behera, B. K. (2018). *Efficient quantum algorithm for solving travelling salesman problem: An IBM quantum experience*. https://arxiv.org/abs/1805.10928

The Economist. (2020). Wall Street's latest shiny new thing: quantum computing. *The Economist*. https://www.economist.com/finance-and-economics/2020/12/19/wall-streets-latest-shiny-new-thing-quantum-computing

Vizzotto, J. K. (2013). Quantum computing: state-of-art and challenges. *Proceedings of the 2nd Workshop-School of Theoretical Computer Science*, 9-13.

What is Quantum Machine Learning? (2021). Retrieved 7 October 2021, from https://pennylane.ai/qml/whatisqml.html

Wiebe, N., Kapoor, A., & Svore, K. (2014). Quantum Algorithms for Nearest-Neighbor Methods for Supervised and Unsupervised Learning. *Quantum Information & Computation, 15*(3), 318–358.

Wittek, P. (2014). *Quantum Machine Learning: What Quantum Computing Means to Data Mining*. Academic Press.

KEY TERMS AND DEFINITIONS

Intelligent Systems: An intelligent system is a machine with an embedded, Internet-connected computer that has the capacity to gather and analyze data and communicate with other systems. Similarly, intelligent systems can also include sophisticated AI-based software systems, such as chatbots, expert systems and other types of software.

Machine Learning: Machine learning (ML) is a type of artificial intelligence (AI) that allows software applications to become more accurate at predicting outcomes without being explicitly programmed to do so. Machine learning algorithms use historical data as input to predict new output values. Machine learning is important because it gives enterprises a view of trends in customer behavior and business operational patterns, as well as supports the development of new products. Many of today's leading companies, such as Facebook, Google, and Uber, make machine learning a central part of their operations. Machine learning has become a significant competitive differentiator for many companies.

Optimization: An optimization problem is the problem of finding the best solution from all feasible solutions. Optimization problems can be divided into two categories, depending on whether the variables are continuous or discrete. An optimization problem with discrete variables is known as a discrete optimization, in which an object such as an integer, permutation or graph must be found from a countable set. A problem with continuous variables is known as a continuous optimization, in which an optimal value from a continuous function must be found. They can include constrained problems and multimodal problems.

Quantum Computing: Quantum computing is an area of computing focused on developing computer technology based on the principles of quantum theory (which explains the behavior of energy and material on the atomic and subatomic levels).

Computers used today can only encode information in bits that take the value of 1 or 0—restricting their ability. Quantum computing, on the other hand, uses quantum bits or qubits. It harnesses the unique ability of subatomic particles that allows them to exist in more than one state (i.e., a 1 and a 0 at the same time).

Simulation: A simulation is the imitation of the operation of a real-world process or system over time. Simulations require the use of models; the model represents the key characteristics or behaviors of the selected system or process, whereas the simulation represents the evolution of the model over time. Often, computers are used to execute the simulation.

Chapter 6
The Potential of Quantum Computing in Healthcare

Prisilla Jayanthi

(iD) https://orcid.org/0000-0002-4961-9010
St. Joseph's Degree and PG College, India

Bharatendra K. Rai
Charlton College of Business, University of Massachusetts, Dartmouth, USA

Iyyanki Muralikrishna
Smart Village Movement in Alliance with Berkeley HAAS, Hyderabad, India

ABSTRACT

The need for IR4 technologies with faster and accurate results for huge health datasets is required. Healthcare has made a lot of advancements with technologies and has certain issues in terms of carbon emission. This in turn sets the patient's life in risk. The study proposes a model for all the healthcare sectors. The study deals with the various quantum neural networks implemented on diabetes retinopathy and COVID-19 images. The quantum computing model outperformed all other machine learning and deep learning models giving more accurate results in less time. The revolution of quantum computing has proven the healthcare in diabetes retinopathy and COVID-19 detection to be faster. It can henceforth be implemented for early warning of the diseases and provide treatment for the patients.

DOI: 10.4018/978-1-7998-9183-3.ch006

INTRODUCTION

The key area in which quantum computing helps optimizing pricing is risk analysis in health care. In this sector of health, triple aim is developed for system performance. It aims at the goal to advance the patient care experience, improve the population health, and minimize per capita health care costs. The approach with 3D in single aim, this model has worked great in guiding the optimization of health systems — improved clinical experience — leading to the creation of the quadruple aim model.

The idea is to achieve better outcome, improved clinical experience, improved patient experience and lower costs. But the authors proposed new model (pentacle aim) which has five goals shown in figure 1 with a zero carbon emission with addition. Since the healthcare generates largest carbon emission. Every mention of health care refers to patient diagnosis but the carbon emitted from this sector pollutes the other area of living, making worst for survival.

Figure 1. Proposed model

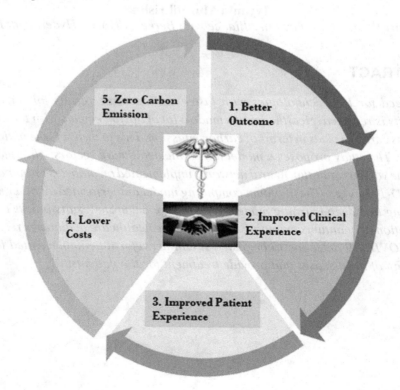

FEW USE CASES - QUANTUM COMPUTING - HEALTHCARE

Healthcare centers obtain lot of benefits from the business and scientific activity in the era of QC. This powerful technology helps to create innovation with next-generation technologies, organization need to take certain steps before implementing QC.

- *Engage quantum champions.*

Every organization identifies, enables, and hires quant champions in its organization—including both technology and healthcare professionals. They serve as focal point to connect quant expertise with healthcare requirements.

- *Explore and prioritize.*

Explore potential QC use cases and prioritize the ones with the largest impact for the organization.

- *Experiment.*

Implement the applications of QC and experiments with real quant computers. This allows driving toward quant advantage and provides the employees with hands-on enablement. It is accelerated by combining a quant ecosystem, a group of industry and technology participants sharing risks and rewards in quant computing (Flöther et al., 2020).

QUANTUM COMPUTING POWERED BY ARTIFICIAL INTELLIGENCE

Quantum computing has enabled and challenged the human intelligence in determining drugs and remedies against diseases which have no medication. The accuracy and precision of medicines for AIDS and Cancer were found to be near future. Till now, there is no medication for few common ailments, but now the diagnosis may be possible by QC powered artificial intelligence based simulations and drug research processes. Hence, QC powered AI can prove to be a boon for researchers across the world. The positive point is the newer potential of drug reactions and future risks would be declined with the help of **Q**uantum **C**omputing **P**owered **A**rtificial **I**ntelligence **R**esearch **C**omputers (QACPAIRC) (Mehta et al., 2019).

One of the major fertile areas for quantum computing (QC) is AI that relies on processing huge amounts of complex datasets (Taulli, 2020). A large scale quant computer can be built using a controllable quant system, provided the physical system meets the following requirements, called as the DiVincenzo criteria (Sahni & Srivastava, 2015). QC promises to deliver quick analysis and integration of huge data sets that improves and transforms the capabilities of machine learning and artificial intelligence (Marr, n.d.).

Rai (2019) highlight that machine learning and DL method has gained in popularity in recent years and is an active area of research and applications. Most computing resources such as machine learning and AI techniques interprets CT scans, aid surgical procedures and help to analyze disease related big data for developing predictive models. Gulshan (2016) implemented ML and DL algorithms on nearly 10,000 retinal images to develop an algorithm that detects diabetic retinopathy with high sensitivity and specificity. Had the programs created by Gulshan used the computational power of QC, one would imagine running an algorithm in real time to help physicians accurately detect retinopathy, at an earlier stage (Gulshan et al., 2016). Solenov (2018) suggests that QC may not replace the doctor-patient relationship, transparency and trust needed for shared decision making. In cancer treatment, QC contributes to improved therapies. For interpreting diagnostic images, QC can be applied using AI (Solenov et al., 2018). The miniature of quantum technologies approves new ways for portable sensor devices to increase their monitoring abilities, accuracy, and system integration in day-to-day usage (Torgler, 2020). However, QC enhances the accuracy of the resultant model by localizing the relevant optimal mix of values and weights (Atik & Jeutner, 2021).

APPLICATIONS- QUANTUM COMPUTING AND AI

QC addresses the various challenges involved in building a comprehensive digital healthcare ecosystem that works with different data sources and establishes correlation among them such as medical records, clinical data and medical imaging data, doctor's prescription, etc. QC has capacity for processing the huge amount of multipurpose data from various data sources, building correlations and inferences to bring a complete view of a particular medical case. Quantum Magnetic Resonance Imaging (Q-MRI) machines can generate enormously exact images that allow the visualization of individual molecules. QC technology can improve MRI technology by providing extremely accurate measurements and allowing doctors to look much deeper into small particles that conventional computing technology would not be able to detect. The use of QC along with AI helps to interpret diagnostic images in its very minute details. The following provide application with the combination of QC and AI as shown in figure 2 (Quantum Computing and AI, 2021).

1. Processing Huge Data Sets

It's a known fact that every day healthcare and various organizations produce huge amount of data equivalent to about 2.5 exabytes. Every minute of every day, 3.2B global internet users feed the data banks with 9722 pins on Pinterest, 4.2M facebook posts, and 347,224 tweets. QC approches are designed to manage such huge amount of data, along with uncovering patterns and spotting anomalies quickly. New developers have made the quantum error correction code better to manage the potential of quantum bits for solving all types of business problems to make better decisions (eHealth, 2020).

2. Solve Complex Problem Faster

QC computes calculations within seconds that take today's computers many years to calculate. QC can take multiple inputs simultaneously and process the amount of data that business generate on a daily basis and carry out fast calculations used to solve very complex problems which can be expressed as quant supremacy.

3. Better Business Insights Models

With piling up of daily data that is generated by various industries, companies are looking for models that process complex data in complex situation. Creating quant technology can lead to better treatment for diseases in the healthcare field such as recent CV -19.

4. Integration of Multiple Data Sets

Integrating multiple number of sets of data from various sources, quantum computers provide great help, making the process quicker, and making the analysis quite easier. QC has an ability for solving business problems in a variety of fields (eHealth, 2020).

QUANTUM ALGORITHM –CT SCAN –COVID 19 PATIENT

Quantum Machine Learning (QML) has evolved from the theory of QC and achieves solution parallelism, and for optimal constraint solving uses Quantum bit (Qb) or qubits. Quantum algorithms are focused on the concept of Boolean algebra i.e OR, AND, and NOT gates and quantum physics. Figure 3 compares ML/DL and Quantum machine learning algorithms. The two responsibilities that QML performs better compared to classical DL techniques include:

Figure 2. Applications of QC and AI

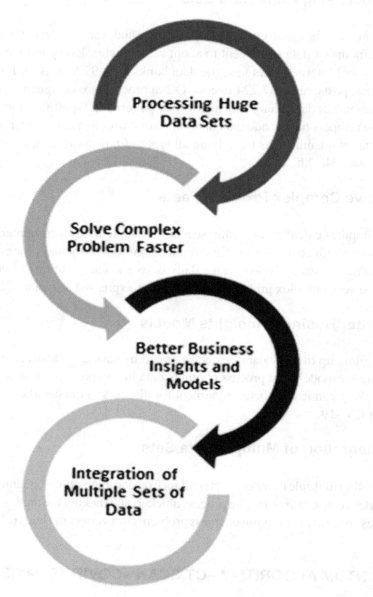

1. Optimization and Gibbs Sampling.
2. Enhance learning algorithms like Bayesian networks, Tensors, and search (Kinshuk Sengupta & Srivastava, 2021).

Figure 3. Execution block diagram of classical ML/DL versus QML algorithms (Kinshuk Sengupta & Srivastava, 2021)

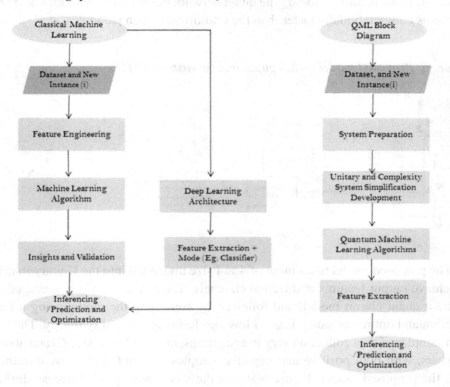

Figure 4. QNN Architecture (Kinshuk Sengupta & Srivastava, 2021)

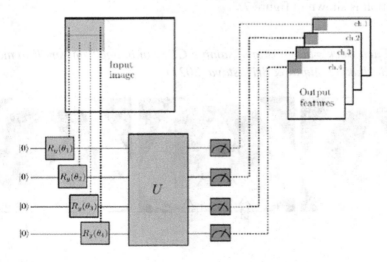

Quantum or Quanvolutional neural network (QNN) modelled by Henderson, 2019 (figure 4) helps in understanding the quant network design that solves classical DL problems computationally faster than the traditional design paradigm.

Figure 5. Proposed model by Sengupta and Srivastava (2021)

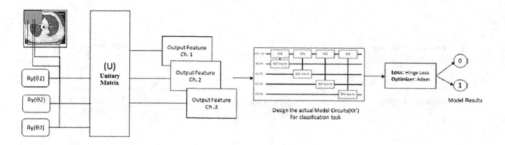

The proposed model takes input of 4×4 size image fed into the Unitary matrix to achieve output features at different channels. These features were leveraged to create a quant circuit model, and followed by compiling the model using a loss function and optimizer using TensorFlow and Keras model utility library. The CT scan samples of data collection vary in age groups, ranging from 20 to 60 and above 60 years, with both positive and negative samples (figure 6 and 7) were trained with the proposed model. Figure 6 shows the week–wise patch increase during diagnostic, a positive CV-19 case with dense mucus concentrated across the lungs for 20-days. The mucus, segmented across a small patch growth across two weeks of observation is shown in figure 7.

Figure 6. Each week's diagnostic of sample CT scan image from small to medium patches (Kinshuk Sengupta & Srivastava, 2021)

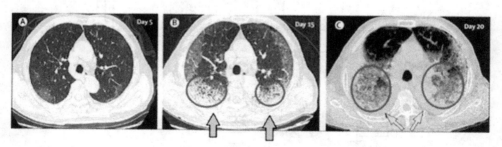

Figure 7. Sample CT scan image of CV-19 diagnosed (Kinshuk Sengupta & Srivastava, 2021)

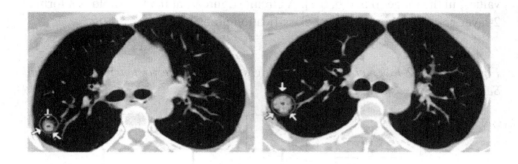

Figure 8. Hybrid Conv with multiple quantum filters (Kinshuk Sengupta & Srivastava, 2021)

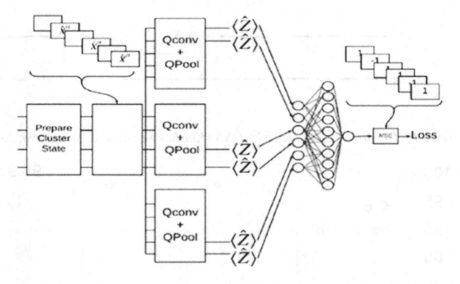

The experimental involves opting a base model for training the image and developing the same using the collected data. The different performance criteria were compared between QNN, QCNN, Hybrid CNN with a single filter and Hybrid CNN with multiple filters (Figure 8) from the circuit design and performance measurement, QNN was chosen for remaining benchmarking during the trials. The experiments were performed using TensorFlow Quantum (TFQ), and a python framework for QML development. D-wave Leap and TensorFlow Quantum Framework are used for training and evaluating the experiment. The estimated wait time for problem

89

submission was 1–10 s on a 2041 qubits system, under 13.5 qubit temperatures (mK). The encoding data into the Quantum circuit was iterated at multiple threshold values, in the range [0.5, 0.6, 0.7]. A circuit (figure 9) at 0.5 threshold is a form of 2-layer circuit design for binary classification problems.

Figure 9. The 2-layer circuit for training samples in the first iteration (Kinshuk Sengupta & Srivastava, 2021)

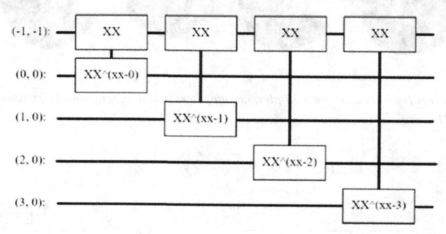

Figure 10. DL models compared with QNN (Kinshuk Sengupta & Srivastava, 2021)

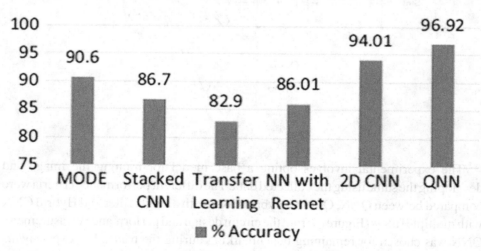

Figure 10 clearly shows that the results achieved by QNN (96.92%) are more accurate than other DL models. This shows that one can implement QNN on medical images to get more proming and accurate results.

The Quantum circuit was built using qubit of length 12 (figure 11) using python, and the circuit is shown in figure 12 and 13 with various combinations of the gates. Figure 14 and 15 are the circuits built with different input values of key length(30).

Figure 11. Qubits defined for the length =12

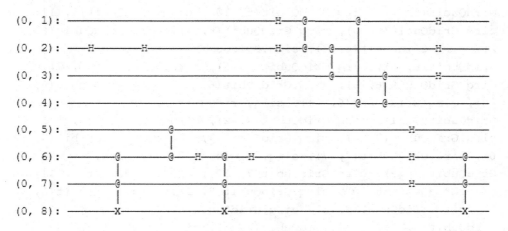

```
[cirq.GridQubit(0, 0), cirq.GridQubit(0, 1), cirq.GridQubit(0,
2), cirq.GridQubit(0, 3), cirq.GridQubit(0, 4), cirq.
GridQubit(0, 5), cirq.GridQubit(0, 6), cirq.GridQubit(0, 7),
cirq.GridQubit(0, 8), cirq.GridQubit(0, 9), cirq.GridQubit(0,
10), cirq.GridQubit(0, 11), cirq.GridQubit(1, 0), cirq.
GridQubit(1, 1), cirq.GridQubit(1, 2), cirq.GridQubit(1, 3),
cirq.GridQubit(1, 4), cirq.GridQubit(1, 5), cirq.GridQubit(1,
6), cirq.GridQubit(1, 7), cirq.GridQubit(1, 8), cirq.
GridQubit(1, 9), cirq.GridQubit(1, 10), cirq.GridQubit(1, 11),
cirq.GridQubit(2, 0), cirq.GridQubit(2, 1), cirq.GridQubit(2,
2), cirq.GridQubit(2, 3), cirq.GridQubit(2, 4), cirq.
GridQubit(2, 5), cirq.GridQubit(2, 6), cirq.GridQubit(2, 7),
cirq.GridQubit(2, 8), cirq.GridQubit(2, 9), cirq.GridQubit(2,
10), cirq.GridQubit(2, 11), cirq.GridQubit(3, 0), cirq.
GridQubit(3, 1), cirq.GridQubit(3, 2), cirq.GridQubit(3, 3),
cirq.GridQubit(3, 4), cirq.GridQubit(3, 5), cirq.GridQubit(3,
6), cirq.GridQubit(3, 7), cirq.GridQubit(3, 8), cirq.
```

```
GridQubit(3, 9), cirq.GridQubit(3, 10), cirq.GridQubit(3, 11),
cirq.GridQubit(4, 0), cirq.GridQubit(4, 1), cirq.GridQubit(4,
2), cirq.GridQubit(4, 3), cirq.GridQubit(4, 4), cirq.
GridQubit(4, 5), cirq.GridQubit(4, 6), cirq.GridQubit(4, 7),
cirq.GridQubit(4, 8), cirq.GridQubit(4, 9), cirq.GridQubit(4,
10), cirq.GridQubit(4, 11), cirq.GridQubit(5, 0), cirq.
GridQubit(5, 1), cirq.GridQubit(5, 2), cirq.GridQubit(5, 3),
cirq.GridQubit(5, 4), cirq.GridQubit(5, 5), cirq.GridQubit(5,
6), cirq.GridQubit(5, 7), cirq.GridQubit(5, 8), cirq.
GridQubit(5, 9), cirq.GridQubit(5, 10), cirq.GridQubit(5, 11),
cirq.GridQubit(6, 0), cirq.GridQubit(6, 1), cirq.GridQubit(6,
2), cirq.GridQubit(6, 3), cirq.GridQubit(6, 4), cirq.
GridQubit(6, 5), cirq.GridQubit(6, 6), cirq.GridQubit(6, 7),
cirq.GridQubit(6, 8), cirq.GridQubit(6, 9), cirq.GridQubit(6,
10), cirq.GridQubit(6, 11), cirq.GridQubit(7, 0), cirq.
GridQubit(7, 1), cirq.GridQubit(7, 2), cirq.GridQubit(7, 3),
cirq.GridQubit(7, 4), cirq.GridQubit(7, 5), cirq.GridQubit(7,
6), cirq.GridQubit(7, 7), cirq.GridQubit(7, 8), cirq.
GridQubit(7, 9), cirq.GridQubit(7, 10), cirq.GridQubit(7, 11),
cirq.GridQubit(8, 0), cirq.GridQubit(8, 1), cirq.GridQubit(8,
2), cirq.GridQubit(8, 3), cirq.GridQubit(8, 4), cirq.
GridQubit(8, 5), cirq.GridQubit(8, 6), cirq.GridQubit(8, 7),
cirq.GridQubit(8, 8), cirq.GridQubit(8, 9), cirq.GridQubit(8,
10), cirq.GridQubit(8, 11), cirq.GridQubit(9, 0), cirq.
GridQubit(9, 1), cirq.GridQubit(9, 2), cirq.GridQubit(9, 3),
cirq.GridQubit(9, 4), cirq.GridQubit(9, 5), cirq.GridQubit(9,
6), cirq.GridQubit(9, 7), cirq.GridQubit(9, 8), cirq.
GridQubit(9, 9), cirq.GridQubit(9, 10), cirq.GridQubit(9,
11), cirq.GridQubit(10, 0), cirq.GridQubit(10, 1), cirq.
GridQubit(10, 2), cirq.GridQubit(10, 3), cirq.GridQubit(10,
4), cirq.GridQubit(10, 5), cirq.GridQubit(10, 6), cirq.
GridQubit(10, 7), cirq.GridQubit(10, 8), cirq.GridQubit(10,
9), cirq.GridQubit(10, 10), cirq.GridQubit(10, 11), cirq.
GridQubit(11, 0), cirq.GridQubit(11, 1), cirq.GridQubit(11,
2), cirq.GridQubit(11, 3), cirq.GridQubit(11, 4), cirq.
GridQubit(11, 5), cirq.GridQubit(11, 6), cirq.GridQubit(11,
7), cirq.GridQubit(11, 8), cirq.GridQubit(11, 9), cirq.
GridQubit(11, 10), cirq.GridQubit(11, 11)]
```

Figure 12. Quantum circuit-1

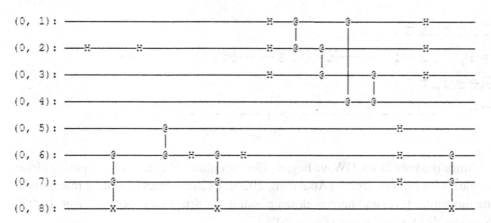

Figure 13. Quantum circuit-2

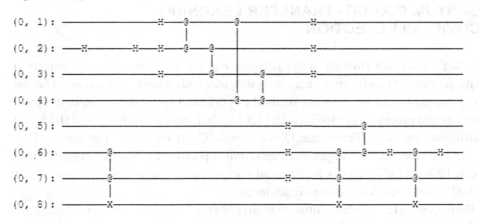

Figure 14. Circuits output with length key =30 for inputs = 1, 2

```
Circuit:
(1, 2): ——X^0.5——M('m')——
Results:
m=0100001001100000010111110001
```

Figure 15. Circuits output with length key =30 for inputs = 4, 12

```
Circuit:
(4, 12): ──X^0.5──M('m')──
Results:
m=001011101101100011100001001101
```

Since the year 2018, DWave began offering enhanced quantum computing cloud service with remote access (Anderson, 2020). QC simulates chemical reactions at the molecular level and narrow down possibly for drugs and vaccines from 10,000 compounds to a few dozen (Press, 2020).

QUANTUM CIRCUIT- TRANSFER LEARNING – COVID- 19 DETECTION

Acar & Yilmaz (2020) in their study of detection of CV-19 from CT images generated the most accurate results, using classical computer and quantum computers. The use of the quantum transfer learning method to perform CV-19 detection in different quantum real processors (IBMQx2, IBMQ-London and IBMQ-Rome) of IBM, and in different simulators (Pennylane, Qiskit-Aer and Cirq). By using a 126 datasets CV-19 and 100 Normal CT images, one can obtain a positive or negative classification of CV-19 with 90% success in classical computers, while a high success rate of 94-100% in quantum computers is achieved.

Performance results and confusion matrix of classical model and hybrid quantum model is shown in figure 16 and in figure 17 is obtained by quantum circuit. Table 1 represents the performance results with 95% CI for classic models and hybrid models on different simulators and IBM Quantum computers.

In another case study of predicting CV-19 severity in patients is proposed by El-Shafeiy et al. (2021). This proposed CQNN approach had two stages; in the first, the QRFS method is implemented to improve its classification performance and, in the second, the QNN predicts the levels of severity of CV-19 in patients.

Table 2 describes the dataset characteristics namely ID, attribute name, type, minimum and maximum value. Table 3 gives the accuracy of CQNN approach for the various input nodes. CQNN achieved an accuracy of 92.33% for the testing dataset, better than those of the other methods.

Figure 16. Confusion matrix for classical model and hybrid quantum models (Acar & Yilmaz, 2020)

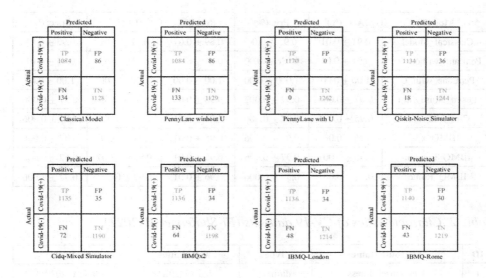

Figure 17. Quantum circuit U(α, β, θ, γ) (Acar & Yilmaz, 2020)

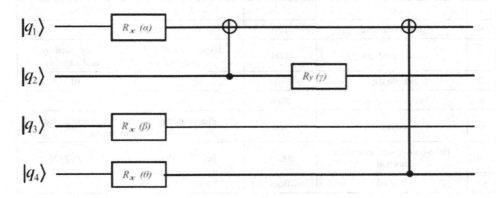

Table 1. The performance results for classical and hybrid model (Acar & Yilmaz, 2020).

Models	Acc. (%)	Pre. (%)	Rec. (%)	F1 (%)	Spec. (%)
Classical_Model	0.91 ± 0.01	0.92 ± 0.00	0.89 ± 0.01	0.91 ± 0.01	0.93 ± 0.01
PenLane_without_U	0.91 ± 0.01	0.926 ± 0.00	0.89 ± 0.01	0.91 ± 0.01	0.93 ± 0.01
PenLane_with_U	1.00 ± 0.00	1.000 ± 0.00	1.00 ± 0.00	1.00 ± 0.00	1.00 ± 0.00
Qiskit_Noise_Sim	0.97 ± 0.006	0.97 ± 0.007	0.98 ± 0.00	0.97 ± 0.05	0.97 ± 0.006
Cirq_Mix_Sim	0.95 ± 0.008	0.97 ± 0.006	0.94 ± 0.01	0.95 ± 0.01	0.97 ± 0.006
IBMQ_x2	0.96 ± 0.008	0.97 ± 0.006	0.95 ± 0.01	0.96 ± 0.01	0.97 ± 0.006
IBMQ_London	0.96 ± 0.007	0.97 ± 0.006	0.96 ± 0.01	0.96 ± 0.007	0.97 ± 0.006
IBMQ_Rome	0.97 ± 0.007	0.97 ± 0.006	0.96 ± 0.01	0.97 ± 0.007	0.97 ± 0.006

Table 2. Characteristics of CV-19 datasets (El-Shafeiy et al. 2021).

ID	Attribute Name	Type	Min. Value	Max. Value
1	Time-onset-illness	dt/time	Jan 16, 2020	Jan 31, 2020
2	Admission_Time	dt/time	Jan 22, 2020	Feb 02, 2020
3	Gender	Text	M or F	
4	Age	Num	22	70
5	Epidemic data	Text	Wahan, China	
6	Comorbidities	Text	Hypertension, diabetics, lg A nephropathy, hypothyroidism and bronchial asthma	
7	Febrile days	Num	1	10
8	Temp before adm	Num	37.3°c	40°c
9	Concomitant sym	Text	Pharyngalgia, dry cough, feebleness and shortness of breath	
10	Time-body-temp-returns-to-normal	dt/time	Jan 27, 2020	Feb 20, 2020
11	O2 uptake	Bool	Y or N	
12	Lopinavir/ ritonavir	Bool	Y or N	
13	Interferon atomization	Bool	Y or N	
14	Arbidol HCL	Bool	Y or N	
15	WBC	Num	2.58	11.75
16.	NEUT	Num	1.3	9.38
17	LYMPH	Num	0.56	1.4
18	NEUT%	Num	42.50%	79.80%
19	LYMPH%	Num	9.60%	45.70%
20	PLT	Num	82	255

Table 2. Continued

ID	Attribute Name	Type	Min. Value	Max. Value
21	HGB	Num	120	169
22	RBC	Num	4.16	5.66
23	ALT	Num	6	85
24	AST	Num	19	54
25	ALB	Num	35.4	52.6
26	TBIL	Num	2.3	26.6
27	DBIL	Num	1.2	9.6
28	CRP	Num	10	38.9
29	PCT	Num	0.022	0.108
30	IL-6	Num	1.5	40.9
31	LYMPH0	Num	0.56	1.4
32	LYMPH3	Num	0.4	1.45
33	LYMPH5	Num	0.37	1.65
34	LYMPH7	Num	0.37	1.91
35	LYMPH9	Num	0.51	2.08
36	LYMPH11	Num	0.32	3.06
37	LYMPH13	Num	0.55	1.98
38	LYMPH15	Num	0.45	2.43

Table 3. Accuracy levels of CQNN (El Shafeiy et al. 2021).

Input nodes	Acc. of CQNN
8	0.72445
10	0.65723
13	0.76945
15	0.79836
18	0.88527
20	0.72877
24	0.91238
30	0.92334

CONCLUSION

The benefits of quantum computing for the development of health care and for the global technology are high. In this study of diabetes retinal fundus images, an algorithm based on deep machine learning generated high sensitivity and specificity. Retinopathy quantum computing improves imaging, diagnosis, and treatment. Quantum computer is seen accessible for daily use in medicine and research. The QNN and CQNN proposed method on large datasets to test its effectiveness and then automatically upload the results to a cloud-based epidemiological and early-warning monitoring for disease surveillance and medical monitoring in institutions at all levels of government. Hence, Quantum computing provides early warnings, analyze the situation and support for decision-making in the state-of-art of the pandemic.

REFERENCES

Acar, E., & Yilmaz, I. (2020). COVID-19 detection on IBM quantum computer with classical-quantum transfer learning. doi:10.1101/2020.11.07.20227306

Anderson, M. (2020). Can Quantum computers Help Us Respond to the Coronavirus. *IEEE Spectrum*.

Atik, J., & Jeutner, V. (2021). Quantum computing and computational law. *Law, Innovation and Technology*, *13*(2), 302–324. Advance online publication. doi:10.1080/17579961.2021.1977216

eHealth. (2020). https://ehealth.eletsonline.com/2020/11/quantumizing-digital-healthcare-arena/

El-Shafeiy, E., Hassanien, A. E., Sallam, K. M., & Abohany, A. A. (2021). Approach for Training Quantum Neural Network to Predict Severity of COVID-19 in Patients. *Computers, Materials, & Continua*, *66*(2), 1745–1755.

Flöther, F., Murphy, J., Murtha, J., & Sow, D. (2020). *Exploring quantum computing use cases for healthcare*. IBM.

Gulshan, V., Peng, L., Coram, M., Stumpe, M. C., Wu, D., Narayanaswamy, A., Venugopalan, S., Widner, K., Madams, T., Cuadros, J., Kim, R., Raman, R., Nelson, P. C., Mega, J. L., & Webster, D. R. (2016). Development and Validation of a Deep Learning Algorithm for Detection of Diabetic Retinopathy in Retinal Fundus Photographs. *Journal of the American Medical Association*, *316*(22), 2402–2410. doi:10.1001/jama.2016.17216 PMID:27898976

Henderson, M., Shakya, S., Pradhan, S., & Cook, T. (2019). *Quanvolutional neural networks: powering image recognition with quantum circuits.* arXiv.org.

Kinshuk Sengupta, K., & Srivastava, P. R. (2021). Quantum algorithm for quicker clinical prognostic analysis: An application and experimental study using CT scan images of COVID-19 patients. *BMC Medical Informatics and Decision Making, 21*(1), 227. doi:10.118612911-021-01588-6 PMID:34330278

Marr, B. (n.d.). *How Quantum Computers Will Revolutionise Artificial Intelligence, Machine Learning And Big Data.* Available at https://bernardmarr.com/

Mehta, D., Paharia, A., Singh, S., & Salman, M. (2019). Quantum computing will enhance the power of Artificial Intelligence. A boon for Research endeavors across the globe. *American Journal of PharmTech Research.*

Press, G. (2020). Calling on AI and Quantum Computing to Fight the Coronavirus. *Forbes.*

Quantum Computing and AI. (2021). *A Transformational Match.* Available at https://www.bbvaopenmind.com/

Rai, B. (2019). *Advanced Deep Learning with R: Become an Expert at Designing, Building, and Improving Advanced Neural Network Models Using R.* Packt Publishing. doi:10.1002/9781119564843.ch5

Sahni, V., & Srivastava, D. P. (2015). Quantum Information and Computation Systems. *CSI Communications.*

Solenov, D., Brieler, J., & Scherrer, J. F. (2018). The Potential of Quantum Computing and Machine Learning to Advance Clinical Research and Change the Practice of Medicine. *Missouri Medicine, 115*(5), 463–467. PMID:30385997

Taulli, T. (2020). *Quantum Computing: What Does It Mean For AI (Artificial Intelligence)?* Available at https://www.forbes.com

Torgler, B. (2020). Big Data, Artificial Intelligence, and Quantum Computing in Sports. Academic Press.

KEY TERMS AND DEFINITIONS

COVID-19: Coronavirus disease (*COVID*-19) is an infectious disease caused by the SARS-CoV-2 virus.

Diabetic Retinopathy: It is an eye condition that can cause vision loss and blindness in people who have diabetes.

Healthcare: It is the various services for the prevention or treatment of illness and injuries. Nobody wants to pay more for health care.

Hybrid CNN: It utilizes a Deep Neural Network (DNN) to effectively memorize global features by one-dimensional (1D) data and utilizes a CNN to generalize local features by two-dimensional (2D) data.

Net Carbon Zero Emissions: It refers to achieving an overall balance between greenhouse gas emissions produced and greenhouse gas emissions taken out of the atmosphere.

Quantum Circuit: In quantum information theory, a quantum circuit is a model for quantum computation, similar to classical circuits, in which a computation is a sequence of quantum gates, measurements, initializations of qubits to known values, and possibly other actions.

Quantum Computing: Quantum computing is an area of computing focused on developing computer technology based on the principles of quantum theory. It uses quantum bits or qubits.

Quantum Machine Learning: Quantum machine learning (QML) is built on two concepts: quantum data and hybrid quantum-classical models.

Quanvolutional Neural Network: Quanvolutional layers operate on input data by locally transforming the data using a number of random quantum circuits, in a way that is similar to the transformations performed by random convolutional filter layers.

TensorFlow Quantum: TensorFlow Quantum (TFQ) is a Python framework for quantum machine learning.

ADDITIONAL NOTES ON WHY NET ZERO CARBON EMISSIONS

Reducing emissions from hospitals and supply chains, there are a number of benefits that health institutions and society can reap from net zero healthcare. The health systems have a accountability to implement *the Hippocratic Oath*, to "do no harm" as it relates to its own climate footprint, while influencing other sectors to do the same. It switches to renewable sources of energy that provides healthcare institutions with a *financial benefit* in the form of reduced utilities and equipment costs. It implements climate mitigation policies that will contribute to *improved health conditions* for healthcare workers and citizens. Net zero emissions can help limit the occurrence of extreme weather events and climate catastrophes that bothers health systems.

Chapter 7
Quantum Software Engineering and Technology

Subramaniam Meenakshi Sundaram
GSSS Institute of Engineering and Technology for Women, India

Tejaswini R. Murgod
GSSS Institute of Engineering and Technology for Women, India

ABSTRACT

Quantum technology works with and relies on sub-atomic particles or physics that operates on the quantum level. Quantum computing has become a mature field, having diversified applications in supply chain and logistics, chemistry, economics and financial services, energy and agriculture, medicine and health, etc. In the recent years, companies have started to incorporate quantum software to benefit the research and the practitioner communities. Software engineering and programming practices need to be brought into the domain of quantum computing. Quantum algorithms provide the ability to analyze the data and offer simulations based on the data. A few of the quantum computing programming languages include QISKit, Q#, Cirq, and forest are used to write and run quantum programs. In this chapter, the authors provide an overall picture of the problems and challenges of developing quantum software and up-to-date software engineering processes, methods, techniques, practices, and principles for the development of quantum software to both researchers and practitioners.

DOI: 10.4018/978-1-7998-9183-3.ch007

INTRODUCTION

Decades have passed since the great minds of physics, including Richard Feynman and David Deutsch, predicted that the laws of quantum mechanics could give rise to a computing paradigm that is superior to classical computing. But controlling fragile quantum systems well enough to construct even the most primitive quantum computing hardware has proved taxing. Quantum software plays a critical role in exploiting the full potential of quantum computing systems. Experimental advances in the past few years have proved the power of quantum computing. Just as programming languages and compilers facilitate interaction with the semiconductor transistors in a classical computer, many layers of software tools will sit between quantum algorithms and hardware. An important component is quantum error-correcting code. The fragility of quantum bits leads to errors during computation, and choices about how to make quantum-computing architectures fault tolerant have a knock-on effect on higher layers of the quantum tool chain. With quantum programming languages and compilers to hand, the quantum software engineer can implement 'killer' software applications, in which the speed afforded by quantum computers will have real-world impact. Factoring using Shor's algorithm is one potential application because it could break current methods of encryption. Yet cryptographers are already devising classical cryptosystems that would guarantee security even if quantum computers achieve factoring at mesmerizing speeds. Perhaps quantum machine learning will also turn out to be a killer application, it has, at least, been an important motivator for IT giant companies to invest in quantum computing.

As the practical relevance of quantum computing becomes clearer, we should not forget the part that foundational thinking played in its inception. Research on the fundamental limits of classical versus quantum computing remains fascinating and may even help to surmount quantum engineering hurdles.

BACKGROUND

A) Evolution of Quantum Computing

As early as 1959 the American physicist and Nobel laureate Richard Feynman noted that, as electronic components begin to reach microscopic scales, effects predicted by quantum mechanics occur—which, he suggested, might be exploited in the design of more powerful computers. During the 1980s and '90s the theory of quantum computers advanced considerably beyond Feynman's early speculations. In 1985 David Deutsch of the University of Oxford described the construction of quantum logic gates for a universal quantum computer, and in 1994 Peter Shor of

AT&T devised an algorithm to factor numbers with a quantum computer that would require as few as six qubits (although many more qubits would be necessary for factoring large numbers in a reasonable time).

In 1998 Isaac Chuang of the Los Alamos National Laboratory, Neil Gershenfeld of the Massachusetts Institute of Technology (MIT), and Mark Kubinec of the University of California at Berkeley created the first quantum computer (2-qubit) that could be loaded with data and output a solution. In 2001 Shor's algorithm was demonstrated for the first time in a real quantum computing experiment, albeit with a very pedestrian problem: 15=3×5. The IBM system employed qubits in nuclear spins, similar to an MRI machine. In 2004, Robert Schoelkopf and his collaborators at Yale University invent circuit QED, a means of studying the interaction of a photon and an artificial quantum object on a chip. Their work established the standard for coupling and reading out superconducting qubits as systems continue to scale. In 2007 Schoelkopf and his collaborators invent a type of superconducting qubit designed to have reduced sensitivity to charge noise, a major obstacle for long coherence. The superconducting qubit has been adopted by many superconducting quantum groups, including at IBM.

In 2012 several important parameters for quantum information processing with transmon qubits are improved. IBM extends the coherence time, which is the duration that a qubit retains its quantum state, up to 100 microseconds. In 2015 the IBM quantum team performs an experiment demonstrating the smallest, almost-quantum error detection code. With a single quantum state stabilized, it's possible to detect both types of quantum errors: bit-flips and phase-flips. The code is realized in a 4-qubit lattice arrangement, which serves as a building block for future quantum computing systems.

Later in 2016 IBM scientists build the IBM Quantum Experience, a first-of-a-kind quantum computing platform delivered via the IBM Cloud and accessible by desktop or mobile devices. It enables users to run experiments on IBM's quantum processor, work with individual qubits, and explore tutorials and simulations of the wondrous possibilities of quantum computing.

2019 was the biggest year for quantum computing since, well, ever. It's the year IBM put a quantum computer in a box and Google claimed its Bristlecone system reached quantum supremacy. But perhaps most exciting was the incredible research happening in universities and think-tanks around the globe. From warp drives to time travel, scientists around the world released one breakthrough paper after another.

B) Quantum Computing and Impact on Engineering

Quantum computers will be faster, meaning they will be able to crack problems, solve equations and enrich our understanding of the universe in ways we can't yet predict.

There is no fully operational quantum computer capable of sustaining a quantum state for a prolonged time. IBM has built a 50-qubit computer that can generate and maintain a quantum state for around 90 seconds, which is currently the record. Quantum machines must be kept at extremely low temperatures near absolute zero to be able to maintain quantum states for extended periods. Quantum technology represent the leap forward in computing necessary to solve the hardest problems in fields like software verification and validation (VV), materials science, and machine learning and artificial intelligence and machine learning. Another potential use of quantum computing is to simulate complex chemical and biological systems. This simulation is key to producing advanced materials (such as metals, polymers, and hybrids), supporting advanced aeronautics, and advancing the state of biotechnology to develop new vaccines and treatments for diseases.

C) Essential Software Components of a Quantum Computer

In addition to creating the hardware functionality to support quantum computing, a functional quantum computer will also require extensive software components. Given the different, and emerging, approaches to building a quantum data plane, early-stage high-level software tools must be particularly flexible, if they are to remain useful in the event of changes in hardware and algorithms. This requirement complicates the task of developing complete software architecture for quantum computing.

For quantum computers, simulation tools, such as universal simulator, can provide a programmer with the ability to model each quantum operation and to track the quantum state that would results, along with its evolution in time. This capability is essential for debugging both programs and newly developed hardware. Optimization tools such as resource estimators would enable rapid estimation of the performance and qubit resources needed to perform different quantum algorithms.

Debugging and verification of quantum programs are also major challenges. Quantum computing programs have an exponentially large state-space that is collapsed by physical qubit measurements, and quantum computing execution cannot be restarted after a mid-run measurement. Thus, design of debugging and verification techniques for quantum programs is an essential and fundamentally challenging requirement to enable progress in quantum computing development. While QC simulation and debugging are truly grand challenge research endeavors, other aspects of the software tool chain such as languages and compilers have seen greater progress, but also remain important.

D) Software for Quantum Computing

Quantum algorithms provide the ability to analyze the data and offer simulations based on the data. These algorithms are written in a quantum-focused programming language. Several quantum languages have been developed by researchers and technology companies.

These are a few of the quantum computing programming languages:

1. QISKit: The Quantum Information Software Kit from IBM is a full-stack library to write, simulate, and run quantum programs.
2. Q#: The programming language included in the Microsoft Quantum Development Kit. The development kit includes a quantum simulator and algorithm libraries.
3. Cirq: A quantum language developed by Google that uses a python library to write circuits and run these circuits in quantum computers and simulators.
4. Forest: A developer environment created by Rigetti Computing that is used to write and run quantum programs.

E) Challenges of Quantum Computing:

Quantum computing is a new and promising technology with the potential of exponentially powerful computation, if only a large-scale one can be built. There are several challenges in building a large-scale quantum computer – fabrication, verification, and architecture. The power of quantum computing comes from the ability to store a complex state in a single bit. This also what makes quantum systems difficult to build, verify, and design. Quantum states are fragile, so fabrication must be precise, and bits must often operate at very low temperatures.

Quantum computers are extremely temperamental machines, which makes them immensely difficult to build and operate. They need to be isolated from the outside environment and kept almost at absolute zero (-273°C) in order to be usable. If not, they produce quantum de coherence, which is essentially the loss of information to the environment. Most quantum computers require temperatures colder than those found in deep space. To reach these temperatures, all the components and hardware are contained within a dilution refrigerator—highly specialized equipment that cools the qubits to just above absolute zero. Because standard electronics don't work at these temperatures, a majority of quantum computers today use room-temperature control. With this method, controls on the outside of the refrigerator send signals through cables, communicating with the qubits inside.

F) Quantum Computing Applications:

As the technology develops, quantum computing could lead to significant advances in numerous fields, from chemistry and materials science to nuclear physics and machine learning.

Top potential applications include: cyber security, drug development, financial modeling, weather forecasting and climate change, artificial intelligence, health care, electronic materials discovery etc.

Quantum computing could enable breakthroughs by:

1. Machine learning: Improved ML through faster structured prediction. Examples include Boltzmann machines, quantum Boltzmann machines, semi-supervised learning, unsupervised learning and deep learning.
2. Artificial intelligence: Faster calculations could improve perception, comprehension, and circuit fault diagnosis/binary classifiers.
3. Chemistry: New fertilizers, catalysts, battery chemistries will all drive improvements in resource utilization
4. Biochemistry: New drugs, tailored drugs, and maybe even hair restorer.
5. Finance: Quantum computing could enable faster, more complex Monte Carlo simulations; for example, trading, trajectory optimization, market instability, price optimization and hedging strategies.
6. Healthcare: DNA gene sequencing, such as radiotherapy treatment optimization/ brain tumor detection, could be performed in seconds instead of hours or weeks.
7. Materials: super strong materials; corrosion proof paints; lubricants; semiconductors
8. Computer science: Faster multidimensional search functions; for example, query optimization, mathematics and simulations

G) Quantum Software Engineering

The fact that quantum computing is reaching the degree of maturity that claims for a Quantum Software Engineering is evidenced by the considerable amount of research works on this subject that has been developed in recent years. The most complete and recent survey on this topic is maybe the one developed by Prof. Jianjun Zhao (Zhao, 2020). It provides a definition of QSE that could be widely accepted by the community: "Quantum software engineering is the use of sound engineering principles for the development, operation, and maintenance of quantum software and the associated document to obtain economically quantum software that is reliable and works efficiently on quantum computers". The software needs processes and processes need methodologies that help carry out each of the activities of the processes whether it is requirements specification, architectural design, detailed design, implementation or testing (Piattini & Pérez-Castillo, 2020) .

Regarding the process for quantum software development, it could be assumed that the basic strategies for classical software development could be valid. They provide a general guide to approach the problem with the aim of getting a piece of software that supports the problem. In any case, quantum software processes, as commonly accepted for classical software today, should be as iterative, incremental and agile as possible. However, the methodologies for carrying out each activity of the process should be reviewed to address the needs of quantum software development. The reason being that the techniques

A key step for having new techniques and methodologies is defining new abstractions for the quantum computing world. We include a class model in an UML class diagram to represent a real-world object. This object exists in the system with the ability to interact with other entities. In this way the entities interact and are modeled in a sequence diagram. Abstract Data Types (ADT) allows data structures to be modeled along with the set of operations to manipulate them. With all the above, maybe one of the most interesting directions to be addressed by quantum software engineering research is to propose adequate abstractions for modeling, designing and building quantum programs. When thinking about these abstractions it is also interesting to think that the type of problems that will be solved with quantum computing are those included in the Bounded-error Quantum Polynomial time (BQP) class.

Currently, quantum programming languages (Garhwal & Ahmad, 2019; Gay, 2006; Miszczak, 2010; Sofge, 2008) work almost at the quantum circuit level. One of the greatest advances towards modern programming languages was the development of structured programming that led to the basic structures for computing: sequence, bifurcation, iteration. It opened the doors to the diverse programming paradigms we have today in classical computing. As with abstractions, we could wonder what should be the basic structures and patterns in the development of quantum programs. Again, to do this, one must assume that the nature of a quantum computer is very different to Von Newman's architecture model

H) Quantum Software Processes and Methodologies

One of the main lessons learned during the evolution of classic software engineering is that software needs processes and processes need methodologies that help carry out each of the activities of the processes whether it is requirements specification, architectural design, detailed design, implementation or testing. Regarding the process for quantum software development, it could be assumed that the basic strategies for classical software development could be valid. They provide a general guide to approach the problem with the aim of getting a piece of software that supports the problem. In any case, quantum software processes, as commonly accepted for classical software today, should be as iterative, incremental and agile as possible. However, the methodologies for carrying out each activity of the process should be reviewed to address the needs of quantum software development. The reason being that the techniques designed for classical computing are based on an underlying model of computing in which a sequence of instructions manipulates a set of data. The final state of the data is the output of the program. For example, the way in which a design is produced from a requirement specification is tightly aligned with such computational model. Nevertheless, such model is radically different to the quantum computational model. We have not such sequence of instructions but a system with the ability of having a set of possible states and being in all of them at the same time. Computation stops when a certain subset of the system state is in a desired state, which will define the state of the whole system by collapse. There are authors who have already approached some methodologies to deal with some activities such as design (Pérez-Delgado & Perez-Gonzalez, 2020) or even re-engineering (Jiménez-Navajas & Piattini, 2020).

I) Abstractions for Quantum Software

A key step for having new techniques and methodologies is defining new abstractions for the quantum computing world. Let's focus now on the mechanisms of abstraction that we use in the design of classic software. For example, when we include a class model in an UML class diagram we are representing a real-world object. This object exists in the system with the ability to interact with other entities. The ways in which entities interact is modeled in a sequence diagram. We use classes because they proved to be much richer than the Abstract Data Types (ADT) that we used previously. They (ADT) basically allowed data structures to be modeled along with the set of operations to manipulate them. The reason to have them was that giving each programmer the responsibility of implementing the operations of a data structure introduced not only duplicate efforts but semantic variations in the structures that made them difficult to reuse. Both, the structures and the operations were hardly portable from one program to another.

Moreover, the functionality code ended up being tangled with the code that implemented the operations on the data structures. Software Engineering Researchers realized then that a data structure was meaningless without the set of operations to manipulate it directly. Before ADTs, we simply used procedures and functions to model pieces of functionality that the programmer could focus on, program, maintain, and evolve in isolation. In any case, all those abstractions correspond to pieces of software functionality as sequences of instructions that eventually manipulate data and that interact with each other by means of a protocol of control transfer from one to another. Again, this is due to classic computers being based on Von Neumann's machine model that expects to execute instructions in a certain sequence and our models must represent reality on that computer model. It is worth remembering at this point what happened with the code written by those programmers born in procedural programming when they went on to the use of classes. It was common to find classes that modeled data structures (the TADs they were used to), classes grouping different sets of modules and a main class which collected the program control flow. This was the case even when object-oriented programming books systematically started explaining the differences between procedural and OOP programming. It was very hard then for programmers to change their way of conceiving software systems even when the underlying computer model was the same.

Thus, the new change we are facing in which the underlying computer model is completely different is expected to be even harder. When we think about taking our abstractions into the quantum environment, many questions arise: For example, Does it make sense to have a class in quantum computing? Is that a proper abstraction? What is the interest of having a class instance in all its possible states? What is the point of modeling a class in which part of its state is entangled with that of another class? What are the best abstractions for doing this? No doubt, we will feel inclined to replicate our techniques and abstractions from classical computing to quantum computing. But then, just as it happened to programmers who moved from procedural to object oriented programming, we may end up using them improperly wanting to do something that is intrinsically different. We will provide programmers with the possibility of generating classic computing solutions that will run on quantum computers, but we will not have generated the opportunity to "think and model in quantum". With all the above, maybe one of the most interesting directions to be addressed by quantum software engineering research is to propose adequate abstractions for modelling, designing and building quantum programs. When thinking about these abstractions it is also interesting to think that the type of problems that will be solved with quantum computing are those included in the *BQP* class. If the typology of these problems can be categorized, domain-specific modeling languages could be designed for them.

J) Quantum Structured Programming

Currently, quantum programming languages (Garhwal & Ahmad, 2019; Gay, 2006; Miszczak, 2010; Sofge, 2008) work almost at the quantum circuit level. Its description is very reminiscent of the wiring work needed by the ENIAC to execute programs. One of the greatest advances towards modern programming languages was the development of structured programming that led to the basic structures for computing: sequence, bifurcation, iteration. It opened the doors to the diverse programming paradigms we have today in classical computing. As with abstractions, we could wonder what should be the basic structures and patterns in the development of quantum programs. Again, to do this, one must assume that the nature of a quantum computer is very different to Von Newman's architecture model. There are researchers who are already concerned about this aspect: (Knill, 1996; Leymann, 2019; Ying & Feng, 2010).

CONCLUSION

The functions of quantum technologies are derived from science that cannot be explained by classical physics, such as Newton's Laws of Motion, thermodynamics or Maxwell's equations of electromagnetism. Despite recent advances in quantum programming tools, there are two major challenges facing quantum software developers. First, there is an understandable fear of betting on a platform or language that ends up being discontinued. Second, quantum computer scientists need to understand current software engineering principles and techniques, or they will spend too much time reinventing the wheel.

With quantum programming languages and compilers, the quantum software engineer can implement 'killer' software applications, in which the speed afforded by quantum computers will have real-world impact. Factoring using Shor's algorithm is one potential application because it could break current methods of encryption. Yet cryptographers are already devising classical cryptosystems that would guarantee security even if quantum computers achieve factoring at mesmerizing speeds. IBM has built a 50-qubit computer that can generate and maintain a quantum state for around 90 seconds, which is currently the record.

For quantum computers, simulation tools, such as a so-called universal simulator, can provide a programmer with the ability to model each quantum operation and to track the quantum state that would results, along with its evolution in time. The software tools needed to create and debug quantum programs are as essential to all scales of quantum computer as the underlying quantum data plane.

Debugging and verification of quantum programs are also major challenges. Most classical computers provide programmers the ability to stop execution at an arbitrary point in the program, and examine the machine state—that is, the values of program variables and other items stored in memory. Programmers can determine whether the state is correct or not, and if not, find the program bug

As the technology develops, quantum computing could lead to significant advances in numerous fields, from chemistry and materials science to nuclear physics and machine learning. Top potential applications include cyber security, drug development, financial modeling, weather forecasting and climate change, artificial intelligence to name a few. Quantum software engineering is the use of sound engineering principles for the development, operation, and maintenance of quantum software and the associated document to obtain economically quantum software that is reliable and works efficiently on quantum computers. Software Engineering researchers realized then that a data structure was meaningless without the set of operations to manipulate it directly When thinking about these abstractions it is also interesting to think that the type of problems that will be solved with quantum computing are those included in the bounded-error quantum polynomial time (BQP)class. If the typology of these problems can be categorized, domain-specific modeling languages could be designed for them.

REFERENCES

Garhwal, S., & Ahmad, A. (2019). Quantum programming language: A systematic review of research topic and top cited languages. *Archives of Computational Methods in Engineering*, 1–22.

Gay, S. J. (2006). Quantum programming languages: Survey and bibliography. *Mathematical Structures in Computer Science*, *16*(4), 581. doi:10.1017/S0960129506005378

How quantum technology will change engineering. (n.d.). https://www.sei.cmu.edu

Jiménez-Navajas, L., & Piattini, M. (2020). Reverse engineering of quantum programs toward KDM models. In *Quality of Information and Communications Technology - 13th International Conference, Faro, Portugal, September 9-11, 2020, Proceedings*. Springer. 10.1007/978-3-030-58793-2_20

Knill, E. (1996). *Conventions for quantum pseudocode, Technical Report*. Los Alamos National Lab. doi:10.2172/366453

Leymann, F. (2019). Towards a pattern language for quantum algorithms. *International Workshop on Quantum Technology and Optimization Problems*, 218–230. 10.1007/978-3-030-14082-3_19

Miszczak, J. A. (2010). Models of quantum computation and quantum programming languages. arXiv preprint arXiv:1012.6035

Pérez-Delgado, C. A., & Perez-Gonzalez, H. G. (2020). Towards a quantum software modeling language. *Proceedings of the IEEE/ACM 42nd International Conference on Software Engineering Workshops*, 442–444. 10.1145/3387940.3392183

Piattini & Pérez-Castillo. (2020). Quantum computing: A new software engineering golden age. *SIGSOFT Softw. Eng. Notes, 45*, 12–14. doi:10.1145/3402127.3402131

Quantum software engineering challenges. (n.d.). https://www.cutter.co

Sofge, D. A. (2008), A survey of quantum programming languages: History, methods, and tools. *Second International Conference on Quantum, Nano and Micro Technologies (ICQNM 2008)*, 66–71. 10.1109/ICQNM.2008.15

Ying, M., & Feng, Y. (2010). Quantum loop programs. *Acta Informatica, 47*(4), 221–250. doi:10.100700236-010-0117-4

Zhao, J. (2020). Quantum software engineering: Landscapes and horizons. arXiv preprint arXiv:2007.07047

KEY TERMS AND DEFINITIONS

Abstract Data Type (ADT): Is a mathematical model for data types. This is defined by its behavior (semantics) from the point of view of a user, of the data, specifically in terms of possible values, possible operations on data of this type, and the behavior of these operations.

Bounded-Error Quantum Polynomial Time (BQP): In computational complexity theory, bounded-error quantum polynomial time (BQP) is the class of decision problems solvable by a quantum computer in polynomial time, with an error probability of at most 1/3 for all instances.

Quantum Algorithm: Runs on a realistic model of quantum computation, the most commonly used model being the quantum circuit model of computation.

Quantum Computer: Can be referred to a machine that consists of a many-particle quantum system for solving complex computational problems. Possibly the most important issue in quantum computers fabrication is making a closed box. In other words, since quantum systems are very fragile, the probability of de coherence and de phasing is very high.

Quantum Computing: Harnesses the phenomena of quantum mechanics to deliver a huge leap forward in computation to solve certain problems. This is a type of computation that harnesses the collective properties of quantum states, such as superposition, interference, and entanglement, to perform calculations. The devices that perform quantum computations are known as quantum computers.

Quantum Engineering: Is a revolutionary discipline that seeks theoretical and practical applications of Quantum Information Science. It encompasses both fundamental physics and the broad engineering skill-set necessary to meet the practical challenges of the future.

Quantum Logic Gates: A quantum logic gate (or simply quantum gate) is a basic quantum circuit operating on a small number of qubits. They are the building blocks of quantum circuits, like classical logic gates are for conventional digital circuits.

Quantum Machine Learning: Is the integration of quantum algorithms within machine learning programs. The most common use of the term refers to machine learning algorithms for the analysis of classical data executed on a quantum computer, i.e. quantum-enhanced machine learning.

Quantum Programming Languages: Are essential to translate ideas into instructions that can be executed by a quantum computer. They are crucial to the programming of quantum computers at scale but also they can facilitate the discovery and development of quantum algorithms even before hardware exists that is capable of executing them. These are used for controlling existing physical devices, for estimating the execution costs of quantum algorithms on future devices, for teaching quantum computing concepts, or for verifying quantum algorithms and their implementations.

Quantum Technology: Is a class of technology that works by using the principles of quantum mechanics (the physics of sub-atomic particles), including quantum entanglement and quantum superposition. This is an emerging field of physics and engineering, which relies on the principles of quantum physics. Quantum computing, quantum sensors, quantum cryptography, quantum simulation, quantum metrology and quantum imaging are all examples of quantum technologies, where properties of quantum mechanics, especially quantum entanglement, quantum superposition and quantum tunneling, are important.

Qubit: Qubit or quantum bit is the basic unit of quantum information. The quantum version of the classic binary bit physically realized with a two-state device. This is a two-state (or two-level) quantum-mechanical system, one of the simplest quantum systems displaying the peculiarity of quantum mechanics.

APPENDIX

1. **Major problems in Quantum Computing** "Quantum Computing is incredibly exciting because it is the only technology that we know of that could fundamentally change what is practically computable, and this could soon change the foundations of chemistry, materials science, biology, medicine, and agriculture." Over the past decade, quantum computing has evolved from a field of scientific research to a full-fledged technology industry.

Industry, governments, and Universities are all experimenting with advanced quantum computing hardware and software to become quantum ready. To achieve quantum advantage using quantum computers that emulate how nature processes information is challenging because quantum computing is so different from classical computing. To solve problems using integrated quantum and classical computations requires innovation and ingenuity. Integrating quantum and classical computations can generate practical solutions for different applications and technology stages by leveraging the strengths of both worlds.

The benefits of quantum computing are promising, but there are huge obstacles to overcome still. Some problems with quantum computing are:

1. Interference - the slightest disturbance in a quantum system can cause a quantum computation to collapse, a process known as de-coherence. A quantum computer must be totally isolated from all external interference during the computation phase. Some success has been achieved with the use of qubits in intense magnetic fields, using ions.

2. Error correction - Qubits are not digital bits of data and cannot use conventional error correction. Error correction is critical in quantum computing, where even a single error in a calculation can cause the validity of the entire computation to collapse. There has been considerable progress in this area, however. With an error correction algorithm developed that utilizes 9 qubits -- 1 computational and 8 correctional. More recently, there was a breakthrough by IBM that makes do with a total of 5 qubits (1 computational and 4 correctional).

3. Output observance - Retrieving output data after a quantum calculation is complete risks corrupting the data. Developments have since been made, such as a database search algorithm that relies on the special "wave" shape of the probability curve in quantum computers. This ensures that once all calculations are done, the act of measurement will see the quantum state decohere into the correct answer.

2. A Quantum Workforce

For most of us, quantum computing, next-generation quantum sensing and quantum networking still belong to the future. But many early-career scientists and students are already preparing for that future.

When there is an infusion of new people and new ideas, there's likely to be a big advance in technology," The realm of quantum technology extends well beyond physics, into any problem for which many potential solutions exist, such as modeling climate and weather, creating new types of molecules, or examining financial markets. To tackle these types of problems, people are working to build useful quantum computers.

Building quantum computers requires a number of interconnected engineering systems. Specialized electronics send precise microwave signals to the processor to control the qubit. Quantum systems require certain lasers, optics, vacuums and cryogenic systems. There is always the push to design these systems in more compact and stable forms. The new generation needs to be trained to work with this technology and advance this field. If we do that right, it will dramatically expand opportunities in this field.

Chapter 8
Simulation of Bloch Sphere for a Single Qubit

Harsha Vardhan Garine
BML Munjal University, India

Atul Mishra
BML Munjal University, India

Anubhav Agrawal
BML Munjal University, India

ABSTRACT

The Bloch sphere is a generalisation of the complex number z with |z|2 = 1 being represented in the complex plane as a point on the unit circle. The goal of the research is to create a simulation that can be used to visualise a Bloch sphere of a single quantum bit, also known as a Qbit. QISKIT (developed by IBM) is an open-source lab for education in the realm of quantum computing, and is used to test and validate this simulator. This study made use of both quantitative and qualitative methods of investigation.

INTRODUCTION

A bit is the fundamental unit of a computer. The essential component allows data to be stored in binary numbers, either 0 or 1. In a similar vein, the smallest unit of a quantum computer capable of storing information is referred to as a quantum bit, or in short, a qubit, for short. It has a complicated two-level mechanical system with two states, $|1>$ and $|0>$, divided into two categories. In the same way, that information stored in a classic bit may be updated to meet our requirements, data

DOI: 10.4018/978-1-7998-9183-3.ch008

or data recorded in a quantum bit can likewise be modified within the confines of quantum mechanics. Different gates, such as XOR, OR, and more, are used in digital electronics to change data and transport bits of information, among other things. In the quantum world, we have a variety of gates to choose from. To better understand how these gates function and how the qubit interacts with gates, we must first understand a few mathematical concepts such as complex numbers, matrices, and vectors. This is analogous to a simulation problem in that it is necessary to comprehend and visualize the process. It is possible to tackle this difficulty by modeling and simulating the procedure. Refer to Figure 1 for a visual understanding of how a physical quantum device is simulated on a real quantum simulator.

This is a discrete event simulation, which means that the outputs are fixed for the specified set of input parameters. The work (which is either one of $|1>$ or $|0>$) is determined by the probability of achieving the desired results. Please keep in mind that this project will only be able to replicate a single qubit at this time. It is possible to simulate several qubits as well.

Figure 1. A simulator of a real quantum computer

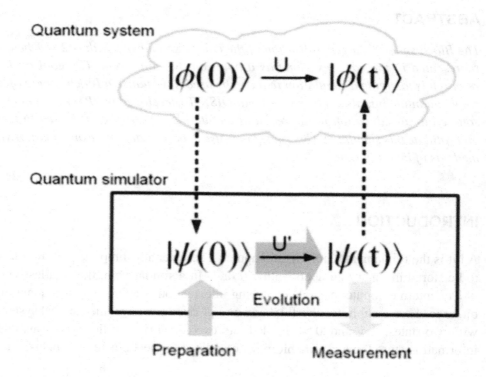

BACKGROUND

It is challenging to visualize a quantum bit's state consistently visually, and the mathematics required is expensive to solve. As the number of qubits increases, they are simulating the difference in a qubit after a gate is applied gets progressively complex. Matrix multiplication in multiple dimensions is essential in this scenario due to using mathematical techniques and concepts such as live vectors. Visualizing or recreating a Bloch sphere in a graphical environment would be beneficial. The conventional bit contains only two gates: a NOT gate that reverses the bit from 1 to 0 and another that changes the bit from 0 to 1. Four unitary operations or gates are matrix multiplied to form a qubit's final state. After converting this final state to polar form, the changed qubit is acquired. Figure 2 here represents different gates and their corresponding matrixes for unitary operations.

$$I := \begin{pmatrix} 1 & 0 \\ 0 & 1 \end{pmatrix}, X := \begin{pmatrix} 0 & 1 \\ 1 & 0 \end{pmatrix}$$

$$Y := \begin{pmatrix} 0 & -i \\ i & 0 \end{pmatrix}, Z := \begin{pmatrix} 1 & 0 \\ 0 & -1 \end{pmatrix}$$

Different gates for a single qubit.

Pasieka (Pasieka et al., 2009) introduces the Bloch sphere interpretation of single qubit quantum channels and operations. This work presents a mathematical technique that begins with an arbitrary mathematical description of a channel and proceeds to identify the geometric aspects of the channel that are relevant for experimentation. The algorithm is implemented in Maple, and the associated code is provided.

Other simulators have also been used for the simulation of the Block sphere. ChangmingHuo (Huo, 2009) a study, a Java simulator and a 3D display based on the Bloch sphere and Bloch ball concepts are used to animate the motion of a qubit or spinor. The simulator may be used to demonstrate a qubit's Larmor precession, the Rabi formula for computing the probability of spin-flip in a time-dependent magnetic field, and the density matrix notion for examining the time evolution of an ensemble of spinors. On the user interface, control panels are developed to le qubit manipulation and change simulation parameters such as external time-independent and time-dependent magnetic fields. Stephen Shary (Shary, 2011) presented simulation software to visually represent a quantum state or qubit based on the Bloch sphere representation. The software uses the Java language and libraries to provide a multi-platform simulator that can be quickly distributed and viewed using the Java web-start technology.

MODEL CONCEPTUALISATION

1. **Modelling a Bloch sphere:** The Bloch sphere equation contains several components that must be considered when simulating it. But first and foremost, we must comprehend the mathematical representation of a qubit and the process of determining the final states following the application of gates. Take note of the equation for the state of a qubit. Because we are dealing with a polar form, there are always two angles θ, φ, (also known as phase) involved. It regulates the displacement of the state vectors and significantly impacts their exile. The state vector is used in conjunction to determine the state of a qubit. Let us comprehend the many components, such as the state vector, phase, and basis.

    a. A state vector: A State vector represents the state of the qubit in the block sphere (Qiskit Development team, 2021). It contains the probability of finding the photon in It is a block sphere representation of the qubit's state. It includes the chance of detecting the photon in the spacetime cavity that we use as information. The state space is denoted by a unit vector extending from the center of the Bloch sphere to its edge. The equation of a quantum state is $|\psi\rangle = c_0 \cdot |0\rangle + c_1 \cdot |1\rangle$. where $(|c_0|^2 + |c_1|^2 = 1)$. It is the representation of the state of a qubit. The image for the two-dimensional representation of a Bloch sphere is shown in Figure 3.

    After rewriting the state equation with phases and amplitudes, states $|0\rangle$ and $|1\rangle$:If these states appear perplexing, consider the cube as a coin, except that the coin is constantly spinning in the case of a quantum bit. Thus, |0> and |1> represent the top and bottom of a spinning coin whose motions are limited to rotation in the same plane. The base states are used to describe any other states. Equation (1) represents the exclusive representation of two states and equatioavailable) is state representation with base states respectively.

$$|0 = \begin{bmatrix} 1 \\ 0 \end{bmatrix} |1\rangle = \begin{bmatrix} 0 \\ 1 \end{bmatrix} \tag{1}$$

$$|q_0 = \frac{1}{\sqrt{2}}|0\rangle + \frac{i}{\sqrt{2}}|l \tag{2}$$

    b. Representing a quantum bit:Felloni S et.al. (Felloni et al., 2009a) (Felloni et al. 2009b) talks about the representation of a quantum system using diagrams. The final state equation can also be re-written in polar

Figure 2. State vector in two dimensions

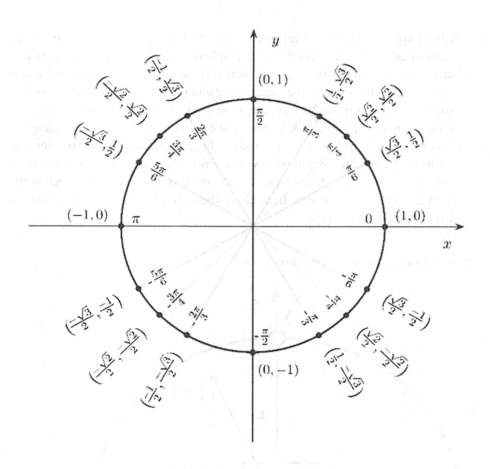

coordinates as in Equation 2, where |0⟩ and |1⟩ are called ground states. If we compare that with a classic bit, these two states are like binary 0 and 1. |0⟩ is located at the north pole of the Bloch sphere and |1⟩ at the south pole. The Euler's form representation of a quantum state is in equation 3 below. The polar form of the quantum state is represented in equation4 below.

$$|\psi\rangle = \cos(\theta/2)|0\rangle + \sin(\theta/2)e^{i\phi_\beta}|1\rangle \qquad (3)$$

$$|\psi\rangle = r_{\alpha}e^{i\phi_{\alpha}}|0\rangle + r_{\beta}e^{i\phi_{\beta}}|1\rangle \qquad (4)$$

2.   **Bloch sphere:** Graphical representation of states is discussed in (Chuang, 2004)(Felloni & Strini, 2006).A Bloch sphere visualizes a quantum state with different components like a Bloch vector; phase angles θ, φ, and amplitude as shown in Figure 4. Here, the state vector and the Bloch vector are other. The state vector helps in the 2D representation of a state. The Bloch vector has three components: amplitude, θ & φ. So, what exactly is the role of visualizing this Bloch sphere? The Bloch vector and the neutral states are used to determine information storage. When we try to measure the state of a quantum bit, it collapses to the nearest neutral states ($|0\rangle$ and $|1\rangle$). Let us say the Bloch vector is in the upper hemisphere. It would collapse to $|0\rangle$ and vice versa with the lower hemisphere to $|1\rangle$.

Figure 3. Bloch sphere in three dimensions

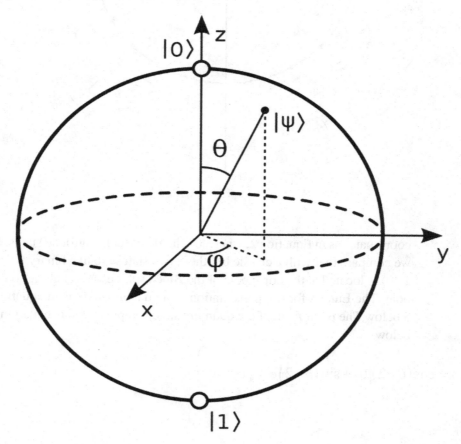

3. **Interaction or change of state by a gate:** Based on conceptual perception, the state of a qubit can be represented in various ways, including polar, Euler, and matrix representations (Chang et al., 2021). Nonetheless, the gates influence quantum mechanical features that are not of interest to our research. All that is required for our modeling and simulation is the mathematics that underpins them. This can be explained using Pauli's X, Y, and Z gates. Pauli's (X, Y, Z), S, H, and T gates are the gates that can be used to change the quantum state of a single qubit (Nielsen & Chuang, 1997). They are used to spin the Bloch vector in different directions, called gates. If we examine the matrix form, the addition of gates is simply the product of multiplication by fixed matrices, as shown in Table 1.

Table 1. Different forms of representations of all the quantum games in our simulator.

Nomenclature	Equations
Comparable	$R_x(\theta) \equiv e^{-i\theta X/2}$ $R_y(\theta) \equiv e^{-i\theta Y/2}$ $R_z(\theta) \equiv e^{-i\theta Z/2}$
Equational Representation	$a_0\lvert 0\rangle + a_1\lvert 1\rangle \rightarrow X-gate \rightarrow a_0\lvert 1\rangle + a_1\lvert 0\rangle$ $a_0\lvert 0\rangle + a_1\lvert 1\rangle \rightarrow Z-gate \rightarrow a_0\lvert 0\rangle - a_1\lvert 1\rangle$ $a_0\lvert 0\rangle + a_1\lvert 1\rangle \rightarrow H-gate \rightarrow a_0\lvert +\rangle + a_1\lvert -\rangle$
Matrix Transformation	$R_x(\xi) = \cos\dfrac{\xi}{2} \cdot I - j\sin\dfrac{\xi}{2} \cdot X = \begin{bmatrix} \cos\dfrac{\xi}{2} & -j\sin\dfrac{\xi}{2} \\ -j\sin\dfrac{\xi}{2} & \cos\dfrac{\xi}{2} \end{bmatrix}$ $R_y(\xi) = \cos\dfrac{\xi}{2} \cdot I - j\sin\dfrac{\xi}{2} \cdot Y = \begin{bmatrix} \cos\dfrac{\xi}{2} & -\sin\dfrac{\xi}{2} \\ \sin\dfrac{\xi}{2} & \cos\dfrac{\xi}{2} \end{bmatrix}$ $R_z(\xi) = \cos\dfrac{\xi}{2} \cdot I - j\sin\dfrac{\xi}{2} \cdot Z = \begin{bmatrix} e^{-j\frac{\xi}{2}} & 0 \\ 0 & e^{j\frac{\xi}{2}} \end{bmatrix}$

SOLUTIONS AND RECOMMENDATIONS

The goal is to create a web-based graphical user interface (GUI) that can be installed on a web server and accessed from anywhere in the world. The model is converted into python code for further analysis with mathematical tools such as math, NumPy, and SciPy. The graphical interface, on the other hand, via which the output and input parameters are provided and taken, was built entirely in JavaScript. The input variables are as follows:

- The initial state of the qubit
- the gates to be applied in a sequence

the result is displayed in the three representations (Polar representation, equational representation, and probability of (|0| and |1|). A combination of JavaScript and Python is used to do this. The input parameters are shown in Figure 4.

Figure 4. Input Parameters

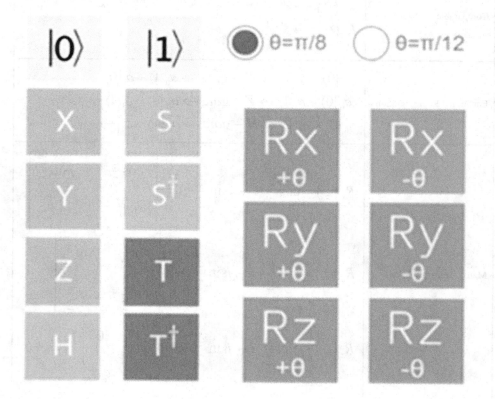

On the left side of the table, input parameters like the state ($|0\rangle$ and $|1\rangle$) and gates X, Y, Z, H, S, T functions can be given while on the right side, angles can be given with the different axes x, y, and z with two options adding an angle of $\pi/8$ or $\pi/12$. Multiple times pressing the button would return in add up.

There are three different ways of understanding our final state: Given the initial state and the gates to be applied; we will end at the end state by using those gates to the state. The following are the 4 result parameters obtained.

1. The state vector 3D visualization is on the sphere itself.
2. The probability of getting either of the states on the left side.
3. The result or final phase angle at the bottom is represented as a shadow of the Bloch sphere at the bottom.
4. The state equation in the polar form at the top.

Figure 5. Output state representation

$$|\psi\rangle = \sqrt{0.80}\,|0\rangle + (\sqrt{0.20}\,)e^{i0.26\pi}\,|1\rangle$$

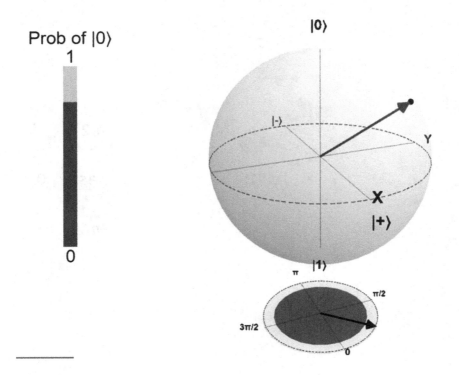

Figure 5 shows the output state representation. The parameters used for visualizing the results are most frequently utilized in related work. Traditionally, the process is accomplished by lengthy mathematical calculations and complicated visualization attempts. The model proposed in this work is an automated system with a simplified graphical user interface for simulation.

Figure 6. Final Bloch sphere obtained with phase by IBM Q.

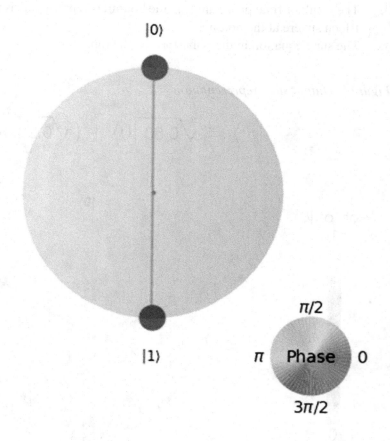

VERIFICATION AND VALIDATION

Many organizations can verify this simulator using different python packages, like the Microsoft Azure quantum computing development kit or the QISKIT by IBM and Amazon bracket. These provide readily available Python functions and visualizers for visualizing gates and qubits. This simulator can be validated by running it over a real quantum computer. We used IBM's quantum experience to validate the project with a simple circuit and the result is shown in Figure 7.We compared the obtained result with the one from our simulator as shown in Figure 8. Both the results are in close coordination which proves the validation of our project. From the development of our simulator, we were able to validate the accuracy of our project.

Figure 7. Final representation of Bloch sphere on our model

$$|\psi\rangle = \sqrt{0.50}\,|0\rangle + (\sqrt{0.50}\,)e^{i0}\quad |1\rangle$$

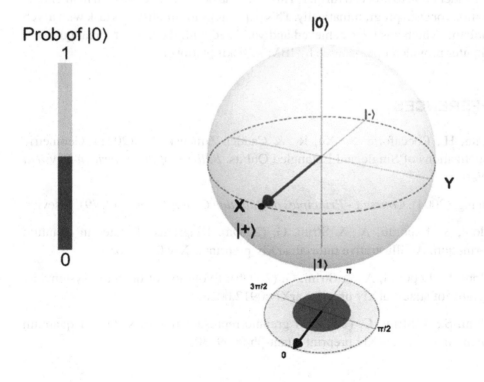

FUTURE RESEARCH DIRECTIONS

With quantum technology growing exponentially in the past decade, there are many branches for this project to spread into. There is no limitation in the simulation space for a quantum circuit. But the physical quantum chip has a limitation in the number of qubits it can have. One can develop a simulation of a multi-qubit state visualizer which would visualize the state of a qubit in a multi-qubit circuit. We can think of adding more gates or even creating custom gates per our requirements.

CONCLUSION

The whole idea of simulating a real-world process is to understand the process and answer complex questions to think and visualize for human cognitive skills. In the quantum computing environment, quantum circuits are the building blocks. Designing an efficient quantum circuit is crucial for the system that is being developed. This development of an efficient quantum circuit requires a few tedious steps in both mathematic and programmatic spaces. At every step, the state of a particular qubit is to be understood to proceed further. This state can be computed through mathematic equations or even programmatically. This paper aims to simplify this task with a web simulator, which has been achieved and validated with the help of a real quantum computer provided open-source by IBM's Qiskit platform.

REFERENCES

Chang, H., Roccaforte, S., Xu, R., & Cadden-Zimansky, P. (2021). Geometric Visualizations of Single and Entangled Qubits. *Bulletin of the American Physical Society*.

Chuang. (2004). *Course 1 - Principles of Quantum Computation* (Vol. 79). Elsevier.

Felloni, S., Leporati, A., & Strini, G. (2009a). Diagrams of states in quantum information: An illustrative tutorial. arXiv preprint arXiv:0904.2656.

Felloni, S., Leporati, A., & Strini, G. (2009b). Evolution of quantum systems by diagrams of states. arXiv preprint arXiv:0912.0026.

Felloni, S., & Strini, G. (2006). A graphic representation of states for quantum copying machines. arXiv preprint quant-ph/0609230.

Huo, C. (2009). *A Bloch Sphere Animation Software using a Three-Dimensional JavaSimulator* (Doctoral dissertation). University of Cincinnati.

Nielsen, M. A., & Chuang, I. L. (1997). Programmable quantum gate arrays. *Physical Review Letters*, *79*(2), 321–324. doi:10.1103/PhysRevLett.79.321

Pasieka, A., Kribs, D. W., Laflamme, R., & Pereira, R. (2009). On the geometric interpretation of single qubit quantum operations on the Bloch sphere. *Acta Applicandae Mathematicae*, *108*(3), 697–707. doi:10.100710440-008-9423-z

Qiskit Development team. (2021). *Representing Qubit States by Qiskit.* Retrieved May 5, 2021, from https://qiskit.org/textbook/ch-states/representing-qubit-states.html

Shary, S. (2011). *Java Simulator of Qubits and Quantum-Mechanical Gates Using the Bloch Sphere Representation* (Doctoral dissertation). University of Cincinnati.

KEY TERMS AND DEFINITIONS

Bloch Sphere: In quantum mechanics and computing, the Bloch sphere is a geometrical representation of the pure state space of a two-level quantum mechanical system (qubit), named after the physicist Felix Bloch. The Bloch sphere is a unit 2-sphere, with antipodal points corresponding to a pair of mutually orthogonal state vectors. The north and south poles of the Bloch sphere are typically chosen to correspond to the standard basis vectors.

Bloch Vector: A Bloch vector is a unit vector $(\cos\varphi\sin\theta, \sin\varphi\sin\theta, \cos\theta)$ used to represent points on a Bloch sphere.

Phase Angles: Phase angle refers to a particular point in the time of a cycle whose measurement takes place from some arbitrary zero and its expression is as an angle. Furthermore, a phase angle happens to be one of the most important characteristics of a periodic wave.

Quantum Bit: It is the primary unit of how information is represented in the quantum computing space. It is similar to that of how information is stored in traditional classical computing, which is a binary bit. In a classical system, a bit would have to be in one state or the other. However, quantum mechanics allows the qubit to be in a coherent superposition of both states simultaneously, a property that is fundamental to quantum mechanics and quantum computing.

Quantum Gates: In quantum computing and specifically the quantum circuit model of computation, a quantum logic gate (or simply quantum gate) is a basic quantum circuit operating on a small number of qubits. They are the building blocks of quantum circuits, like classical logic gates are for conventional digital circuits.

Unlike many classical logic gates, quantum logic gates are reversible. However, it is possible to perform classical computing using only reversible gates. For example, the reversible Toffoli gate can implement all Boolean functions, often at the cost of having to use ancilla bits. The Toffoli gate has a direct quantum equivalent, showing that quantum circuits can perform all operations performed by classical circuits.

Quantum States: In quantum physics, a quantum state is a mathematical entity that provides a probability distribution for the outcomes of each possible measurement on a system. Knowledge of the quantum state together with the rules for the system's evolution in time exhausts all that can be predicted about the system's behavior. A mixture of quantum states is again a quantum state. Quantum states that cannot be written as a mixture of other states are called pure quantum states, while all other states are called mixed quantum states. A pure quantum state can be represented by a ray in a Hilbert space over the complex numbers, while mixed states are represented by density matrices, which are positive semidefinite operators that act on Hilbert spaces.

State Vector: In the mathematical formulation of quantum mechanics, pure quantum states correspond to vectors in a Hilbert space, while each observable quantity (such as the energy or momentum of a particle) is associated with a mathematical operator. The operator serves as a linear function which acts on the states of the system.

APPENDIX

Basic understanding of Quantum computers. We discovered that 'bits' are the simplest alphabet in the world and can represent any data. Additionally, we found that all current computers store and operate on bits. Until now, we've thought of bits as abstract units of information, but to build a functional computer, we need to fabricate our bits out of physical objects. Therefore, how can we earn a living in the actual world? Both cards and compact discs exhibit behavior clearly described using classical physics: Physics is fundamentally a description of the world around us; we conduct experiments to observe how the world acts and then attempt to deduce the rules that govern the universe. "Classical physics" refers to the set of laws devised by scientists before the early 1900s. It is highly accurate at predicting the behavior of objects such as cricket balls and automobile engines.

However, the electron orbiting an atom is somewhat unique. Around the turn of the twentieth century, scientists learned to study atomic size objects. They discovered that small entities, such as atoms, behave differently than the objects we interact with daily and that in some situations, the principles of classical physics were incorrect. Because the physics they had required modification, the scientists devised a more specific set of principles that became known as "quantum physics."

A logical issue for computer scientists is, "What if our bits obeyed quantum physics laws rather than classical physics constraints?" These bits are referred to as "qubits" for "quantum bit," and computers that can operate on them are referred to as "quantum computers." To investigate quantum behavior, it's necessary to refresh our memory on probabilities. If you read the preceding chapter, you will recall that all operations discussed thus far have been deterministic. Something is deterministic if its behavior is devoid of randomness, and this means it will always produce the same output state when acting on the same input state. Consider a new operation that operates exclusively on quantum bits: the Hadamard.

This process (which we sometimes refer to as a 'transformation') was called after Jacques Hadamard's gate, which we will abbreviate as the "H-gate."

Probabilities are essential when there are numerous possible outcomes, and we lack sufficient knowledge to determine which one will occur, like with a dice roll or coin flip. We assign probabilities to each possibility and use them to assess the chance of anything happening. Probabilities work exceptionally well for most things we observe in the world, but with "quantum" objects (such as qubits), this technique fails, and we must update it to account for the observed behavior..

Chapter 9
Hidden Treasures of Semiconducting Materials for Quantum Computing:
An Upcoming Fortune for Supercomputing

Dillip Kumar Pattanayak
GIET University, India

Lokesh Kumar Prusty
GIET University, India

Arun Kumar Padhy
GIET University, India

Ranjan Kumar Bhuyna
Government College, Anugul, India

Samita Pattanayak
Odisha University of Technology and Research, Bhubaneswa, India

ABSTRACT

Quantum computing is based on physical materials. The choice of material is important, and semiconductor materials have become a widely trailed choice in recent years. A lot of initial research into quantum computing only manifested that it could operate at temperatures close to absolute zero. However, because semiconductors are now used in the construct of these systems, it has enabled researchers to utilize quantum computers in room temperature conditions. This is one of the major reasons why quantum computing is close to commercial realization, so the role played by semiconductors is of major importance. It is true that the implementation of semiconductors has been challenging in its own way. Many semiconducting materials can exhibit many quantum degrees of freedom, and this causes the qubits to interact with each and decode quickly. Here the authors try to project a systematic study of different semiconducting materials used for quantum computing.

DOI: 10.4018/978-1-7998-9183-3.ch009

1. INTRODUCTION

1.1. Background

Recent advances in quantum computation pulled in worldwide consideration, making this subject again under the spot light since it was first proposed by Richard Feynman and Yuri Manin (Feynman, 1982) in1982. The epicentre of quantum processing is to store data in quantum state and to utilize quantum gate operation to register on that data, by tackling and figuring out how to "program" in quantum state execute. An early instance of programming impedance to take care of an issue thought to be challenging for our normal computers was finished by Peter Shor in 1994 for an issue known as factoring. Addressing and figuring carries with it the capacity to break a significant number of our public key cryptosystems which is the basic in the security of internet business today, including RSA (Rivest-Shamir-Adleman) and Elliptic Curve Cryptography. Since that time, quick and productive quantum computer calculations have been created for a large number of our hard traditional assignments like simulating physical system in chemistry, physical science, and materials science, looking through an unordered information, and machine learning.

In 1996, Lov Grover developed a quantum information base calculation that introduced a quadratic speedup for an assortment of issues. Any issue which must be tackled by arbitrary or beast power search should now be possible 4x quicker.

In 1998, a functioning 2-qubit quantum computer was constructed and settled first quantum calculations like Grover's calculation. The race into another time of computer power started and that's just the beginning and more applications were created.

In 1998 Isaac Chuang of the Los Alamos National Laboratory, Neil Gershenfeld of the Massachusetts Institute of Technology (MIT), and Mark Kubinec of the University of California at Berkeley made the main quantum computer (2-qubit) that could be stacked with data and output a solution. In spite of the fact that their system was coherent for a couple of nanoseconds and unimportant according to the point of view of taking care of significant issues, it showed the standards of quantum calculation. Rather than attempting to confine a couple of subatomic particles, they broke up countless chloroform atoms (CHCL3) in water at room temperature and applied a magnetic field to arrange the spin of the carbon and hydrogen cores in the chloroform. (Since standard carbon has no attractive twist, their answer utilized an isotope, carbon-13.) A spin corresponding to the outer magnetic field could then be deciphered as a 1 and an antiparallel spin as 0, and the hydrogen cores and carbon-13 cores could be dealt with altogether as a 2-qubit system. Notwithstanding the external magnetic field, radio frequency beats were applied to cause spin states to "flip," in this way making superimposed parallel and antiparallel states. Further pulse were applied to execute a basic calculation and to analyze the system's last state. This sort of quantum computer can be reached out by utilizing atoms with all the more exclusively addressable cores. Indeed, in March 2000 Emanuel Knill, Raymond Laflamme, and Rudy Martinez of Los Alamos and Ching-Hua Tseng of MIT reported that they had made a 7-qubit quantum computer utilizing transcrotonic acid. Be that as it may, numerous scientists are incredulous about expanding magnetic technique much past 10 to 15 qubits due to decreasing coherence among the nucleus.

Physicist David Wineland et.al at the U.S. Public Institute for Standards and Technology (NIST) reported that they had made a 4-qubit quantum computer by entrapping four ionized beryllium molecules utilizing an electromagnetic "trap." After keeping the particles in a linear arrangement, a laser cooled the particles nearly to absolute zero and synchronized their twist states. At last, a laser was utilized to trap the particles, making a superposition of both spin up and turn down states all the while for every one of the four particles. Once more, this methodology showed fundamental standards of quantum computing, yet increasing the strategy to viable aspects stays hazardous. After twenty years, in 2017, IBM introduced the main financially usable quantum computer, raising the rush to another level.

1.2 Objectives of the Chapter

In the competition to assemble a quantum computer, a few concepts arise like superconducting circuits (Devoret & Schoelkopf, 2013; Wendin, 2017), trapped iron (Häffner et al., 2008; Monroe & Kim, 2013), semiconductors (Awschalom et al., 2013; Xin et al., 2018), nitrogen-vacancy centres (Childress & Hanson, 2013; Weber et al., 2010), nuclear magnetic resonance (Vandersypen & Chuang, 2005) etc. Among them, semiconductor is one of the strong competitor for its critical job in the field of classical computer. They have not just completely changed ourselves with the computers, advanced mobile phone, Internet and man-made reasoning yet in addition helped the financial overall like the introduction of Silicon Valley in the United States of America. With a conviction of advancing innovation unrest by the quantum field, somewhat recently, a few huge leap forwards in quantum data handling have been made based on semiconductors. These advances thus affirm the confidence to assemble a quantum computer out of semiconductor.

Because quantum computing is based on physical materials, the choice of material is important and semiconductor materials have become a widely trailed choice in recent years. A lot of initial research into quantum computing only manifested that could operate at temperatures close to absolute zero. However, because semiconductors are now used in the construct of these systems, it has enabled researchers to utilize quantum computers in room temperature conditions. This is one of the major reasons why quantum computing is close to commercial realization, so the role played by semiconductors is of major importance. It is true that the implementation of semiconductors has been challenging in its own way. Many semiconducting materials can exhibit many quantum degrees of freedom and this causes the qubits to interact with each and decode quickly. Here we try to project a systematic study of different semiconducting materials used for quantum computing.

2. GENERAL CONSIDERATION

2.1. What is Quantum Computing?

Commercial computers tasks utilize a bit also called a binary bit which is the littlest unit of information in a computer and it takes on a 0 or 1. Quantum computing uses a comparative bit system known as a qubit. In any case, qubit qualities can be superimposed, so rather than having the option to take on two qualities, they can, indeed, take on one of three. Just like bits in normal computing, qubits are the building block and all function emerge from how the qubits act (Loss & DiVincenzo, 1998). Qubits store data in quantum state precisely and in a two-state system and uses the ½ spin condition of electrons, which appear as up or down, and through the polarization of a photon which can be perused as either a vertical or horizontal polarization (DiVincenzo, 2000; Petta et al., 2005).

Quantum computing depends on specific actual qualities and actual directions to give the ideal processing power. It isn't programming, it is hardware technology, and hence the kinds of materials used to build the quantum PC is significant. There are a couple of necessities that are vital for a quantum PC to be effective. The materials utilized normally need to have enduring spin states.

2.2 Qubits

As we explore in our open step on qubits, traditional computers are built on bits. These bits (short for binary digits) are the basic units of information in computing, where two distinct configurations can be measured. They can be thought of as on or off, up or down, or, as encoded in binary, as either 0s or 1s (Medford et al., 2013). In quantum computing, quantum bits or qubits form the basics of how these computers work. These qubits can be made from quantum-mechanical systems that can have two states. For example, the spin of an electron can be measured as up or down, or a single photon is either vertically or horizontally polarized.

2.3 Superfluid

Your desktop computer likely uses a fan to get cold enough to work. Quantum processors need to be very cold – about a hundredth of a degree above absolute zero (Kim et al., 2014). To achieve this, we use super-cooled superfluid to create superconductors (Shulman et al., 2012).

2.4 Superconductors

At those ultra-low temperatures certain materials in our processors exhibit another important quantum mechanical effect: electrons move through them without resistance (Angus et al., 2007; Simmons et al., 2007). This makes them "superconductors." When electrons pass through superconductors they match up, forming "Cooper pairs." These pairs can carry a charge across barriers, or insulators, through a process known as quantum tunneling (Veldhorst et al., 2014). Two superconductors placed on either side of an insulator form a Josephson junction.

2.5 Control

Quantum computers use Josephson junctions as superconducting qubits. By firing microwave photons at these qubits, we can control their behavior and get them to hold, change, and read out individual units of quantum information.

2.6 Superposition

A qubit itself isn't very useful. But it can perform an important trick: placing the quantum information it holds into a state of superposition, which represents a combination of all possible configurations of the qubit. Groups of qubits in superposition can create complex, multidimensional computational spaces. Complex problems can be represented in new ways in these spaces.

2.7 Entanglement

Entanglement is a quantum mechanical effect that correlates the behavior of two separate things (Yoneda et al., 2018). When two qubits are entangled, changes to one qubit directly impact the other. Quantum algorithms leverage those relationships to find solutions to complex problems.

3. THE ROLE OF SEMICONDUCTING MATERIALS IN QUANTUM COMPUTING

Since quantum computing relies on real substances, fabric selection is huge and semiconductor substances have become a commonly examined selection in recent times. Numerous introductory quantum processing tests simply confirmed structures they would paint at temperatures close to absolute zero. In any case, for the reason that semiconductors are currently applied with inside the construct of those system, it has empowered analysts to apply quantum computers in room temperature conditions. This is one of the enormous motivations at the back of why quantum computing is close to commercial enterprise acknowledgment, so the pretended via way of means of semiconductors is critical. It is certainly the case that the execution of semiconductors has been attempting via way of means of its very own doing. Many semiconductor substances can exhibit different ranges of quantum opportunities, causing qubits to communicate with each other and quickly decay. Nonetheless, progresses in atomic engineering and stepped forward semiconductor manufacture advances have faded those impacts.

There are 3 predominant methods wherein semiconductors are fabricated to construct quantum computing systems. These are heterostructures, SRT-embedded heterostructures, and quantum dot arrays (Veldhorst et al., 2015). Heterostructures often incorporate many unique semiconductor layers, all with the same elemental composition, however with various elemental ratios in order that the asset of every layer is barely unique. This is frequently capped with a semiconducting barrier layer on pinnacle, accompanied through a chain of doped gates. The qubits exist in heterostructures and paints along one side a magnetized layer and a pretty quantum layer heterostructure. The heterostructure is laid on pinnacle of a semiconducting floor aircraft and a buffer layer, all on pinnacle of a silicon substrate (Samkharadze et al., 2018). In those systems, the qubits are person however indistinguishable, and capacitance measurements are taken to peer whether or not the nuclear spin of a qubit evolves right into a singlet or triplet state. This is the maximum simple configuration; however many others are tailored from it.

4. DIFFERENT TYPES OF SEMICONDUCTING MATERIALS USED IN QUANTUM COMPUTING

4.1 Gallium arsenide

Spin qubits in gate-defined quantum dots were first exhibited in GaAs because of positive band structure properties what's more the development of MBE development of heterostructures dependent on III–V compounds. In a commonplace balance doped GaAs/AlGaAs heterostructure the conduction-band offset at the GaAs/AlGas interface upholds a two-dimensional electron gas (2DEG), populated from a close by Si-doped AlGaAs layer(Flentje et al., 2017). GaAs and AlGaAs are almost grid coordinated, so GaAs/AlGas heterostructures have a remarkable underlying quality, taking into account huge electron mobility (10^6–10^7 cm^2) also low percolation density ($< 10^{10}$cm^{-2}/Vs)(Huang et al., 2019). Subsequently, quantum dots of around $1/\sqrt{np}$= 100 nm in size, useful with regards to the normal distance between traps, are basically jumble free. To characterize quantum dots, the 2DEG is privately drained by Schottky gates. The shortfall of dielectrics safeguards the low issue of the unblemished heterostructure and builds gadget yield. The single conduction-band valley and low effective mass (m* =0.067me) empower quantum dabs that have huge energy spacing and are somewhat simple to fabricate. The sizable spin-orbit interaction takes into account nearby all-electrical control of single spins. The primary disadvantage of GaAs is the hyperfine coupling to the atomic spin shower, causing extreme qubit de coherence (Huang et al., 2019). Furthermore, the difficult combination of GaAs on a Si wafer restricts the possibility of incorporating enormous quantities of qubits into a reasonable quantum processor.

4.2 Silicon

The two primary restrictions of GaAs become the fundamental drivers to seek after spin qubits in Si. The most well-known isotope,[28]Si, has zero nuclear spin, altogether lessening hyperfine-prompted dephasing, giving long quantum coherence(Vandersypen et al., 2017). Moreover, there is the guarantee to use progressed semiconductor producing for the mix of qubits in the enormous numbers needed for shortcoming quantum computing. Spin qubits in Si are executed in metal oxide semiconductor (Si-MOS) structures or in Si/ SiGe heterostructures (Ono et al., 2002). In Si-MOS, a 2DEG is bound at the interface among Si and SiO2, the two of which can be isotopically refined. Different layers of gates, protected by dielectrics, aggregate and restrict race into quantum dots.

These gates have a fairly close pitch in view of the huge effective mass (0.19me), requiring quantum dots in Si to be a lot more modest than in GaAs. Following the accessibility of [28]SiH$_4$ gas for [28]Si deposition, isotopically decontaminated SiMOS spin qubits were created in a 300-mm semiconductor producing office utilizing all-optical lithography and completely modern processing. In these qubits, Si fnFETs give leading channels, and gates on top characterize quantum spots along the fn. The presence of various conduction groups is a constraint of Si, since the small energy separation (valley parting) between the ground state and the most reduced energized state entangles quantum activities. Notwithstanding, because of the solid restriction at the sharp semiconductor/oxide interface, valley parting in Si-MOS can be substantial (up to 1 meV), making it conceivable to work Si qubits at "hot" temperatures of 1 K (Koppens et al., 2006). This is empowering for cointegration of CMOS-based cryogenic control circuits and silicon quantum processors. The primary downside of Si-MOS is the vicinity of the qubit to the exceptionally disordered oxide interface. Versatility is somewhat low ($\approx 10^4$ cm^2/Vs at best) and the permeation density high ($\approx 10^{11}$ cm^{-2}). Because low disorder is particularly significant for multi-quantum-dot frameworks, these remaining parts a significant thought. Disorder is significantly moderated in Si/SiGe heterostructures, in the fact that the 2DEG is aggregated at the covered point of interaction between a Si quantum well under tensile strain and a Si$_{1-x}$Ge$_x$ barrier (Ge fixation x ≈ 0.3). Similar Si-MOS, the Si quantum well can be isotopically enhanced to ^{28}Si for long quantum coherence. Differently than GaAs, Si/SiGe heterostructures for quantum-dot spin qubits are undoped, furthermore electrons populate the quantum well through voltages applied to top gate. Excellent Si/SiGe represents extra difficulties contrasted with GaAs/AlGaAs as a result of the 4.2% cross section mismatch among Si and Ge. The Si quantum well is stored on a strain loosened up SiGe cushion acquired by step by step expanding the Ge fixation in the SiGe combination to oblige the lattice mismatch among Si and Ge. After decades of advancements, Si/SiGe heterostructures, developed by modern reduced pressure chemical vapor deposition (RP-CVD), maybe developed stage with high mobility ($\approx 10^5$ cm^2/Vs) and low permeation density ($\approx 10^{10}$ cm^{-2}), expected to further improve by utilizing progressed semiconductor fabricating processes for enhancing the gate stack. Creation of quantum dots in Si/SiGe depends on covering gate structures for firmly dispersed quantum dots with gate tunable passage boundaries. Because of the low disorder, gadget yield is high, making it conceivable to characterize and control huge direct varieties of quantum dots. The current significant test with Si/SiGe is the lower valley parting (50 to 200 μeV), contrasted with Si-MOS, due to the atomistic defect and synthetic problem at the epitaxial Si/SiGe interface. In any case, initial steps are being taken to work on the heterostructures by consolidating more perplexing Ge fixation profiles for expanded the valley parting.

4.3 Germanium

While most investigations have focused on electrons, holes in stressed Ge/SiGe heterostructures have as of late arisen as a convincing stage that offers low issue, all-electrical qubit control, and roads for scaling. Ge joins numerous benefits of Si and GaAs while defeating a large portion of their limits. Ge is a CMOS-foundry material and can be isotopically designed for long quantum coherence (Nowack et al., 2007). The high versatility, low effective mass, and sizable spin orbit coupling suggest enormous energy separating for simple creation of quantum dots with full electrical qubit control (Shor, 1994). In a typical Ge/SiGe heterostructure openings are restricted at the connection point between a compressively stressed Ge quantum well and a $Si_{1-x}Ge_x$ barrier ($x \approx 0.8$). Strain and size quantization eliminate the valence-band decline, so holes in Ge/SiGe are a solitary band system, conquering the fundamental restriction of electrons in Si. Beginning from a Si wafer, a strain-relaxed Ge layer is developed, trailed by an evaluated $Si_{1-x}Ge_x$ layer in which the Ge focus is dynamically decreased to ≈ 0.8. The strain relaxed SiGe support fills in as a virtual substrate for the reasonable deposition of the Ge quantum well, the SiGe barrier, and a last conciliatory Si cap. Modulation doping is avoided away from, and charge careers populate the quantum well through voltages applied to top gates. Improved Ge/SiGe stacks are developed by RP-CVD and have comparable degrees of turmoil as Si/SiGe, with $\mu \approx 10^5$ cm^2/Vs and np$\approx 10^{10}$ cm^{-2}

Notwithstanding the tremendous advancement in both the development and utilizations of crystalline materials for quantum computing, challenges remain. As to semiconductor heterostructures spin qubits, it is yet indistinct which material will drive an enormous scope spin qubit quantum processor. However, the most critical advancement in the field can be followed back to jumps in materials improvements. Silicon acquired prevalence over GaAs in fact that the mix of ^{28}Si empowered long quantum coherence. Germanium has stood out since hole spin qubits have advanced at a remarkable speed. The Ge qubit count has multiplied generally each year and bigger systems are not too far off. The Ge quantum data course is ready to hold many benefits of GaAs and Si while conquering a portion of their separate long-standing difficulties. Despite the material of decision, progressively quick input cycles are needed to speed up the improvement of quantum materials. Significant stages toward this path have been taken. Cryo-multiplexing technology mitigates the interconnect bottleneck present in cryostats working at mK temperatures. Accordingly, we can access with high-throughput the low-temperature quantum transport properties of 2D electrons or openings significant for turn qubits. Ideally, high-throughput portrayal will likewise apply to charge clamour estimations. Quick streamlining of the material and door stack boundaries is fundamental as we are moving into the following period of designing qubit system in the enormous numbers needed for valuable quantum computing.

5. MANIPULATION OF MATERIAL PROPERTIES FOR SUPER COMPUTING

5.1 Antimony Doped with Ge

Metal–semiconductor changes in consolidated matter regularly happen simultaneously with underlying changes. There is a longstanding and much discussed issue regarding whether the main thrust in these changes is essentially electronic or underlying in beginning. This issue is especially difficult in situations where the semiconducting stage is a shiny one, as in the class of the mechanically significant stage change materials. These are normally alloys of Ge, Sb, and Te, which in certain structure ranges, like a standard compound $Ge_2Sb_2Te_5$, can be changed over between the leading crystalline stage and a semiconducting amorphous stage (Grover, 1997; Shor, 1996).

For this situation, eutectic GeSb films (regularly 100 nm thick) were stored at room temperature, by utilizing dc magnetron faltering from a normally Ge (15%) Sb(85%) focus, onto either thermally oxidized Si wafers for transport and optical temperature filters, or onto oppose covered wafers, with ensuing take off to get unattached movies for calorimetry furthermore pressure studies (Loss & DiVincenzo, 1998). Raman studies were performed under isotropic pressure, by utilizing a symmetric cylinder chamber precious stone iron block cell (DAC) furnished with 400-µm culet precious stone iron blocks. The tension was not really set in stone from the notable tension shift of the R1 ruby fluorescence line (694.2 nm under encompassing conditions) with a precision of ±0.05 GPa from ruby (Cr_3-doped - Al_2O_3) chips set inside the gasket test chamber. The Raman spectra were gathered in the scope of 100 – 400 cm^{-1}, covering all of the huge Raman dynamic methods of GeSb. X-beam diffraction spectra (at 30.55 keV; λ= 0.4066 nm) were gathered from GeSb in the equivalent DAC at the high-energy, extreme focus superconducting-wiggler X-beam shaft line X17C of the National Synchrotron Light Source at Brookhaven National Lab. Spectroscopic ellipsometry was utilized to acquire complex optical constants of formless (as stored) and glasslike GeSb films on cleaned Si and (out-of-plane c-hub situated) sapphire substrates. We utilized an ellipsometry arrangement connected to a Michelson interferometer to gather information in infrared reach 25 meV–1 eV; in apparent UV ranges, we utilized a norm pivoting analyser ellipsometer.

5.2 Supercomputer Turns its Back on Silicon

The primary business supercomputer made without silicon chips was discovered. All things considered, its processors are made altogether with gallium arsenide, the semiconductor material that was once tipped to supplant silicon. Just the memory chips of Convex's C3800 PC are made of silicon. Its appearance could proclaim a future conflict in the supercomputer market, as the customary creators of regular supercomputers like Cray.

Gallium arsenide (GaAs) chips utilize less power than silicon chips and are quicker, on the grounds that electrons can move all the more openly in the material. Be that as it may troubles in building them make them costly and has restricted their use to particular applications, like military and space gadgets. Their speed makes them alluring in processing applications which need to process immense amounts of information, like climate forecasting, seismic investigation also picture handling. The C3800 ascertains at a pace of 2,000 million numerical tasks each second, however, has a nearly unassuming most extreme power prerequisite of 40 kW. Notwithstanding the higher speed of GaAs, the plan and assembling cycle of the circuits influences the speed and power proficiency of the chip. Maybe the most broadly involved method in silicon is known as complementary metal oxide semiconductor, or CMOS (Yilmaz et al., 2001). An elective plan known as emitter coupled logic is a lot quicker, yet in addition more complicated and exorbitant to make. The chips in the C3800 utilize a plan called direct coupled field effect transistor logic (Yilmaz et al., 2001).

The PC has 30 specially crafted GaAs chips which contain a sum of 45000 logic gates. These chips are less difficult than those utilized by Cray Computer, the more youthful of the two organizations established by Seymour Cray. The other, Cray Research, has been making strong supercomputers for a long time. Cray Computer is additionally fostering a GaAs supercomputer, however utilizing the GaAs likeness the more expensive silicon circuit plan, producer coupled logic. Cray's configuration involves generally a similar power as a comparable silicon form yet works out at three to multiple times the speed.

5.3 The New Material: A Novel Ultrahigh Thermal-Management Material

To beat heat concentration issues, analysts developed a novel ultrahigh thermal management material, a deformity free boron, which was generally more viable as far as drawing and dispersing heat when contrasted with other recognizable metals or semiconductor materials, similar to silicon carbide and diamond. Interestingly, presently in 2021, the analysts have effectively uncovered the viability of the new material by fusing it into powerful device. The group utilized computer chips with advanced wide band gap transistors composed of gallium nitride, known as high-electron-mobility transistors (HEMTs) (Diddams et al., 2002; Heberle et al., 1995). At the point when the processors were run at close most extreme limit, the computer chips involving boron arsenide as a heat spreader had the most elevated heat increment to around 188 °F, which is a lot of lower than the chips utilizing diamond or silicon carbide to disperse heat (Diddams et al., 2002; Heberle et al., 1995).

"These outcomes plainly show that boron-arsenide devices can support a lot higher activity power than processors utilizing traditional thermal management materials. Also, the analyses were done under conditions where latest innovations would fall flat," "This advancement addresses another benchmark execution and shows incredible potential for applications in high-power hardware and future devices bundling"

As per the specialists, the vital component in the boron arsenide material is its extremely low warm limit obstruction.

5.4 Oxide Semiconducting Material

The actual prerequisites for versatile quantum calculation are overwhelming. Deprived of their extraordinary power, e.g., quantum calculations with outstanding or on the other hand quadratic speedups over their traditional partners, quantum computers would scarcely merit building. One of the trial challenges in developing a quantum PC is the administration of decoherence, the unavoidable trap between actual quantum bits and the environment. Enhancement of decoherence times is basically, a materials issue, and the ID and measurement of decoherence a significant hypothetical and exploratory movement (Levy, 2002). A second trial challenge connects with the "simple" character of quantum rationale. While quantum PCs process qubits similarly as traditional computer process bits, quantum advanced logic (one-qubit and two-qubit door activities) even more intently looks like that of simple PCs. That is, both the gate strength and the time are basically persistent boundaries that should be controlled with a serious level of precision. The hypothesis of issue lenient mistake amendment has shown that both decoherence and door errors can be made due, if they are adequately little.

The essential design of the proposed quantum data processor is delineated in Figure 1. Ge quantum dots are filled in a controlled straight cluster on the surface of Si. The dots are dispersed to such an extent that each can be optically tended to. An epitaxial ferroelectric oxide is become on top of the semiconductor. The necessities for the ferroelectric are that it be uniaxial with an unconstrained polarization pointing opposite to the plane. What's more, there should be an adequately low thickness of point of interaction traps so that the static polarization of the ferroelectric can have a field impact in the semiconductor.

The top view, displayed in Figure 1(b) delineates how the ferroelectric can be captivated to make bound districts for electrons. As well as giving static imprisonment to electrons and their twist, the ferroelectric assumes a fundamental part in gating electron turn collaborations interceded by Heisenberg trade. Figure 2 outlines how optical amendment can adjust the static polarization in the ferroelectric. Figure 2(a) shows a circumstance in which two electrons dwell in a potential distinct by the static ferroelectric polarization. A little obstruction (~10 nm) isolates the ferroelectrically-characterized quantum dabs. Upon uniform brightening of the ferroelectric, the greatness of the polarization is diminished, bringing about a lower possible boundary for the two electrons. Coming about cross-over of electron orbitals prompts notable Heisenberg trade between the twist levels of opportunity.

At the point when the light is switched off once more, the hindrance gets back to its previous tallness. A couple of comments ought to be made with regards to the optical amendment process. To begin with, the frequency of light can be picked so that immediate assimilation in the semiconductor or ferroelectric don't happen. If not, the presentation of free transporters would unavoidably disturb the framework. Second, the optical goal needed for controlling the potential boundary for trade is restricted not by diffraction, but rather by the capacity to compose areas in slim ferroelectric films. At last, it ought to be noticed that comparative gating plans in view of optical Stark moves has as of now been applied effectively for the optical control of electron turns in III-V material on femtosecond time scales(Levy, 2002).

6. RECENT ADVANCES

6.1 Quantum Computing Device Fabricated with Atomic Precision

The extreme sensitivity to device fluctuation of the quantum computer structures talked about here is clearly a significant barrier to versatile quantum figuring. It is absolutely conceivable that elective plans can be fostered that are characteristically less delicate to vacillations, and it might be conceivable that plans will be fostered that will make it conceivable to proficiently tune each gadget in a huge quantum computer.

At long last, calculations can be fostered that limit the commitment of gadget fluctuation to quantum computer activity. In any case, it is likely that the improvement of materials and creation methods yielding minuscule gadget varieties will be totally important to the possible development of a largescale quantum PC in strong state materials. Somewhat, this objective is moreover significant for scaling ordinary hardware, yet the imperatives will unavoidably be significantly more tough for quantum processing: for instance, the advancement of materials with high isotopic immaculateness may be vital for turn based quantum computers, however are probably not going to be applicable for any predictable ordinary electronic gadgets.

One illustration of an example of overcoming adversity in the improvement of new materials that permitted new classes of quantum gadgets to be made was the turn of events and flawlessness of high-versatility GaAs/AlGaAs heterostructures, made conceivable by the creation of modulation doping. Improvement of these gadgets over a time of 25 years prompted upgrades in portability of north of four orders of magnitude and empowered the revelation of novel corresponded conditions of the electrons at low temperatures, for example, the partial quantum Hall impact, and the inevitable improvement of new classes of electronic gadgets with an exceptional level of flawlessness(Bennett et al., 1984). While this cycle started with a new knowledge, a significant part of the proceeding with progress has been the consequence of meticulous and continuous up gradation in the innovation of sub-atomic shaft epitaxial of these materials.

Eventually, the best way to keep gadget variety from being a hindrance to enormous scope quantum registering is to be ready to create gadgets at the nuclear scale: gadgets built with the specific same nuclear arrangement will innately have indistinguishable properties. While such a mechanical accomplishment will be remarkably troublesome, it is practically the certain endpoint of the mechanical headway made throughout the most recent 50 years focused on making ever-more modest semiconductor gadgets with progressively all around controlled properties. The work done at IBM over the previous decade, where nuclear structures40 and even atom scale devices have been created one particle at a time with an examining scanning tunnelling microscope (STM), has set up that designing at this scale is conceivable(DiVincenzo & Loss, 1998). These outcomes have prodded endeavours to utilize comparable STM strategies to definitively put phosphorus benefactors into a silicon host to deliver the building blocks for a silicon quantum computer. While early outcomes are extremely uplifting, it still needs to be demonstrated that the situation of benefactors should be possible with the wonderful accuracy important to forestall huge gadget changeability.

Atom scale fabrication methods positively those including STM control are inherently incapable to proficiently produce gadgets in the volumes normally needed for the huge scope mix of traditional hardware. This weak may not be a deadly insufficiency for quantum rationale gadgets, where moderately little numbers of gadgets, by the principles of customary processing (hundreds or thousands of gadgets), would in any case be a gigantic development in the best in class for quantum figuring. It is conceivable that techniques for exceptionally equal manufacture of atom scale gadgets might be created later on or that compound strategies for self-gathering will be important. The possibility of enormous scope quantum processing in semiconductors is a long way from certain: the early sense that strong state ways to deal with quantum rationale will enjoy huge innovative upper hands over elective methodologies should be tempered with the way that gadget inconstancy is pervasive in semiconductor materials what's more that a large portion of the proposed advancements for semiconductor quantum processing are very touchy to these varieties. It is possible that these downfalls will barely matter in the following not many years, when tests will be centred on a tiny number of gadgets. At last, in any case, these issues may end up being unequivocal and feature the need to start investigating materials and creation strategies that are at a definitive breaking point of nuclear flawlessness.

6.2 Implementations of Quantum Logic in Semiconductor

There are right now a wide scope of recommendations for semiconductor-based quantum computers. In the accompanying, will focus on "every single electronic" proposal, where applied voltages are utilized to control the trade collaboration between electrons, since these designs have maybe the most likeness to regular electronic gadgets and thus get the most consideration. Optical control has been fused into a few structures, be that as it may, these methodologies will have extra hindrances to scaling. To utilize the trade collaboration to perform quantum logic in semiconductors, two things are required: a technique should be contrived to make a variety of disengaged single electrons, and a gate should be consolidated to turn on and off the trade communications between adjoining electrons.

The most punctual proposition, and the one that is presently getting the best consideration from experimentalists. They proposed restricting electrons in quantum dots made in GaAs/AlGaAs heterostructures. Restricting single electrons in this way has as of late been accomplished tentatively in balance doped heterostructures. Normally, numerous electrons are disseminated at the GaAs/AlGaAs connection point, and negative voltages are applied to the gate to exhaust the electrons underneath them (Kane, 1998). Disconnected electrons can be created in districts between doors if suitable inclinations move a significant wellspring of de coherence in turn frameworks. Additionally, Si (and carbon-based) semiconductors have a lot more modest twist\ circle coupling qualities than GaAs and other III-V semiconductors, which for the most part converts into longer spin lifetimes(Kikkawa et al., 1997). I proposed the main design for a quantum PC that exploits of the positive properties of Si. Quantum tasks are cultivated by controlling the trade collaborations between single electrons. The key contrast is that the electrons are bound at segregated phosphorus benefactors in Si, rather than gate characterized quantum dots. Benefactors are normally characterized single-electron quantum dots, restricting unequivocally one electron in the 30 Å neighbourhood of the P particle in the Si lattice. The electron wave work has a little plentifulness broadening two or three hundred angstroms from the donor, so it is conceivable to control the trade communication between givers by applying a voltage to a gate situated between the benefactor locales. A characteristic of this proposition is that the quantum lifetimes of electrons and atomic twists related with P in Si have been completely read up for right around 50 years and are known to be remarkably long. A self-evident inconvenience is that building a contributor based quantum PC will require a new innovation for putting single P contributors into a Si gem at recommended destinations. Doping of semiconductors is an omnipresent also full grown cycle in the semiconductor industry, yet current cycles include are applied. Obviously, the elements of the gate should be tiny to create these sorts of gadgets effectively. To carry out an activity in these quantum-dot gadgets, a heartbeat is applied to an entryway lying between two electrons. This beat quickly turns on the trade communication, and in the event that it is ruined the suitable time allotment an activity is performed on the two twists. Broad demonstrating has been performed on this framework to decide the voltages and spans of heartbeats applied to the gate that are important to deliver a rationale activity. Since the tails of the electron wave work tumble off quickly away from the potential minima, the quantum spots should be extremely near one another, and the strength of the trade communication is exceptionally touchy to the voltage applied.

With practical quantum dot calculations, in any case, it is feasible to accomplish quantum rationale activities in less than 1 ns, significantly not exactly the unwinding season of the electron turns, assessed to be on the request for 1 ms (Gordon & Bowers, 1958; Gupta et al., 2001). This way to deal with quantum logic might possibly be applied to any material wherein it is feasible to apply voltage to gates to prompt single-electron quantum wells. While it is most likely most appropriate to GaAs/AlGaAs heterostructures, where the best in class in single-electron gadget nanofabrication is the most progressive, it has additionally been examined in different frameworks, including Si/SiGe heterostructures and carbon nanotubes. According to a materials point of view, Group IV semiconductors have a few significant benefits over their III-V partners: Bunch IV semiconductors all have stable turn 0 atomic isotopes, conceivably permitting the refinement of these materials to once again introducing numerous givers into a semiconductor either by dissemination or particle implantation-processes that unavoidably bring numerous contributors into irregular areas in the silicon grid. In any case, the creation and investigation of single-dopant gadgets is presently a functioning area of examination, and the outcomes are extremely reassuring.

Conflict of Interest

The authors declare no conflict of interest.

ACKNOWLEDGMENT

The authors would like to thank GIET management and authorities & NIT Rourkela for providing the necessary support.

REFERENCES

Angus, S. J., Ferguson, A. J., Dzurak, A. S., & Clark, R. G. (2007). Gate-Defined Quantum Dots in Intrinsic Silicon. *Nano Letters*, *7*(7), 2051–2055. doi:10.1021/nl070949k PMID:17567176

Awschalom, D. D., Bassett, L. C., Dzurak, A. S., Hu, E. L., & Petta, J. R. (2013). Quantum Spintronics: Engineering and Manipulating Atom-Like Spins in Semiconductors. *Science*, *339*(6124), 1174–1179. doi:10.1126cience.1231364 PMID:23471400

Bennett, C. H., Brassard, G., & Breidbart, S. (1984). Article. *IBM Tech. Discl. Bull.*, *26*, 4363.

Childress, L., & Hanson, R. (2013). Diamond NV centers for quantum computing and quantum networks. *MRS Bulletin*, *38*(2), 134–138. doi:10.1557/mrs.2013.20

Devoret, M. H., & Schoelkopf, R. J. (2013). Superconducting Circuits for Quantum Information: An Outlook. *Science*, *339*(6124), 1169–1174. doi:10.1126cience.1231930 PMID:23471399

Diddams, S. A., Hollberg, L., Ma, L.-S., & Robertsson, L. (2002). Femtosecond-laser-based optical clockwork with instability $\leq 63 \times 10^{-16}$ in 1 s. *Optics Letters*, *27*(1), 58. doi:10.1364/OL.27.000058 PMID:18007715

DiVincenzo, D. P. (2000). The Physical Implementation of Quantum Computation. *Fortschritte der Physik*, *48*(9-11), 771–783. doi:10.1002/1521-3978(200009)48:9/11<771::AID-PROP771>3.0.CO;2-E

DiVincenzo, D. P., & Loss, D. (1998). Quantum information is physical. *Superlattices and Microstructures*, *23*(3-4), 419–432. doi:10.1006pmi.1997.0520

Feynman, R. P. (1982). Simulating physics with computers. *International Journal of Theoretical Physics*, *21*(6-7), 467–488. doi:10.1007/BF02650179

Flentje, H., Mortemousque, P.-A., Thalineau, R., Ludwig, A., Wieck, A. D., Bäuerle, C., & Meunier, T. (2017). Coherent long-distance displacement of individual electron spins. *Nature Communications*, 8(1), 501. doi:10.103841467-017-00534-3 PMID:28894092

Gordon, J. P., & Bowers, K. D. (1958). Microwave Spin Echoes from Donor Electrons in Silicon. *Physical Review Letters*, 1(10), 368–370. doi:10.1103/PhysRevLett.1.368

Grover, L. K. (1997). Quantum Mechanics Helps in Searching for a Needle in a Haystack. *Physical Review Letters*, 79(2), 325–328. doi:10.1103/PhysRevLett.79.325

Gupta, J. A., Knobel, R., Samarth, N., & Awschalom, D. D. (2001). Ultrafast Manipulation of Electron Spin Coherence. *Science*, 292(5526), 2458–2461. doi:10.1126cience.1061169 PMID:11431559

Häffner, H., Roos, C. F., & Blatt, R. (2008). Quantum computing with trapped ions. *Physics Reports*, 469(4), 155–203. doi:10.1016/j.physrep.2008.09.003

Heberle, A. P., Baumberg, J. J., & Kohler, K. (1995). Ultrafast Coherent Control and Destruction of Excitons in Quantum Wells. *Physical Review Letters*, 75(13), 2598–2601. doi:10.1103/PhysRevLett.75.2598 PMID:10059352

Huang, W., Yang, C. H., Chan, K. W., Tanttu, T., Hensen, B., Leon, R. C. C., Fogarty, M. A., Hwang, J. C. C., Hudson, F. E., Itoh, K. M., Morello, A., Laucht, A., & Dzurak, A. S. (2019). Fidelity benchmarks for two-qubit gates in silicon. *Nature*, 569(7757), 532–536. doi:10.103841586-019-1197-0 PMID:31086337

Kane, B. E. (1998). A silicon-based nuclear spin quantum computer. *Nature*, 393(6681), 133–137. doi:10.1038/30156

Kikkawa, J. M., Smorchkova, I. P., Samarth, N., & Awschalom, D. D. (1997). Room-Temperature Spin Memory in Two-Dimensional Electron Gases. *Science*, 277(5330), 1284–1287. doi:10.1126cience.277.5330.1284

Kim, D., Shi, Z., Simmons, C. B., Ward, D. R., Prance, J. R., Koh, T. S., Gamble, J. K., Savage, D. E., Lagally, M. G., Friesen, M., Coppersmith, S. N., & Eriksson, M. A. (2014). Quantum control and process tomography of a semiconductor quantum dot hybrid qubit. *Nature*, 511(7507), 70–74. doi:10.1038/nature13407 PMID:24990747

Koppens, F. H. L., Buizert, C., Tielrooij, K. J., Vink, I. T., Nowack, K. C., Meunier, T., Kouwenhoven, L. P., & Vandersypen, L. M. K. (2006). Driven coherent oscillations of a single electron spin in a quantum dot. *Nature*, 442(7104), 766–771. doi:10.1038/nature05065 PMID:16915280

Levy, J. (2002). *Oxide – Semiconductor Materials for Quantum Computation.* Academic Press.

Loss, D., & DiVincenzo, D. P. (1998). Quantum computation with quantum dots. *Physical Review A, 57*(1), 120–126. doi:10.1103/PhysRevA.57.120

Medford, J., Beil, J., Taylor, J. M., Rashba, E. I., Lu, H., Gossard, A. C., & Marcus, C. M. (2013). Quantum-Dot-Based Resonant Exchange Qubit. *Physical Review Letters, 111*(5), 050501. doi:10.1103/PhysRevLett.111.050501 PMID:23952375

Monroe, C., & Kim, J. (2013). Scaling the Ion Trap Quantum Processor. *Science, 339*(6124), 1164–1169. doi:10.1126cience.1231298 PMID:23471398

Nowack, K. C., Koppens, F. H. L., Nazarov, Y. V., & Vandersypen, L. M. K. (2007). Coherent Control of a Single Electron Spin with Electric Fields. *Science, 318*(5855), 1430–1433. doi:10.1126cience.1148092 PMID:17975030

Ono, K., Austing, D. G., Tokura, Y., & Tarucha, S. (2002). Current Rectification by Pauli Exclusion in a Weakly Coupled Double Quantum Dot System. *Science, 297*(5585), 1313–1317. doi:10.1126cience.1070958 PMID:12142438

Petta, J. R., Johnson, A. C., Taylor, J. M., Laird, E. A., Yacoby, A., Lukin, M. D., Marcus, C. M., Hanson, M. P., & Gossard, A. C. (2005). Coherent Manipulation of Coupled Electron Spins in Semiconductor Quantum Dots. *Science, 309*(5744), 2180–2184. doi:10.1126cience.1116955 PMID:16141370

Samkharadze, N., Zheng, G., Kalhor, N., Brousse, D., Sammak, A., Mendes, U. C., Blais, A., Scappucci, G., & Vandersypen, L. M. K. (2018). Strong spin-photon coupling in silicon. *Science, 359*(6380), 1123–1127. doi:10.1126cience.aar4054 PMID:29371427

Shor, P. W. (1994). Article. In *Proc. 1st Internat. Symp., Algorithmic Number Theory.* Springer-Verlag.

Shor, P. W. (1996). Article. In *Proc. 37th Conf. Foundations of Computer Science.* IEEE Comput. Soc. Press.

Shulman, M. D., Dial, O. E., Harvey, S. P., Bluhm, H., Umansky, V., & Yacoby, A. (2012). Demonstration of Entanglement of Electrostatically Coupled Singlet-Triplet Qubits. *Science, 336*(6078), 202–205. doi:10.1126cience.1217692 PMID:22499942

Simmons, C. B., Thalakulam, M., Shaji, N., Klein, L. J., Qin, H., Blick, R. H., Savage, D. E., Lagally, M. G., Coppersmith, S. N., & Eriksson, M. A. (2007). Single-electron quantum dot in Si/SiGe with integrated charge sensing. *Applied Physics Letters, 91*(21), 213103. doi:10.1063/1.2816331

Vandersypen, L. M. K., Bluhm, H., Clarke, J. S., Dzurak, A. S., Ishihara, R., Morello, A., Reilly, D. J., Schreiber, L. R., & Veldhorst, M. (2017). Interfacing spin qubits in quantum dots and donors—Hot, dense, and coherent. *NPJ Quantum Information*, *3*(1), 34. doi:10.103841534-017-0038-y

Vandersypen, L.M.K., & Chuang, I.L. (2005). NMR techniques for quantum control and computation. *Rev. Mod. Phys., 76*, 1037-69.

Veldhorst, M., Hwang, J. C. C., Yang, C. H., Leenstra, A. W., de Ronde, B., Dehollain, J. P., Muhonen, J. T., Hudson, F. E., Itoh, K. M., Morello, A., & Dzurak, A. S. (2014). An addressable quantum dot qubit with fault-tolerant control-fidelity. *Nature Nanotechnology*, *9*(12), 981–985. doi:10.1038/nnano.2014.216 PMID:25305743

Veldhorst, M., Yang, C. H., Hwang, J. C. C., Huang, W., Dehollain, J. P., Muhonen, J. T., Simmons, S., Laucht, A., Hudson, F. E., Itoh, K. M., Morello, A., & Dzurak, A. S. (2015). A two-qubit logic gate in silicon. *Nature*, *526*(7573), 410–414. doi:10.1038/nature15263 PMID:26436453

Weber, J. R., Koehl, W. F., Varley, J. B., Janotti, A., Buckley, B. B., Van de Walle, C. G., & Awschalom, D. D. (2010). Quantum computing with defects. *Proceedings of the National Academy of Sciences of the United States of America*, *107*(19), 8513–8518. doi:10.1073/pnas.1003052107 PMID:20404195

Wendin, G. (2017). Quantum information processing with superconducting circuits: A review. *Rep. Prog. Phys., 80*(24).

Xin, Z., Hai-Ou, L., & Ke, W. (2018). Qubits based on semiconductor quantum dots. *Chinese Physics B*, *27*(2), 020305. doi:10.1088/1674-1056/27/2/020305

Yilmaz, T., DePriest, C. M., & Delfyett, P. J. Jr. (2001). Complete noise characterisation of external cavity semiconductor laser hybridly modelocked at 10 GHz. *Electronics Letters*, *37*(22), 1338. doi:10.1049/el:20010919

Yoneda, J., Takeda, K., Otsuka, T., Nakajima, T., Delbecq, M. R., Allison, G., Honda, T., Kodera, T., Oda, S., Hoshi, Y., Usami, N., Itoh, K. M., & Tarucha, S. (2018). A quantum-dot spin qubit with coherence limited by charge noise and fidelity higher than 99.9%. *Nature Nanotechnology*, *13*(2), 102–106. doi:10.103841565-017-0014-x PMID:29255292

KEY TERMS AND DEFINITIONS

Entanglement: Entanglement is a quantum mechanical effect that correlates the behavior of two separate things. When two qubits are entangled, changes to one qubit directly impact the other. Quantum algorithms leverage those relationships to find solutions to complex problems.

Quantum Computing: Is an area of computing focused on developing computer technology based on the principles of quantum theory. It saddles the exceptional capacity of subatomic particles that permits them to exist in more than one state.

Qubits: Qubit or quantum bit is a unit of computing information that is represented by a state of an atom or elementary particle (such as the spin) and can store multiple values at once due to the principles of quantum mechanics. In quantum computing the information is encoded in qubits. A qubit is a two-level quantum system where the two basis qubit states are usually written as $|0\rangle$ and $|1\rangle$. A qubit can be in state $|0\rangle$, $|1\rangle$ or (unlike a classical bit) in a linear combination of both states.

Semiconducting Materials: Is a crystal material whose ability to conduct electricity rises as its temperature goes up. That is, it sometimes acts as a conductor and sometimes as an insulator. Its conducting ability can be much increased by chemical treatment. A manufactured chip of silicon, less than half an inch square, may contain millions of microscopic transistors, which can serve control and memory functions when installed in a computer.

Superconductors: A superconductor is any material that can conduct electricity with no resistance. In most cases, materials such as metallic elements or compounds offer some resistance at room temperature but offer less resistance at a temperature known as its critical temperature. The transport of electrons from one atom to another is often done by these certain materials after achieving the critical temperature, thus making the material superconductive.

Superfluids: Computer likely uses a fan to get cold enough to work. Quantum processors need to be very cold – about a hundredth of a degree above absolute zero. To achieve this, we use super-cooled superfluids to create superconductors.

APPENDIX

Future of Quantum Computing-Quantum computing has a dynamic nature, acting as a useful solution for complex mathematical models, such as:

- Encryption methods have been designed to take centuries to solve even for supercomputers. However, these problems could possibly be solved within minutes with quantum computing.
- Even though the modelling of a molecule does not seem to happen in the near future with classical computing, quantum computing can make it possible by solving equations that impede advances in extracting an exact model of molecules. This development has the potential to transform biology, chemistry and material science. There are different approaches in the implementation of quantum computing. Since quantum computerization and quantum circuits create high investment costs, trial and error of all different approaches will be costly in both time and financial terms. Different approaches for different applications seem to be the most likely solution now. Currently, some approaches explored by QC companies are analog quantum model, universal quantum gate model and quantum annealing. • For example, Microsoft's approach is called topological qubit method under the quantum gate model for mass production of qubits.
- D-wave built the first commercial hardware solution for quantum annealing. Quantum annealing is the most likely approach to be commercialized in the near term for solving complex mathematical problems.

Chapter 10
Tunable Attenuator Based on Hybrid Metal–Graphene Structure on Spoof Surface Plasmon Polaritons Waveguide

Aymen Hlali
University of Carthage, Tunisia

Hassen Zairi
ENICarthage, University of Carthage, Tunisia

ABSTRACT

A novel type of tunable attenuator on spoof surface plasmon polaritons (SSPP) waveguide based on hybrid metal-graphene structure for terahertz applications is proposed in this chapter. Two structures are analyzed and designed, where the first is composed of a graphene sheet at only one cell of the SSPP waveguide and the second at all cells. By varying the graphene chemical potential via a biased voltage, the surface conductivity of graphene can be adjusted. Therefore, the attenuation can also be adjusted. Moreover, an equivalent circuit model is proposed to facilitate the designs of the proposed attenuator and offer the general understanding of the attenuation mechanism. Numerical simulation results with the CST simulator and WCIP method have a good agreement with the theoretical results. The simulated results show that the attenuator can obtain adjustment range from 6.02 to 14.32 dB for the first structure and from 1.58 to 30.93 dB for the second, as the chemical potential rises from 0 to 0.5 eV.

DOI: 10.4018/978-1-7998-9183-3.ch010

INTRODUCTION

In the past few years, Spoof Surface Plasmon Polaritons (SSPPs) have attracted increasing attention due to their exceptional capability of guiding electromagnetic waves, flexibility enhancement and mutual coupling reduction (Chen et al., 2018; Tang et al., 2019). Several groups developed many microwave components and devices based on SSPP concept, such as antennas, waveguides, sensors, filters, splitters and couplers (Kianinejad et al., 2015; Kianinejad et al., 2018; Zhang et al., 2017). A reconfigurable SSPP waveguide attenuator is a fundamental component for the microwave applications. Graphene, as a two-dimensional material with its several interesting characteristics, has been widely used in the manufacture of microwave and terahertz components. In fact, it is considered to be an electronically tunable component thanks to one of its key characteristics which is its ability to change its conductivity. A number of graphene-based tunable attenuators have been proposed in (Zhang et al., 2019a; Zhang et al., 2019b; Zhang et al., 2018; Zhang et al., 2019). Similarly, the tunable substrate integrated waveguide attenuator using graphene mentioned in (Zhang et al., 2018), were obtained by depositing two graphene sandwich structures inside a Substrate Integrated Waveguide (SIW). The attenuator in reference (Zhang et al., 2019a) consists of a microstrip line and two graphene sandwich structures. In fact, these graphene sandwich structures are placed on the substrate of the micro strip line, close to the signal strip over the propagation direction. Reference (Zhang et al., 2019) has proposed and realized a flexible and tunable attenuator construct on graphene-based spoof surface plasmon polaritons waveguide. This attenuator is built by making a graphene sandwich structure on a SSPP waveguide. All of these structures operate in the bands 7-14, 10-40 and 6-9 GHz, respectively. However, though it has not been developed a terahertz tunable attenuator is a fundamental device for an RF system. To our knowledge, no work has been developed a tunable attenuator based on SSPP designs in THz band. In this work a novel type of tunable attenuator based on hybrid metal-graphene structure on spoof surface plasmon polaritons waveguide is proposed, this type of attenuator is developed to operate in terahertz band. The theoretical analysis of the graphene-based attenuator demonstrated that the attenuation can be adjusted by adding graphene cells over the SSPP waveguide and by varying the graphene chemical potential. In order to validate the accuracy and efficiency of our study, the extracted analytic results are comprehensively compared with the simulated results with Wave Concept Iterative Process (WCIP) method and CST simulator. This paper is organized as follows. In section II, the theoretical analysis of the structures and some theoretical aspects about the graphene and WCIP method are presented. Subsequently, numerical results are introduced in section III to demonstrate the effect of graphene chemical potential variation and the number of cells on attenuation. Eventually, conclusions are provided at the end of this paper.

Theory and formulation

Figure 1 illustrates a schematic configuration of the proposed SSPP waveguide, which is composed of a metal strip with periodic square cells. The golden area represents the metal, the gray area stands for graphene, and the white area describes the dielectric substrate. Here, we choose Arlon as the substrate with thickness of 2.8 µm and relative permittivity of 3.

Figure 1. Schematic configuration of the proposed attenuator.

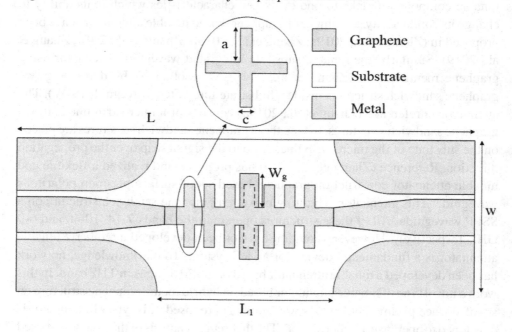

As shown in Fig. 1, the graphene layer is placed on the SSPP waveguide. The parameters of the proposed attenuator are designed as: L = 66, L1 = 26.2, W = 23.4, Wg = 2.7, h = 2.8, a = 2.7, c = 1, all in micrometers.

An equivalent circuit model is proposed to offer a general understanding and facilitate the designs and optimizations with desired performance. The equivalent circuit of the attenuator with a graphene sheet at only one cell of the SSPP waveguide is shown in Fig. 2.

Figure 2. Equivalent circuit of the attenuator with a graphene sheet at only one cell of the SSPP waveguide.

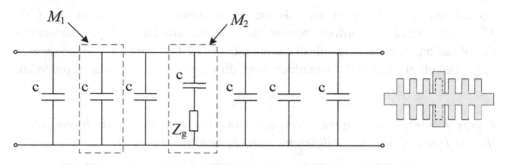

To include the graphene in the equivalent circuit model, we add loading impedance to the shunt lines. In the range of frequency below 8 THz, the intraband conductivity dominates the overall conductivity and the interband conductivity has no impact on the total conductivity within this band (Hlali et al., 2019a). The attenuator is a reciprocal (S21=S12) and symmetrical network (S11=S22). Thus, its S21 can be obtained by the matrix conversion from the ABCD matrix (Pozar, 2011). Fig. 3 depicts the equivalent circuit of the attenuator with a graphene sheet at all cells of the SSPP waveguide.

The WCIP method has been described in various articles (Hlali et al., 2018; Hlali et al., 2019a; Hlali et al., 2019b). Graphene is implemented in the WCIP method as boundary condition via the electric field and the current density using the surface conductivity. It has been fully explained in these articles (Hlali et al., 2018; Hlali et al., 2019a). In the case where a layer of metal is placed below a layer of graphene, the scattering matrix of this hybrid form considers the boundary conditions of graphene in medium 1 and the boundary conditions of metal in medium 2.

Figure 3. Equivalent circuit of the attenuator with a graphene sheet at all cells of the SSPP waveguide.

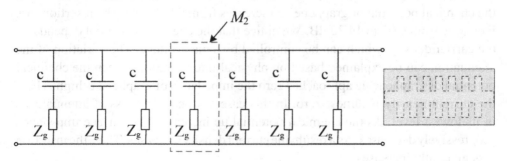

NUMERICAL RESULTS AND DISCUSSION

To validate the theoretical analysis presented above, WCIP method and CST Microwave Studio are utilized here to perform the simulation. Fig. 4 shows the calculated and simulated results of the attenuator at 2 THz with a graphene sheet at only one cell of the SSPP waveguide versus different values of chemical potential.

Figure 4. Insertion loss of the attenuator with a graphene sheet at only one cell of the SSPP waveguide versus different values of chemical potential.

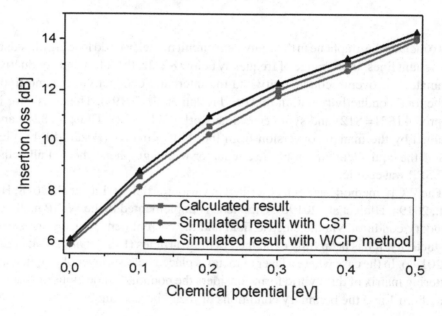

As shown in Fig. 4, there is a good agreement between the calculated results and the simulated results obtained by the WCIP method and the CST simulator. We also note that the graphene conductivity has an important effect on the attenuation. As the chemical potential of graphene μc increases from 0 to 0.5 eV, the insertion loss increases from 6.02 to 14.32 dB. We notice that the chemical potential depends on the carrier density, which can be controlled by a bias voltage. The variation of the attenuation can be explained based on physical interpretation. When the chemical potential of graphene μc approaches zero the impedance of graphene is high. Then, the current density is almost zero. In this case, the insertion loss of attenuator is in its lowest level. As the chemical potential μc increases, the surface impedance progressively decreases. As a result, the current density increases. Thus, the insertion loss gradually increases.

Figure 5. Insertion loss of the attenuator with a graphene sheet at all cells of the SSPP waveguide versus different values of chemical potential.

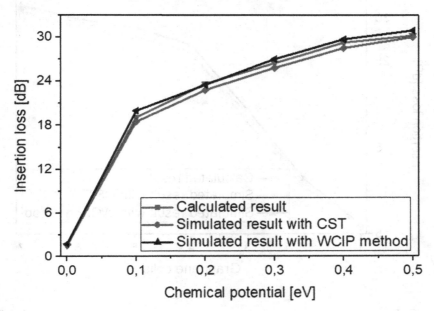

It can be clearly demonstrated that this attenuator can achieve an attenuation range from 1.58 to 30.93 dB while the chemical potential of graphene is changing from 0 to 0.5 eV. In order to demonstrate the effect of the graphene cells number on attenuation, Fig. 6 shows the calculated and simulated insertion loss as a function of the number of graphene cells, where the graphene chemical potential is 0.5 eV.

We can note that the insertion loss increases when the number of graphene cells increases; thus, the regulation band rises. In addition, the effect of the width of the graphene sheet at 2 THz is studied in Figure 7.

The result shows that by increasing the width of graphene sheet Wg the insertion loss increases as the width of graphene Wg increases from 0 μm to Wg ' a. After this value, the insertion loss remains almost unchanged. Table 1 presents the comparison results of the performance comparison of the proposed attenuator with a graphene sheet at only one cell and at all cells of the spoof surface plasmon polaritons waveguide, and without graphene.

According to the results obtained above, it can be obviously seen that the proposed attenuator with a graphene sheet at all cells gives a wider tunable attenuation range which increases from 6.02-14.32 dB to 1.58-30.93 dB, and a low return loss when compared with the attenuator with a graphene sheet at one cell. Further, Fig. 8 shows the variation of the reflection and transmission coefficients of the attenuator with a graphene sheet at all cells operating from 1 to 4 THz for different chemical potentials.

Figure 6. Insertion loss of the attenuator versus the number of graphene cells.

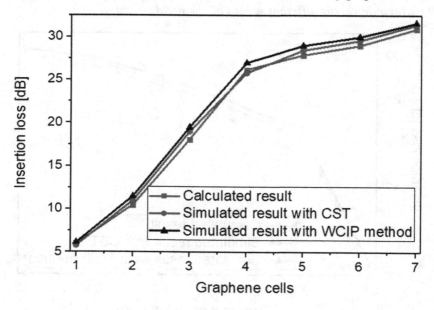

Figure 7. Insertion loss of the attenuator with a graphene sheet at all cells of the SSPP waveguide versus width of graphene sheet.

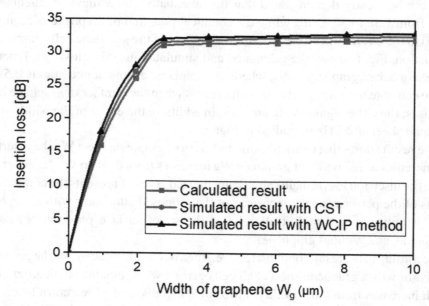

Table 1. Performance characteristics of the three configurations.

$|S_{21}|$rangeStructure		$|S_{11}|$	Frequency band
	(dB)	(dB)	(THz)
Without graphene	non-tunable	<-15	2 – 4
Graphene at one cell	6.02 - 14.32	<-40	2 – 4
Graphene at all cells	1.58 - 30.93	<-50	2 – 4

Figure 8a.

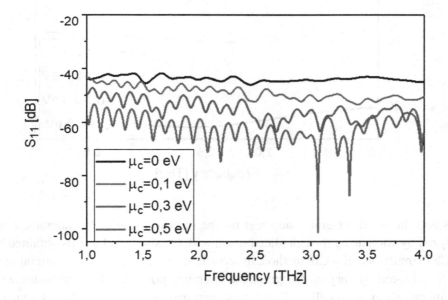

As shown in Fig. 8 (b), the magnitude of transmission coefficient can be tuned from 1.58 to 30.9 dB with reflection below 40 dB, when the chemical potential µc increases from 0 to 0.5 eV. The return loss characteristics decrease by increasing the chemical potential.

CONCLUSION

A novel type of tunable attenuator on spoof surface plasmon polaritons waveguide based on hybrid metal-graphene structure for terahertz applications is discussed in this paper. We produce this attenuator by depositing a graphene sheet at only one cell of the SSPP waveguide or at all cells. Equivalent circuit models for the two structures are provided to analyze the performance of this attenuator. Based in these models, the influences of the graphene chemical potential, the number of graphene

Figure 8b. Simulated results for different chemical potentials: (a) Reflection coefficient and (b) transmission coefficient.

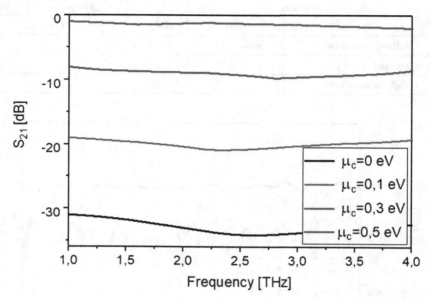

cells and the width of graphene sheet on the insertion loss of the attenuator are analyzed by comparing the calculated result with the simulated results obtained by the CST simulator and WCIP method. In accordance with the analysis, the attenuation can be adjusted by varying the graphene chemical potential. The attenuator with a graphene sheet at all cells exhibits good performance than the other attenuator, where it gives a wider tunable attenuation range which increases from 6.02-14.32 dB to 1.58-30.93 dB and low return loss.

REFERENCES

Chen, H., Lu, W. B., Lui, Z. G., Zhang, J., & Huang, B. H. (2018). Efficient Manipulation of Spoof Surface Plasmon Polaritons Based on Rotated Complementary H-Shaped Resonator Metasurface. *IEEE Transactions on Antennas and Propagation*, 65(12), 7383–7388. doi:10.1109/TAP.2017.2763175

Hlali, A., Houaneb, Z., & Zairi, H. (2018). Dual-Band Reconfigurable Graphene-Based Patch Antenna in Terahertz Band: Design, Analysis and Modeling Using WCIP Method. *Progress In Electromagnetics Research C*, 87, 213–226. doi:10.2528/PIERC18080107

Hlali, A., Houaneb, Z., & Zairi, H. (2019a). Tunable filter based on hybrid metal-graphene structures over an ultrawide terahertz band using an improved Wave Concept Iterative Process method. *International Journal for Light and Electron Optics*, *181*, 423–431. doi:10.1016/j.ijleo.2018.12.091

Hlali, A., Houaneb, Z., & Zairi, H. (2019b). Effective Modeling of Magnetized Graphene by the Wave Concept Iterative Process Method Using Boundary Conditions. *Progress In Electromagnetics Research C*, *89*, 121–132. doi:10.2528/PIERC18111514

Kianinejad, A., Chen, Z. N., & Qiu, Ch. W. (2015). Design and Modeling of Spoof Surface Plasmon Modes-Based Microwave Slow-Wave Transmission Line. *IEEE Transactions on Microwave Theory and Techniques*, *63*(6), 1817–1825. doi:10.1109/TMTT.2015.2422694

Kianinejad, A., Chen, Z. N., & Qiu, Ch. W. (2018). Full Modeling, Loss Reduction, and Mutual Coupling Control of Spoof Surface Plasmon-Based Meander Slow Wave Transmission Lines. *IEEE Transactions on Microwave Theory and Techniques*, *66*(8), 3764–3772. doi:10.1109/TMTT.2018.2841857

Pozar, D. M. (2011). Microwave Engineering. New York: John Wiley & Sons.

Tang, W. L., Zhang, H. Ch., Ma, H. F., Jiang, W. X., & Cui, T. J. (2019). Concept, Theory, Design, and Applications of Spoof Surface Plasmon Polaritons at Microwave Frequencies. *Advanced Optical Materials, 7*, 1–22.

Zhang, A. Q., Liu, Z. G., Lu, W. B., & Chen, H. (2019a). Dynamically Tunable Attenuator on a Graphene-Based Microstrip Line. *IEEE Transactions on Microwave Theory and Techniques*, *67*(2), 746–753. doi:10.1109/TMTT.2018.2885761

Zhang, A. Q., Liu, Z. G., Lu, W. B., & Chen, H. (2019b). Graphene-Based Dynamically Tunable Attenuator on a Coplanar Waveguide or a Slotline. *IEEE Transactions on Microwave Theory and Techniques*, *67*(1), 70–77. doi:10.1109/TMTT.2018.2875078

Zhang, A. Q., Lu, W. B., Liu, Z. G., Chen, H., & Huang, B. H. (2018). Dynamically Tunable Substrate Integrated Waveguide Attenuator Using Graphene. *IEEE Transactions on Microwave Theory and Techniques*, *66*(6), 3081–3089. doi:10.1109/TMTT.2018.2809577

Zhang, A. Q., Lu, W. B., Liu, Z. G., Wu, B., & Chen, H. (2019). Flexible and Dynamically Tunable Attenuator Based on Spoof Surface Plasmon Polaritons Waveguide Loaded With Graphene. *IEEE Transactions on Antennas and Propagation*, *67*(8), 5582–5589. doi:10.1109/TAP.2019.2911590

Zhang, X., Zhang, H. Ch., Tang, W. X., Liu, J. F., Fang, Z., Wu, J. W., & Cui, J. W. (2017). Loss Analysis and Engineering of Spoof Surface Plasmons Based on Circuit Topology. *IEEE Antennas and Wireless Propagation Letters*, *16*, 3204–3207. doi:10.1109/LAWP.2017.2768551

Conclusion

In this book we have included ten book chapters related to Quantum computing, Quantum technology, Quantum Engineering and many more. Objective of each chapter is discussed in the Preface section. Self-explanatory chapters are arranged here for the reader's easy understanding.

As learning is a never-ending process, so we will organize an International Conference and one online workshop on Advances in Quantum Computing and Engineering to bring together quantum professionals, researchers, educators, entrepreneurs, champions and enthusiasts to exchange and share their experiences, challenges, research results, innovations, applications, pathways and enthusiasm on all aspects of Quantum Computing and Engineering. Its outcome will be the 2nd edition of this book.

Glossary

Abstract Data Type (ADT): Is a mathematical model for data types. This is defined by its behavior (semantics) from the point of view of a user, of the data, specifically in terms of possible values, possible operations on data of this type, and the behavior of these operations.

Bloch Sphere: In quantum mechanics and computing, the Bloch sphere is a geometrical representation of the pure state space of a two-level quantum mechanical system (qubit), named after the physicist Felix Bloch. The Bloch sphere is a unit 2-sphere, with antipodal points corresponding to a pair of mutually orthogonal state vectors. The north and south poles of the Bloch sphere are typically chosen to correspond to the standard basis vectors.

Bloch Vector: A Bloch vector is a unit vector $(\cos\varphi\sin\theta, \sin\varphi\sin\theta, \cos\theta)$ used to represent points on a Bloch sphere.

Bounded-Error Quantum Polynomial Time (BQP): In computational complexity theory, bounded-error quantum polynomial time (BQP) is the class of decision problems solvable by a quantum computer in polynomial time, with an error probability of at most 1/3 for all instances.

COVID-19: Coronavirus disease (COVID -19) is an infectious disease caused by the SARS-CoV-2 virus.

Diabetic Retinopathy: It is an eye condition that can cause vision loss and blindness in people who have diabetes.

Entanglement: Entanglement is a quantum mechanical effect that correlates the behavior of two separate things. When two qubits are entangled, changes to one qubit directly impact the other. Quantum algorithms leverage those relationships to find solutions to complex problems.

Evolutionary Algorithm: The evolutionary algorithm (EA) emulates the behavior of living organisms by using mechanisms inspired by nature to solve problems. Both evolutionary computing and bio-inspired computing incorporate EA. Evolutionary algorithms are modeled after Darwin's concepts.

Healthcare: It is the various services for the prevention or treatment of illness and injuries. Nobody wants to pay more for health care.

Hybrid CNN: It utilizes a Deep Neural Network (DNN) to effectively memorize global features by one-dimensional (1D) data and utilizes a CNN to generalize local features by two-dimensional (2D) data.

Intelligent Systems: An intelligent system is a machine with an embedded, Internet-connected computer that has the capacity to gather and analyze data and communicate with other systems. Similarly, intelligent systems can also include sophisticated AI-based software systems, such as chatbots, expert systems and other types of software.

Ion Trap: In ion traps, the qubits are atoms that are missing some electrons and therefore have a net positive charge. We can then trap these ions in electromagnetic fields, and use lasers to move them around and entangle them. Such ion traps are comparable in the size to the qubit chips. They also need to be cooled but not quite as much, "only" to temperatures of the few Kelvins.

Machine Learning: Machine learning (ML) is a type of artificial intelligence (AI) that allows software applications to become more accurate at predicting outcomes without being explicitly programmed to do so. Machine learning algorithms use historical data as input to predict new output values. Machine learning is important because it gives enterprises a view of trends in customer behavior and business operational patterns, as well as supports the development of new products. Many of today's leading companies, such as Facebook, Google, and Uber, make machine learning a central part of their operations. Machine learning has become a significant competitive differentiator for many companies.

Net Carbon Zero Emissions: It refers to achieving an overall balance between greenhouse gas emissions produced and greenhouse gas emissions taken out of the atmosphere.

Nitrogen-Vacancy System: In the nitrogen-vacancy system, the qubits are placed in the structures of a carbon crystal where a carbon atom is replaced by a nitrogen atom.

Noisy Intermediate Scale Quantum: A noisy intermediate-scale quantum (NISQ) processor contains 50 to a few hundred qubits, but are neither sufficiently advanced nor large enough to profit sustainably from quantum supremacy. This term describes the current state of the art in quantum processor fabrication. The term 'noisy' refers to quantum processors that are very sensitive to their environment and may lose their quantum state due to quantum decoherence. During the era of NISQ, quantum processors are not advanced enough to continuously use quantum error correction.

Optimization: An optimization problem is the problem of finding the best solution from all feasible solutions. Optimization problems can be divided into two categories, depending on whether the variables are continuous or discrete. An optimization problem with discrete variables is known as a discrete optimization, in which an object such as an integer, permutation or graph must be found from a countable set. A problem with continuous variables is known as a continuous optimization, in which an optimal value from a continuous function must be found. They can include constrained problems and multimodal problems.

Phase Angles: Phase angle refers to a particular point in the time of a cycle whose measurement takes place from some arbitrary zero and its expression is as an angle. Furthermore, a phase angle happens to be one of the most important characteristics of a periodic wave.

Photonic Gate: In photonic quantum computing, the qubits are properties related to photons. That may be the presence of the photon itself or the uncertainty in a particular state of the photon.

Quantum Algorithm: Runs on a realistic model of quantum computation, the most commonly used model being the quantum circuit model of computation.

Quantum Annealing: Quantum annealing is the process of finding the minimum energy state of something where instead of focusing on trying to find the minimum energy state, a sample from any low energy state is taken and try and characterize the shape of the energy landscape. This is useful for applications like machine learning where we try to build a probabilistic representation of the world and these samples give us information about what the model looks like now and these models can be used over time.

Quantum Bit: It is the primary unit of how information is represented in the quantum computing space. It is similar to that of how information is stored in traditional classical computing, which is a binary bit. In a classical system, a bit would have to be in one state or the other. However, quantum mechanics allows the qubit to be in a coherent superposition of both states simultaneously, a property that is fundamental to quantum mechanics and quantum computing.

Quantum Circuit: In quantum information theory, a quantum circuit is a model for quantum computation, similar to classical circuits, in which a computation is a sequence of quantum gates, measurements, initializations of qubits to known values, and possibly other actions.

Quantum Clustering: Quantum Clustering refers to a class of algorithms that use concepts and mathematical tools from quantum mechanics to cluster data. Clusters are defined by higher densities of data points, and QC belongs to the family of density-based clustering algorithms.

Quantum Computer: Can be referred to a machine that consists of a many-particle quantum system for solving complex computational problems. Possibly the most important issue in quantum computers fabrication is making a closed box. In other words, since quantum systems are very fragile, the probability of de coherence and de phasing is very high.

Quantum Computing: A quantum computing system is a computer technology based on quantum theory (which explains how energy and matter behave at atomic and subatomic levels). Modern computers can only encode information in bits that have a value of 1 or 0, which limits their capabilities. Qubits, on the other hand, are an essential part of quantum computing. It takes advantage of the unique property of subatomic particles, which allows them to exist in more than one state at once (i.e., as a 1 and a 0).

Quantum Computing: Quantum computing is an area of computing focused on developing computer technology based on the principles of quantum theory (which explains the behavior of energy and material on the atomic and subatomic levels). Computers used today can only encode information in bits that take the value of 1 or 0—restricting their ability. Quantum computing, on the other hand, uses quantum bits or qubits. It harnesses the unique ability of subatomic particles that allows them to exist in more than one state (i.e., a 1 and a 0 at the same time).

Quantum Computing: Quantum computing is an area of computing focused on developing computer technology based on the principles of quantum theory. It uses quantum bits or qubits.

Quantum Computing: Harnesses the phenomena of quantum mechanics to deliver a huge leap forward in computation to solve certain problems. This is a type of computation that harnesses the collective properties of quantum states, such as superposition, interference, and entanglement, to perform calculations. The devices that perform quantum computations are known as quantum computers.

Quantum Computing: Is an area of computing focused on developing computer technology based on the principles of quantum theory. It saddles the exceptional capacity of subatomic particles that permits them to exist in more than one state.

Quantum Engineering: Is a revolutionary discipline that seeks theoretical and practical applications of Quantum Information Science. It encompasses both fundamental physics and the broad engineering skill-set necessary to meet the practical challenges of the future.

Quantum Entanglement: Quantum entanglement comes into play when there is more than one particle is participating in the computation. When the quantum particles are in an entangled state, they are linked in the strongest possible way even if they are far apart from each other. once they are entangled, an invisible link is generated among them irrespective of how far apart they are. The entanglement among these quantum particles gives rise to the enormous number of possibilities of states for quantum communication.

Quantum Gates: In quantum computing and specifically the quantum circuit model of computation, a quantum logic gate (or simply quantum gate) is a basic quantum circuit operating on a small number of qubits. They are the building blocks of quantum circuits, like classical logic gates are for conventional digital circuits. Unlike many classical logic gates, quantum logic gates are reversible. However, it is possible to perform classical computing using only reversible gates. For example, the reversible Toffoli gate can implement all Boolean functions, often at the cost of having to use ancilla bits. The Toffoli gate has a direct quantum equivalent, showing that quantum circuits can perform all operations performed by classical circuits.

Quantum Logic Gates: A quantum logic gate (or simply quantum gate) is a basic quantum circuit operating on a small number of qubits. They are the building blocks of quantum circuits, like classical logic gates are for conventional digital circuits.

Quantum Machine Learning: Quantum machine learning is the integration of quantum algorithms into machine learning programs. Quantum algorithms can be used to analyze quantum states instead of analyzing classical data. Furthermore, quantum algorithms can be used to analyze quantum states instead of classical data. These routines can be more complex in nature and executed more quickly on a quantum computer.

Quantum Mechanics: Fundamental to physics, quantum mechanics describes the physical properties of matter on an atomic level and at a subatomic scale. Among its many applications are quantum chemistry, quantum field theory, quantum technology, and quantum information science.

Quantum Neural Network: The quantum neural network is a computational neural network that is based on quantum mechanics. Machine learning algorithms and quantum neural networks (QNN) combine concepts from quantum computing and artificial neural networks. In the past decade, the term has been applied to describe a variety of ideas, ranging from quantum computers that emulate the exact functions of neural nets to general trainable quantum circuits that bear little resemblance to the multilayer structure of perceptron.

Quantum Optimization: A quantum optimization algorithm is used to solve a problem of optimization. From a set of possible solutions, mathematical optimization aims to find the most optimal solution. Most optimization problems are presented as minimization problems, where one attempts to minimize an error which is a function of the solution: the optimal solution has the smallest error. There are many optimization techniques used in fields like mechanics, economics, and engineering, and as the complexity and amount of data involved rise, it becomes increasingly important to find more efficient solutions to optimization problems. There is a possibility that quantum computing may allow problems which are beyond the capabilities of classical computers to be resolved, or may suggest a significant speedup over the fastest known classical algorithm.

Quantum Programming Languages: Are essential to translate ideas into instructions that can be executed by a quantum computer. They are crucial to the programming of quantum computers at scale but also they can facilitate the discovery and development of quantum algorithms even before hardware exists that is capable of executing them. These are used for controlling existing physical devices, for estimating the execution costs of quantum algorithms on future devices, for teaching quantum computing concepts, or for verifying quantum algorithms and their implementations.

Quantum States: In quantum physics, a quantum state is a mathematical entity that provides a probability distribution for the outcomes of each possible measurement on a system. Knowledge of the quantum state together with the rules for the system's evolution in time exhausts all that can be predicted about the system's behavior. A mixture of quantum states is again a quantum state. Quantum states that cannot be written as a mixture of other states are called pure quantum states, while all other states are called mixed quantum states. A pure quantum state can be represented by a ray in a Hilbert space over the complex numbers, while mixed states are represented by density matrices, which are positive semidefinite operators that act on Hilbert spaces.

Quantum Technology: Is a class of technology that works by using the principles of quantum mechanics (the physics of sub-atomic particles), including quantum entanglement and quantum superposition. This is an emerging field of physics and engineering, which relies on the principles of quantum physics. Quantum computing, quantum sensors, quantum cryptography, quantum simulation, quantum metrology and quantum imaging are all examples of quantum technologies, where properties of quantum mechanics, especially quantum entanglement, quantum superposition and quantum tunneling, are important.

Quanvolutional Neural Network: Quanvolutional layers operate on input data by locally transforming the data using a number of random quantum circuits, in a way that is similar to the transformations performed by random convolutional filter layers.

Qubit: Qubit or quantum bit is the basic unit of quantum information. The quantum version of the classic binary bit physically realized with a two-state device. This is a two-state (or two-level) quantum-mechanical system, one of the simplest quantum systems displaying the peculiarity of quantum mechanics.

Semiconducting Materials: Is a crystal material whose ability to conduct electricity rises as its temperature goes up. That is, it sometimes acts as a conductor and sometimes as an insulator. Its conducting ability can be much increased by chemical treatment. A manufactured chip of silicon, less than half an inch square, may contain millions of microscopic transistors, which can serve control and memory functions when installed in a computer.

Semiconducting Qubits: Semiconducting qubits are very similar to superconducting qubits, but here the qubits are either the spin or charge of a single electron.

Simulation: A simulation is the imitation of the operation of a real-world process or system over time. Simulations require the use of models; the model represents the key characteristics or behaviors of the selected system or process, whereas the simulation represents the evolution of the model over time. Often, computers are used to execute the simulation.

State Vector: In the mathematical formulation of quantum mechanics, pure quantum states correspond to vectors in a Hilbert space, while each observable quantity (such as the energy or momentum of a particle) is associated with a mathematical operator. The operator serves as a linear function which acts on the states of the system.

Superconducting Gate: Superconducting qubits are the most widely used and most advanced type of qubits. They are basically small currents on a chip. The two-state qubits can be physically realized either by the distribution of the charge or by the flux of the current.

Superconductors: A superconductor is any material that can conduct electricity with no resistance. In most cases, materials such as metallic elements or compounds offer some resistance at room temperature but offer less resistance at a temperature known as its critical temperature. The transport of electrons from one atom to another is often done by these certain materials after achieving the critical temperature, thus making the material superconductive.

Superfluids: Computer likely uses a fan to get cold enough to work. Quantum processors need to be very cold – about a hundredth of a degree above absolute zero. To achieve this, we use super-cooled superfluids to create superconductors.

TensorFlow Quantum: TensorFlow Quantum (TFQ) is a Python framework for quantum machine learning.

Topological Quantum Computing: In topological quantum computers, information will be stored in conserved properties of "quasi-particles," which are collective motions of particles. The great thing about this is that this information would be very robust to decoherence.

Compilation of References

Abbas, A., Sutter, D., Zoufal, C., & Lucchi, A. (2020). The power of quantum neural networks. arXiv. https://arxiv.org/abs/2011.00027

Abbasnejad, B., Moeinzadeh, S., Ahankoob, A., & Wong, P. S. (2021). The Role of Collaboration in the Implementation of BIM-Enabled Projects. In J. Underwood & M. Shelbourn (Eds.), Handbook of Research on Driving Transformational Change in the Digital Built Environment (pp. 27–62). IGI Global. https://doi.org/10.4018/978-1-7998-6600-8.ch002

Abdelgaber, N., & Nikolopoulos, C. (2020). Overview on Quantum Computing and its Applications in Artificial Intelligence. 2020 IEEE Third International Conference on Artificial Intelligence and Knowledge Engineering (AIKE), 198-199. 10.1109/AIKE48582.2020.00038

Abdulrahman, K. O., Mahamood, R. M., & Akinlabi, E. T. (2022). Additive Manufacturing (AM): Processing Technique for Lightweight Alloys and Composite Material. In K. Kumar, B. Babu, & J. Davim (Ed.), Handbook of Research on Advancements in the Processing, Characterization, and Application of Lightweight Materials (pp. 27-48). IGI Global. https://doi.org/10.4018/978-1-7998-7864-3.ch002

Acar, E., & Yilmaz, I. (2020). COVID-19 detection on IBM quantum computer with classical-quantum transfer learning. doi:10.1101/2020.11.07.20227306

Agrawal, R., Sharma, P., & Saxena, A. (2021). A Diamond Cut Leather Substrate Antenna for BAN (Body Area Network) Application. In V. Singh, V. Dubey, A. Saxena, R. Tiwari, & H. Sharma (Eds.), Emerging Materials and Advanced Designs for Wearable Antennas (pp. 54–59). IGI Global. https://doi.org/10.4018/978-1-7998-7611-3.ch004

Ahmad, F., Al-Ammar, E. A., & Alsaidan, I. (2022). Battery Swapping Station: A Potential Solution to Address the Limitations of EV Charging Infrastructure. In M. Alam, R. Pillai, & N. Murugesan (Eds.), Developing Charging Infrastructure and Technologies for Electric Vehicles (pp. 195–207). IGI Global. doi:10.4018/978-1-7998-6858-3.ch010

Aikhuele, D. (2018). A Study of Product Development Engineering and Design Reliability Concerns. International Journal of Applied Industrial Engineering, 5(1), 79–89. doi:10.4018/IJAIE.2018010105

Compilation of References

Al-Khatri, H., & Al-Atrash, F. (2021). Occupants' Habits and Natural Ventilation in a Hot Arid Climate. In R. González-Lezcano (Ed.), Advancements in Sustainable Architecture and Energy Efficiency (pp. 146–168). IGI Global. https://doi.org/10.4018/978-1-7998-7023-4.ch007

Al-Shebeeb, O. A., Rangaswamy, S., Gopalakrishan, B., & Devaru, D. G. (2017). Evaluation and Indexing of Process Plans Based on Electrical Demand and Energy Consumption. International Journal of Manufacturing, Materials, and Mechanical Engineering, 7(3), 1–19. doi:10.4018/IJMMME.2017070101

Albrecht, S. M., Higginbotham, A. P., Madsen, M., Kuemmeth, F., Jespersen, T. S., Nygard, J., Krogstrup, P., & Marcus, C. M. (2016). Exponential protection of zero modes in Majorana islands. Nature, 531(7593), 206–209. doi:10.1038/nature17162 PMID:26961654

Alfares, F. S., & Esat, I. I. (2006, November). Real-coded quantum inspired evolution algorithm applied to engineering optimization problems. In Second International Symposium on Leveraging Applications of Formal Methods, Verification and Validation (isola 2006) (pp. 169-176). IEEE. 10.1109/ISoLA.2006.12

Altaisky, M. V., Zolnikova, N. N., Kaputkina, N. E., Krylov, V. A., Lozovik, Y. E., & Dattani, N. S. (2016). Towards a feasible implementation of quantum neural networks using quantum dots. Applied Physics Letters, 108(10), 103108. doi:10.1063/1.4943622

Alvarez-Rodriguez, U., Sanz, M., Lamata, L., & Solano, E. (2016). Artificial life in quantum technologies. Scientific Reports, 6(1), 20956. doi:10.1038rep20956 PMID:26853918

Amuda, M. O., Lawal, T. F., & Akinlabi, E. T. (2017). Research Progress on Rheological Behavior of AA7075 Aluminum Alloy During Hot Deformation. International Journal of Materials Forming and Machining Processes, 4(1), 53–96. doi:10.4018/IJMFMP.2017010104

Amuda, M. O., Lawal, T. F., & Mridha, S. (2021). Microstructure and Mechanical Properties of Silicon Carbide-Treated Ferritic Stainless Steel Welds. In L. Burstein (Ed.), Handbook of Research on Advancements in Manufacturing, Materials, and Mechanical Engineering (pp. 395–411). IGI Global. https://doi.org/10.4018/978-1-7998-4939-1.ch019

Anderson, M. (2020). Can Quantum computers Help Us Respond to the Coronavirus. IEEE Spectrum.

Angus, S. J., Ferguson, A. J., Dzurak, A. S., & Clark, R. G. (2007). Gate-Defined Quantum Dots in Intrinsic Silicon. Nano Letters, 7(7), 2051–2055. doi:10.1021/nl070949k PMID:17567176

Anikeev, V., Gasem, K. A., & Fan, M. (2021). Application of Supercritical Technologies in Clean Energy Production: A Review. In L. Chen (Ed.), Handbook of Research on Advancements in Supercritical Fluids Applications for Sustainable Energy Systems (pp. 792–821). IGI Global. https://doi.org/10.4018/978-1-7998-5796-9.ch022

Arafat, M. Y., Saleem, I., & Devi, T. P. (2022). Drivers of EV Charging Infrastructure Entrepreneurship in India. In M. Alam, R. Pillai, & N. Murugesan (Eds.), Developing *Charging Infrastructure and Technologies for Electric Vehicles* (pp. 208–219). IGI Global. https://doi.org/10.4018/978-1-7998-6858-3.ch011

Araujo, A., & Manninen, H. (2022). Contribution of Project-Based Learning on Social Skills Development: An Industrial Engineer Perspective. In A. Alves & N. van Hattum-Janssen (Eds.), Training *Engineering* Students for Modern Technological Advancement (pp. 119–145). IGI Global. https://doi.org/10.4018/978-1-7998-8816-1.ch006

Armutlu, H. (2018). Intelligent Biomedical Engineering Operations by Cloud Computing Technologies. In U. Kose, G. Guraksin, & O. Deperlioglu (Eds.), Nature-Inspired Intelligent Techniques for Solving Biomedical *Engineering Problems (pp. 297–317). Hershey, PA: IGI Global. doi:10.4018/978-1-5225-4769-3.ch015*

Asher, P. (1995). Quantum Theory: Concepts and Methods. Kluwer Academic Publishers.

Ather, F. (2021). Knocking on T*uring's* door: Quantum Computing and Machine Learning. The Gradient.

Atik, J., & Jeutner, V. (2021). Quantum computing and computational law. Law, Innovation and Technology, 13*(2), 302–324. Advance online publication. doi:10.1080/17579961.2021.1977216*

Atik, M., Sadek, M., & Shahrour, I. (2017). Single-Run Adaptive Pushover Procedure for Shear Wall Structures. In V. Plevris, *G. Kremmyda, & Y. Fa*hjan (Eds.), Performance-Based Seismic Design of Concrete Structures and Infrastructures (pp. 59–83). Hershey, PA: IGI Global. doi:10.4018/978-1-5225-2089-4.ch003

Attia, H. (2021). Smart Power Microgrid Impact on Sustai*nable Buildi*ng. In R. González-Lezcano (Ed.), Advancements in Sustainable Architecture and Energy Efficiency (pp. 169–194). IGI Global. https://doi.org/10.4018/978-1-7998-702*3-4.ch008*

Awschalom, D. D., Bassett, L. C., Dzurak, A. S., Hu, E. L., & Petta, J. R. (2013). Quantum Spintronics: Engineering and Manipulating Atom-Like Spins in Semiconductors. Science, 339(6124), 1174–1179. doi:10.1*126cience.1231364 PMID:23471400*

Aydin, A., Akyol, E., Gungor, M., Kaya, A., & Tasdelen, S. (2018). Geophysical Surveys in Engineering Geo*logy Investig*ations With Field Examples. In N. Ceryan (Ed.), Handbook of Research on Trends and Digital Advances in Engineering Geology (pp. 257–280). Hershey, PA: IGI Global. doi:10.4018/978-*1-5225-2709-1.ch007*

Ayoobkhan, M. *U.* D., Y., A., J., Easwaran, B., & R., T. (2021). Smart Connected Digital Products and IoT Platform With the Digital Twin. In P. Vasant, G. Weber, & W. Punurai (Ed.), Research Advancements in Smart Technology, Optimization, and Renewable Energy *(pp. 330-350). IGI Globa*l. *h*ttps://doi.org/ doi:10.4018/978-1-7998-3970-5.ch016

Bacon, D., & van Dam, W. (2010). Rec*ent progress in* qu*a*ntum algorithms. Communications of the ACM, 53(2), 84–93. doi:10.1145/1646353.1646375

Baeza Moyano, D., & González Lezcano, R. A. (2021). The Importance of Light *in Our Lives:* Towards New Lighting in Schools. In R. González-Lezcano (Ed.), Advanc*ements in Sustainable Architecture and Ener*gy Efficiency (pp. 239–256). IGI Global. https://doi.org/10.4018/978-1-7998-7023-4.ch011

Bagdadee, A. H. (2021). A Brief Assessment of the Energy Sector of Bangladesh. International Journal of Energy Optimization and Engineering, 10*(1), 36–55. doi:10.4018/IJEOE.2021010103*

Baklezos, A. T., & Hadjigeorgiou, N. G. (2021). Magnetic Sensor*s for Space Applications and Magnetic Cleanliness Considerations. In C. Nikolopoulos (Ed.), Recent Trends on Electromagnetic* Environmental Effects for Aeronautics and Space Applications (pp. 147–185). IGI Global. https://*doi.org/10.4018/978-1-7998-4879-0.ch006*

Ball, P. (2016). Google moves closer to a universal quantum computer. NATNews. Advance online publication. doi:10.1038/nature.2016.20032

Barenco, A., Bennett, C. H.*, Cleve, R., DiVincenzo, D. P., Margolus, N., Shor, P., Sleator, T., Smolin, J. A., & Weinfur*ter, H. (1995). Elementary gates for quantum computation. Physical Review A, 52(5), 3457–3467. doi:10.1103/PhysRevA.52.3457 PMID:9912645

Bas, T. G. (2017). Nutraceutical Industry with the Collaboration of B*iotechnology and Nutrigenomics* Engineering: The Significance of Intellectual Property in the Entrepreneurship and Scientific Resea*rch Ecosystems. In T. Bas & J. Zhao (Eds.),* Comparative Approaches to Biotechnology Development and Use in Developed and Emerging Nations (pp. *1–17). Hershey, PA: IGI Global. doi:10.4018/978-1-5225-1040-6.ch001*

Bazeer Ahamed, B., & Periakaruppan, S. (2021). Taxonomy of Influence Maximization Techniques in Unknown Social Networks. In P. Vasant, G. Weber*, & W. Punurai (Eds.),* Resea*rch* Advancements in Smart Technology, Optimization, and Renewable Energy (pp. 351-363). IGI Global. https://doi.org/10.4018/978-1-7998-3970-5.ch017

Beale, R., & André, J. (2017). Design Solutions and Innovations in Temporary *Structures. Hershey, PA: IGI* Global. doi:10.4018/978-1-5225-2199-0

Behnam, B. (2017). Simulating Post-E*arthquake Fire Loading in Conventional RC Structures. In P. Samui*, S. Chakraborty, & D. Kim (Eds.), Modeling and Simulation Techniques in Structural Engineering (pp. 425–444). Hershey, PA: IGI Global. doi:10.4018/978-1-5225-0588-4.ch015

Ben Hamida, I., Salah, S. B., Msahli, F., & Mimouni, *M. F. (2018). Distri*bution Network Reconfiguration Using SPEA2 for Power Loss Minimization and Reliability Improvem*ent. International Journal of Energy Optimization and Engineering, 7(1), 50–65. doi:10.4018/* IJEOE.2018010103

Benioff, P. (1980). The computer as a physical system: A microscopic quantum mechanical Hamiltonian model of computers as represented by Turing machines. Journal of Statistical Physics, 22(5), 563–591. doi:10.1007/BF01011339

Bennett, C. H., Brassard, G.*, & Breidbart, S. (1984).* Article. IBM Tech. Discl. Bull., 26, 4363.

Bentarzi, H. (2021). Fault Tree-Based Root Cause Analysis Used to Study Mal-Operation of a Protective Relay in a Smart Grid. In A. *Recioui & H. Bentarzi* (Eds.), Optimizing and Measuring Smart Grid Operation and Control (pp. 289–308). IGI Global. https://doi.org/10.4018/978-1-7998-4027-5.ch012

Bernstein, E., & Vazirani, U. (1993, Ju*ne). Quantum complex*ity theory. ACM Digital Library. https://dl.acm.org/doi/10.1145/167088.167097

Bettelli, S., Calarco, T., & Serafini, L. (2003). Toward an architecture for quantum programming. The European Physical Journal D-Atomic, Molecular, Optical and Plasma Physics, 25(2), 181–200.

Beysens, D. A., Garrabos, Y., & Zappoli, B. (2021). Thermal Effects in Near-Critical Fluids: Piston Effect and Related Phenomena. In L. Chen (Ed.), Handbook of Research on Advancements in Supercritical Fluids *Applications for Sustai*nable En*e*rgy Systems (pp. 1–31). IGI Global. https://doi.org/10.4018/978-1-7998-5796-9.ch001

Bhaskar, S. V., & Kudal, H. N. (2017). Effect of TiCN and AlCrN Coating on Tribological Behaviour of Plasma-nitrided AISI 4140 Steel. International *Journal* of *Su*rface Engineering and Interdisciplinary Materials Science, 5(2), 1–17. doi:10.4018/IJSEIMS.2017070101

Bhuyan, D. (2018). Desi*gning of a Twin Tube Shock Absorber:* A *S*tudy in Reverse Engineering. In K. Kumar & J. Davim (Eds.), Design and Optimization of Mechanical Engineering Products (pp. 83–104). Hershey, PA: IGI Global. doi:10.4018/978-1-5225-3401-3.ch005

Biamonte, J., Wittek, P., Pancotti, N., Rebentrost, *P., Wiebe, N., & Lloyd, S. (*2017). Quantum machine learning. Nature, 549(7671), 195–202. doi:10.1038/nature23474 PMID:28905917

Blumberg, G. (2021). Blockchains for Use in Construction and Engineering Projects. In J. Underwood & M. Shelbourn *(Eds.), Handbook of* Re*s*earch on Driving Transformational Change in the Digital Built Environment (pp. 179–208). IGI Global. https://doi.org/10.4018/*978-1-7998-6600-8.ch008*

Bova, F., Goldfarb, A., & Melko, R. G. (2021). Commercial applications of quantum computing. EPJ Quantum Technology, 8(1), 2. doi:10.1140/epjqt40507-021-00091-1 PMID:33569545

Bravyi, S., Gosset, D., & Koenig, R. (2017*). Quan*tum a*d*vantage with shallow circuits. arXiv:1704.00690.

Brecht, T., Pfaff, W., Wang, C., Chu, Y., Frunzio, L., Devoret, M. H., & Schoelkopf, R. J. (2016). Multilayer microwave integrated quantum circuits for scalable quantum computing. NPJ Quantum Information, 2(2), 16002. doi:10.1038/npjqi.2016.2

Bremner, M. J., Montanaro, A., & Shepherd*, D. J. (2*016). Average-case complexity versus approximate simulation of commuting quantum computations. Physical Review Letters, 080501(117). do*i:10.1103/PhysRevL*ett.117.080501 PMID:27588839

Brown, K. R., Kim, J., & Monroe, C. (2016). Co-designing a scalable quantum computer with trapp*ed atomic ions. arXiv:1602.02840.*

Burstein, L. (2021). Simulation Tool for Cable Design. In L. Burstein (Ed.), Handbook of Research on Advancements in Manufacturing, Materials, and Mechanical Engineering (pp. 54–74). IGI Global. https://doi.org/10.4018/978-1-7998-4939-1.ch003

Cai, X., Wu, D., Su, Z., Chen, M., Wang, X., Li, L., Liu, N., Lu, *C., & Pan, J. (2015).* Entanglement-based machine learning on a quantum computer. Physical Review Letters, 114(11), 110504.

Calderon, F. A., Giolo, E. G., Frau, C. D., Rengel, M. G., Rodriguez, H., Tornello, M., ... Gallucci, R. (2018). Seismic Microzonation and Site Effects Detection Through Microtremors Measures: A Review. In N. Ceryan (Ed.), Handbook of Research on Trends *and Digital Advance*s in Engineering Geology (pp. 326–349). Hershey, PA: IGI Global. doi:10.4018/978-1-5225-2709-1.ch009

Ceryan, N., & Can, N. K. (2018). Prediction of The Uniaxial Compressive *Strength of Rocks Materials. In N. Ceryan (Ed.), Handbook of Research* on Trends and Digital Advances in Engineering Geology (pp. 31–96). Hershey, PA: IGI Global. doi:10.4018/978-1-5225-2709-1.ch002

Ceryan, S. (2018). Weathering Indices Used in Evaluation of the Weathering State of Rock Material. In N. Ceryan (Ed.), Handbook of Rese*arch on Tre*nds and Digital Advances in Engineering Geology (pp. 132–186). Hershey, PA: IGI Global. doi:10.4018/978-1-5225-2709-1.ch004

Chang, H., Roccaforte, S., Xu, R., & Cadden-Zimansky, P. (2021). Geome*tric Visualizations of Single and Entangled Qubits. Bu*lletin of the American Physical Society.

Chen, H., Lu, W. B., Lui, Z. G., Zhang, J., & Huang, B. H. (2018). Efficient Manipulation of Spoof Surface Plasmon Polaritons Based on Rotated Complementary H-Shaped Resonator Metasurface. IEEE Transactions on Antennas and Propagation, 65(12), 7383–7388. doi:10.1109/TAP.2017.2763175

Chen, H., Padilla, R. V., & Besarati, S. (2017). *Supercritical Flui*ds and Their Applications in Power Generation. In L. Chen & Y. Iwamoto (Eds.), Advanced Applications of Supercritical Fluids in Energy Systems (pp. 369–402). Hershey, PA: IGI Global. doi:10.4018/*978-1-5225-2047-4.ch012*

Chen, H., Padilla, R. V., & Besarati, S. (2021). Supercritical Fluids and Their Applications in Power Generation. In L. Chen (Ed.*), Handbook of R*esearch on Advancements in Supercritical Fluids Applications for Sustainable Energy Systems (pp. 566–599). IGI Global. https://doi.org/10.4018/978-1-7998-5796-9.ch016

Chen, L. (2017). *Principles, Experiments, and Numeri*cal Studies of Supercritical Fluid Natural Circulation System. *In L. Chen & Y. Iwamoto (Eds.), Advance*d Applications of Supercritical Fluids in Energy Systems (pp. 136–187). Hershey, PA: IGI Global. doi:10.4018/978-1-5225-2047-4.ch005

Chen, L. (2021). Principles, Experiments, and *Numerical Studies of S*upercritical Fluid Natural Circulation System. In L. Chen (Ed.), Handbook of *Research on Advancements in Supercritical Fluids* Applications for Sustainable Energy Systems (pp. 219–269). IGI Global. https://doi.org/10.4018/978-1-7998-5796-9.ch007

Chen, X., Tang, Z., & Li, S. (2005). An modified error function for the complex-value back*propagation. Neural Information Processing-Le*tters and Reviews, 8(1).

Chiba, Y., Marif, Y., Henini, N., & Tlemcani, A. (2021). Modeling of Magnetic Refrigeration Device by Using Artificial Neural *Networks Approach. International Journal of Energy Optimization and Engineering, 10(4)*, 68–76. https://doi.org/10.4018/IJEOE.2021100105

Childress, L., & Hanson, R. (2013). Diamond NV centers for quantum comp*uting* a*nd qu*antum networks. MRS Bulletin, 38(2), 134–138. doi:10.1557/mrs.2013.20

Child*s, A. M., & van Dam, W. (2010). Quantum algorithms for algebraic problems*. Reviews of Modern Physics, 82(1), 1–52. doi:10.1103/RevModPhys.82.1

Chuang. (2004). Course 1 - Principles of Quantum Computation (Vol. 79). Elsevier.

Clementi, F., Di Sciascio, G., Di Sciascio, S., & Lenci, S. (2017). Infl*uence of the Shear-Bending Interaction* on the Global Capacity of Reinforced Concrete Frames: A Brief Overview of the New Perspectives. *In V. Plevris, G. Kremmyda, & Y.* Fahjan (Eds.), Performance-Based Seismic Design of Concrete Structures and Infrastructures (pp. 84–111). Hershey, PA: IGI Global. doi:10.4018/978-1-5225-2089-4.ch004

Codinhoto, R., Fialho, B. C., Pinti, L., & Fabricio, M. M. (2021). BIM and IoT for Facilities Management: Under*standing Key Maintenan*ce Issues. In J. Underwood & M. Shelbourn (Eds.), Handbook of Research on Driving Transformational Change in the Digital Built Environment (pp. 209*–231). IGI Global. doi*:10.4018/978-1-7998-6600-8.ch009

Corcoles, A. D., Magesan, E., Srinivasan, S. J., Cross, A. W., Steffen, M., Gambetta, J. M., & *Chow, J. M. (2015). De*mon*s*tration of a quantum error detection code using a square lattice of four superconducting qubits. Nature Communications, 6(6), 6979. doi:10.1038/ncomms7979 PMID:25923200

Cortés-Polo, D., Calle-Cancho, J., Carmona-Murillo, J*., & González-Sánchez, J. (2017). Future Trends in Mobile-Fixed Integration for Next Gen*eration Networks: Classification and Analysis. International Journal of Vehicular Telematics and Infotainment Systems, 1(1), 33–53. doi:10.4018/IJVTIS.2017010103

Costa, H. *G., Sheremetie*ff, F. H., & Araújo, E. A. (2022). Influence of Game-Based Methods in Developing Engineering Competences. In A. Alves & N. van Hattum-Janssen (Eds.), Training Engineering Students f*or Modern Technological Advancement (pp. 69–88). IGI Global. https://doi.org/10.*4018/978-1-7998-8816-1.ch004

Cross, A. W., Bishop, L. S., Smolin, J. A., & Gamb*etta, J. M. (2017). Open quantum assembly language*. arXiv preprint arXiv:1707.03429.

Cui, X., Zeng, S., Li, Z., Zheng, Q., Yu, X., & Han, B. (2018). Advanced Comp*osites for Civil Engineering Infrastructures. In K. Kumar & J. Davim (E*ds.), Composites and Advanced Materials for Industrial Applications (pp. 212–248). Hershey, PA: IGI Global. doi:10.4018/978-1-5225-5216-1.ch010

Dalgıç, S., & Kuşku, İ. (*2018*). *Geological and* Geotechnical Investigations in Tunneling. In N. Ceryan (Ed.), Handbook of Research on Trends and Digital Advances in Engineering Geology (pp. 482–529). *Hershey, PA: IGI Global. d*oi:10.4018/978-1-5225-2709-1.ch014

Dang, C., & Hihara, E. (2021). Study on Cooling Heat Transfer of Supercritical Carbon Dioxide Applied to Transcritical Carbon Dioxide Heat Pump. In L. Chen (Ed.), Handbook of Research on Advanc*ements in S*upercritical Fluids Applications for Sustainable Energy Systems (pp. 451–493). IGI Global. https://doi.org/10.4018/978-1-7998-5796-9.ch013

Daus, Y., Kharchenko, V., & Yudaev, I. (2021). Optimizing Layout of Distribut*ed Generation Source*s of Power Supply System of Agricultural Object. International Journal of Energy Optimization and Engineering, 10(3), 70–84. https://doi.org/10.4018/IJEOE.2021070104

Daus, Y., Kharchenko, V., & Yudaev, I. (2021). Resear*ch of Solar Energy Pote*ntial of Photovoltaic Installations on Enclosing Structures of Buildings. International Journal of Energy Optimization and Engineering, 10(4), 18–34. https://doi.org/10.*4018/IJEOE.2021100102*

D*eb*, S., Ammar, E. A., AlRajhi, H., Alsaidan, I., & Shariff, S. M. (2022). V2G Pilot Projects: Review and Lessons Learnt. In M. Alam, R. Pillai, & N. Murugesan (Eds.), Developing Charging Infrastructure and Techno*logies for Elec*tric Vehicles (pp. 252–267). IGI Global. https://doi. org/10.4018/978-1-7998-6858-3.ch014

Dehollain, J.P. (2016). Bell'states inequality violation with spins in silicon. Nat. Nano, 11(3), 242–246.

Dekhandji, F. Z., & Ra*is, M.* C. *(2021)*. A Comparative Study of Power Quality Monitoring Using Various Techniques. In A. Recioui & H. Bentarzi (Eds.), Optimizing and Measuring Smart Grid Operation and C*ontrol (pp. 259–288)*. IGI Global. https://doi.org/10.4018/978-1-7998-4027-5.ch011

de *la Varga, D., Soto, M., Arias, C. A., van Oirschot, D.,* Kilian, R., Pascual, A., & Álvarez, J. A. (2017). Constructed Wetlands for Indus*trial Wastewater Treat*ment and Removal of Nutrients. In Á. Val del Río, J. Campos Gómez, & A. Mosquera Corral (Eds.), Technologies for the Treatment and Recovery of Nutrients from Industrial Wastewater (pp. 202–230). *Hershey, PA: IGI G*lobal. doi:10.4018/978-1-5225-1037-6.ch008

Deperlioglu, O. (2018). Intelligent Techniques Inspired by Nature and Used i*n Biomedical Engineering. In U. K*ose, G. Guraksin, & O. Deperlioglu (Eds.), Nature-Inspired Intelligent Techniques for Solving Biomedical Engineering Prob*lems (pp. 51–77). Hershey, PA: IGI Global.* do*i:*10.4018/978-1-5225-4769-3.ch003

Deutsch, D. (1985). Quantum theory, the Church–*Turing principle and the universal quantum compu*ter. Proceedings of the Royal Society of London. A. Mathematical and Physical Sciences, 400(1818), 97-117.

Devoret, M. H., & Schoelkopf, R. J. (2013). Superconducting *Circuits for Quantum Information: An Outlook. Scienc*e, 339(6124), 1169–1174. doi:10.1126cience.1231930 PMID:23471399

Dhurpate, P. R., & Tang, H. (2021). *Quantitative Analysis of the Impact of Inter-Line Conveyor* Capacity for Throughput of Manufacturing Systems. International Journal of Manufacturing, Materials, and Mechanical Engineering, 11(1), 1–17. https://doi.org/*10.4018/ IJMMME.2021010101*

Diddams, S. A., Hollberg, L., Ma, L.-S., & Robertsson, L. (2002). Femtosecond-laser-based optical clockwor*k with instability ≤63 × 10^–16 in 1 s. Optics Letters, 27(1), 58. doi:*10.1364/ OL.27.000058 PMID:18007715

Dinkar, S., & Deep, K. (2021). A Survey of Recent Variants and Applications of Antlion Optim*izer. International* Journal of Energy Optimization and Engineering, 10(2), 48–73. doi:10.4018/ *IJEOE.2021*040103

DiVincenzo, D. P. (2000). The Physical Implementation of Quantum Computation. Fortschritte der Physik, 48(9-11), 771–783. doi:10.1002/1521-3978(200009)48:9/11<771::AID-*PROP771>3.0.*CO;2-E

DiVincenzo, D. P., & Loss, D. (1998). Quantum information is physical. Superlattices and Microstructures, 23(3-4), 419–432. doi:10.1006pmi.*1997.0520*

Dixit, A. (2018). Application of Silica-Gel-Reinforced Aluminium Composite on the Piston of Internal Combustion Engine: Comparative Study of Silica-Gel-Reinforced Aluminium Comp*osite Piston* With Aluminium Alloy Piston. In K. Kumar & J. Davim (Eds.), Composites and Advanced Materials for Industrial Applications (pp. 63–98). Hershey, PA: IGI Global. doi:10.4018/978-1-5225-5216-1.ch004

Drabecki, M. P., & Kułak, K. B. (2021). Global Pandemics on European Electrical *Energy Markets: Lesso*ns Learned From the COVID-19 Outbreak. International Journal of Energy Optimization and Engineering, 10(3), 24–46. https://doi.org/10.4018/IJEOE.2021070102

Dutta, M. M. (2021). Nanomaterials for Food and Agriculture. In M. Bhat, I. Wani, & S. Ashraf (Eds.), Applications of Nanomateria*ls in Agricultu*re, Food Science, and Medicine (pp. 75–97). IGI Global. doi:10.4018/978-1-7998-5563-7.ch004

Dutta, M. M., & Goswami, M. (2021). Coating Materials: Nano-Materials. In S. Roy & G. Bose (Eds.), Advanced Surface Coating Techniques for M*odern Industrial Applications (pp. 1–30). IGI Global. do*i:10.4018/978-1-7998-4870-7.ch001

eHealth. (2020). https://ehealth.eletsonline.com/2020/11/quantumizing-digital-h*ealthcare*-arena/

El-Shafeiy, E., Hassanien, A. E., Sallam, K. M., & Abohany, A. A. (2021). Approach for Training Quantum Neural Networ*k to Predict Seve*rity of COVID-19 in Patients. Computers, Materials, & Continua, 66(2), 1745–1755.

Elsayed, A. M.*, Dakkama, H. J., Mahmoud, S., Al-Dadah, R., & Kaialy, W. (2017). Sustainable Cooli*ng Research Using Activated Carbon Adsorbents and Their Environmental Impact. In T. Kobayashi (Ed.), A*pplied* Environmental Materials Science for Sustainability (pp. 186–221). Hershey, PA: IGI Global. doi:10.4018/978-1-5225-1971-3.ch009

Ercanoglu, M., & Sonmez, H. (2018). General Trends and New Perspectives on Landslide Mapping and Assessment Methods. In N. Ceryan (Ed.), Handbook of Research on Trends and Digital Advances in Engineering Geology (pp. 350–379). Hershey, PA: IGI Global. doi:10.4018/978-1-5225-2709-1.ch010

Farhi, E., & Neven, H. (2018). Classification with quantum neural networks on near term processors. arXiv:1802.06002v1.

Farhi, E., Goldstone, J., Gutmann, S., & Neven, H. (2017). Quantum algorithms for fixed qubit architectures. arXiv:1703.06199v1.

Faroz, S. A., Pujari, N. N., Rastogi, R., & Ghosh, S. (2017). Risk Analysis of Structural Engineering Systems Using Bayesian Inference. In P. Samui, S. Chakraborty, & D. Kim (Eds.), Modeling and Simulation Techniques in Structural Engineering (pp. 390–424). Hershey, PA: IGI Global. doi:10.4018/978-1-5225-0588-4.ch014

Fastovets, D. V., Bogdanov, Y. I., Bantysh, B. I., & Lukichev, V. F. (2019). Machine learning methods in quantum computing theory. In International Conference on Micro-and Nano-Electronics 2018 (Vol. 11022). International Society for Optics and Photonics. 10.1117/12.2522427

Fekik, A., Hamida, M. L., Denoun, H., Azar, A. T., Kamal, N. A., Vaidyanathan, S., Bousbaine, A., & Benamrouche, N. (2022). Multilevel Inverter for Hybrid Fuel Cell/PV Energy Conversion System. In A. Fekik & N. Benamrouche (Eds.), Modeling and Control of Static Converters for Hybrid Storage Systems (pp. 233–270). IGI Global. https://doi.org/10.4018/978-1-7998-7447-8.ch009

Fekik, A., Hamida, M. L., Houassine, H., Azar, A. T., Kamal, N. A., Denoun, H., Vaidyanathan, S., & Sambas, A. (2022). Power Quality Improvement for Grid-Connected Photovoltaic Panels Using Direct Power Control. In A. Fekik & N. Benamrouche (Eds.), Modeling and Control of Static Converters for Hybrid Storage Systems (pp. 107–142). IGI Global. https://doi.org/10.4018/978-1-7998-7447-8.ch005

Felloni, S., & Strini, G. (2006). A graphic representation of states for quantum copying machines. arXiv preprint quant-ph/0609230.

Felloni, S., Leporati, A., & Strini, G. (2009a). Diagrams of states in quantum information: An illustrative tutorial. arXiv preprint arXiv:0904.2656.

Felloni, S., Leporati, A., & Strini, G. (2009b). Evolution of quantum systems by diagrams of states. arXiv preprint arXiv:0912.0026.

Fernando, P. R., Hamigah, T., Disne, S., Wickramasingha, G. G., & Sutharshan, A. (2018). The Evaluation of Engineering Properties of Low Cost Concrete Blocks by Partial Doping of Sand with Sawdust: Low Cost Sawdust Concrete Block. International Journal of Strategic Engineering, 1(2), 26–42. doi:10.4018/IJoSE.2018070103

Ferro, G., Minciardi, R., Parodi, L., & Robba, M. (2022). Optimal Charging Management of Microgrid-Integrated Electric Vehicles. In M. Alam, R. Pillai, & N. Murugesan (Eds.), Developing Charging Infrastructure and Technologies for Electric Vehicles (pp. 133–155). IGI Global. https://doi.org/10.4018/978-1-7998-6858-3.ch007

Feynman, R. P. (1982). Simulating physics with computers. International Journal of Theoretical Physics, 21(6-7), 467–488. doi:10.1007/BF02650179

Feynman, R. P., Hey, T., & Allen, R. W. (2018). Feynman lectures on computation. CRC Press. doi:10.1201/9780429500442

Flentje, H., Mortemousque, P.-A., Thalineau, R., Ludwig, A., Wieck, A. D., Bäuerle, C., & Meunier, T. (2017). Coherent long-distance displacement of individual electron spins. Nature Communications, 8(1), 501. doi:10.103841467-017-00534-3 PMID:28894092

Flumerfelt, S., & Green, C. (2022). Graduate Lean Leadership Education: A Case Study of a Program. In A. Alves & N. van Hattum-Janssen (Eds.), Training Engineering Students for Modern Technological Advancement (pp. 202–224). IGI Global. https://doi.org/10.4018/978-1-7998-8816-1.ch010

Flöther, F., Murphy, J., Murtha, J., & Sow, D. (2020). Exploring quantum computing use cases for healthcare. IBM.

Fowler, A.G. (2015). Minimum weight perfect matching of fault-tolerant topological quantum error correction in average o(1) parallel time. Quant. Inf. Comp., 15.

Fujii, K. (2015). Quantum Computation with Topological Codes. From Qubits to Topological Fault-Tolerance. doi:10.1007/978-981-287-996-7

Galli, B. J. (2021). Implications of Economic Decision Making to the Project Manager. International Journal of Strategic Engineering, 4(1), 19–32. https://doi.org/10.4018/IJoSE.2021010102

Garhwal, S., & Ahmad, A. (2019). Quantum programming language: A systematic review of research topic and top cited languages. Archives of Computational Methods in Engineering, 1–22.

Garnerone, S., Zanardi, P., & Lidar, D. A. (2012). Adiabatic Quantum Algorithm for Search Engine Ranking. Physical Review Letters, 108(23), 230506. doi:10.1103/PhysRevLett.108.230506 PMID:23003933

Gay, S. J. (2006). Quantum programming languages: Survey and bibliography. Mathematical Structures in Computer Science, 16(4), 581. doi:10.1017/S0960129506005378

Gento, A. M., Pimentel, C., & Pascual, J. A. (2022). Teaching Circular Economy and Lean Management in a Learning Factory. In A. Alves & N. van Hattum-Janssen (Eds.), Training Engineering Students for Modern Technological Advancement (pp. 183–201). IGI Global. https://doi.org/10.4018/978-1-7998-8816-1.ch009

Ghosh, S., Mitra, S., Ghosh, S., & Chakraborty, S. (2017). *Seismic Reliability Analysis* in the Framework of Metamodelling Based Monte Carlo Simulation. In P. Samui, S. Chakraborty, & D. Kim *(Eds.)*, *Mode*ling and Simulation Techniques in Structural Engineering (pp. 192–208). Hershey, PA: IGI Global. doi:10.4018/978-1-5225-0588-4.ch006

Gil, M., & Otero, B. (2017). Learning Engineering Skills through Creativi*ty and Collabor*ation: A Game-Based Proposal. In R. Alexandre Peixoto de Queirós & M. Pinto (Eds.), Gamification-Based E-Learning Strategies for Computer *Programming Education (pp. 14–29). Hershey, PA: IGI Global. doi:10.4018/978-1-5225-1034-5.ch*002

Gill, J., Ayre, M., & Mills, J. (2017). Revisioning the Engineering Profession: How to Make It Happen! In M. Gray & K. Thomas (Eds.), Strategies for Increasing Diversity in *Engineering Majors and Careers (pp. 156–175). Hershe*y, *P*A: IGI Global. doi:10.4018/978-1-5225-2212-6.ch008

Gill, S. S., Kumar, A., Singh, H., Singh, M., Kaur, K., Usman, M., & Buyya, R. (2020). Quantum computing: A taxonomy, systematic review and future directions. arXiv preprint arXiv:2010.15559.

Godzhaev, Z., Senkevich, S., Kuzmin, V., & Melikov, I. (2021). Use of the Neural Network Controller of Sprung Mas*s to Reduce Vibrations From Road Irregularities. In P. Vasant, G. Weber, & W. Punurai (E*d.), Research Advancements in Smart Technology, Optimization, and Renewable Energy (pp. 69-87). IGI Global. https://doi.org/10.4018/978-1-7998-3970-5.ch005

Gomes de Gusmão, C. M. (2022). Digital C*ompetencies and Transformation in Higher Education: Upskilling With Extension Actions. In A. Alves & N.* van Hattum-Janssen (Eds.), Training Engineering Students for Modern Technological Advancement (pp. 313–328). IGI Global. https://doi.org/10.4018/978-1-7998-8816-1.ch015A

Gordon, J. P., & Bowers, K. D. (1958). Microwave Spin Echoes from *Donor Electrons in Silicon. Physical Review Letters, 1(10), 368–370. doi:10.1103/PhysRevLett.1.368*

Goyal, N., Ram, M., & Kumar, P. (2017). Welding Process under Fault Coverage Approach for Reliability and MTTF. In M. Ram & J. Davim (Eds.), Mathematical Concepts and Applications in Mechanical Engineering and Mechatronics (pp. 222–245). Hershey, PA: IGI Global. doi:10.4018/978-1-5225-1639-2.ch011

Gray, M., & Lundy, C. (2017). Engineering Study Abroad: High Impact Strategy for Increasing Access. In M. Gray & K. Thomas (Eds.), Strategies for Increasing Diversity in Engineering Majors and Careers (pp. 42–59). Hershey, PA: IGI Global. doi:10.4018/978-1-5225-2212-6.ch003

Grilo, A. B., & Kerenidis, I. (2017). Learn*ing with errors is easy with quantum samples. arXiv:1702.08255.*

Grover, L. K. (1997). Quantum Mechanics Helps in Searching for a Needle in a Haystack. Physical Review Letters, 79(2), 325–328. doi:10.1103/PhysRevLett.79.325

Gulshan, V., Peng, L., Coram, M., Stumpe, M. C., Wu, D., Narayanaswamy, A., Venugopalan, S., Widner, K., Madams, T., Cuadros, J., Kim, R., Raman, R., Nelson, P. C., Mega, J. L., & Webster, D. R. (2016). Development and Validation of a Deep Learning Algorithm for Detection of Diabetic Retinopathy in Retinal Fundus Photographs. Journal of the American Medical Association, 316(22), 2402–2410. doi:10.1001/jama.2016.17216 PMID:27898976

Gupta, J. A., Knobel, R., Samarth, N., & Awschalom, D. D. (2001). Ultrafast Manipulation of Electron Spin Coherence. Science, 292(5526), 2458–2461. doi:10.1126cience.1061169 PMID:11431559

Guraksin, G. E. (2018). Internet of Things and Nature-Inspired Intelligent Techniques for the Future of Biomedical Engineering. In U. Kose, G. Guraksin, & O. Deperlioglu (Eds.), Nature-Inspired Intelligent Techniques for Solving Biomedical Engineering Problems (pp. 263–282). Hershey, PA: IGI Global. doi:10.4018/978-1-5225-4769-3.ch013

Guta, M., & Kotlowski, W. (2010). Quantum learning: Asymptotically optimal classification of qubit states. New Journal of Physics, 12(12), 123032. doi:10.1088/1367-2630/12/12/123032

Gyongyosi, L., Bacsardi, L., & Imre, S. (2019). A survey on quantum key distribution. Infocommunications J, 11(2), 14–21. doi:10.36244/ICJ.2019.2.2

Güler, O., & Varol, T. (2021). Fabrication of Functionally Graded Metal and Ceramic Powders Synthesized by Electroless Deposition. In S. Roy & G. Bose (Eds.), Advanced Surface Coating Techniques for Modern Industrial Applications (pp. 150–187). IGI Global. https://doi.org/10.4018/978-1-7998-4870-7.ch007

Hamida, M. L., Fekik, A., Denoun, H., Ardjal, A., & Bokhtache, A. A. (2022). Flying Capacitor Inverter Integration in a Renewable Energy System. In A. Fekik & N. Benamrouche (Eds.), Modeling and Control of Static Converters for Hybrid Storage Systems (pp. 287–306). IGI Global. https://doi.org/10.4018/978-1-7998-7447-8.ch011

Harrow, A. W., Hassidim, A., & Lloyd, S. (2009). Quantum Algorithm for Linear Systems of Equations. Physical Review Letters, 15(15), 150502. doi:10.1103/PhysRevLett.103.150502 PMID:19905613

Hasegawa, N., & Takahashi, Y. (2021). Control of Soap Bubble Ejection Robot Using Facial Expressions. International Journal of Manufacturing, Materials, and Mechanical Engineering, 11(2), 1–16. https://doi.org/10.4018/IJMMME.2021040101

Heberle, A. P., Baumberg, J. J., & Kohler, K. (1995). Ultrafast Coherent Control and Destruction of Excitons in Quantum Wells. Physical Review Letters, 75(13), 2598–2601. doi:10.1103/PhysRevLett.75.2598 PMID:10059352

Hechenbichler, K., & Schliep, K. (2004). Weighted k-nearest-neighbor techniques and ordinal classification. Academic Press.

Hejazi, T., & Akbari, L. (2017). A Multiresponse Optimization Model for Statistical Design of Processes with Discrete Variables. In M. Ram & J. Davim (Eds.), Mathematical Concepts and *Applications in Mechanical Engineering and Mechatronics (pp. 17–37). Hershey,* PA: IGI Global. doi:10.4018/978-1-5225-1639-2.ch002

Hejazi, T., & Hejazi, A. (2017). Monte Carlo Simulation for Reliability-Based Design of Automotive Complex Subsystems. In M. *Ram & J. Davim (Eds.), Mathematical Concepts and Applications* in Mechanical Engineering and Mechatronics (pp. 177–200). Hershey, PA: IGI Global. doi:10.4018/978-1-5225-1639-2.ch009

Hejazi, T., & Poursabbagh, H. (2017). Reliability Analysis of Engineering Systems: An Accelerated Life Testing for Boiler *Tubes. In M. Ram & J. Davim (Eds.), Mathematical Concepts and Applications* in Mechanical Engineering and Mechatronics (pp. 154–176). Hershey, PA: IGI Global. doi:10.4018/978-1-5225-1639-2.ch008

Henao, J., & Sotelo, O. (2018). Surface Engineering at High Temperature: Thermal Cycling and Corrosion Resistance. In A. Pakseresht (Ed.), Production, Properties, and Applications of High Temperature Coatings (pp. 131–159). Hershey, PA: IGI Global. doi:10.4018/978-1-5225-4194-3.ch006

Henao, J., Poblano-Salas, C. A., Vargas, F., Giraldo-Betancur, A. L., Corona-Castuera, J., & Sotelo-Mazón, O. (2021). Principles and Applications of Thermal Spray *Coatings. In S. Roy & G. Bose (Eds.), Advanced Surface Coating* Techniques for Modern Industrial Applications (pp. 31–70). IGI Global. https://doi.org/10.4018/978-1-7998-4870-7.ch002

Henderson, M., Shakya, S., Pradhan, *S., & Cook, T. (2019). Quanvolutional neural networks: power*ing image recognition with quantum circuits. arXiv.org.

Hey, T. (1999). Quantum computing: An introduction. Computing & Control Engineering Journal, 10(3), 105–112. doi:10.1049/cce:19990303

Hill, C. *D., Peretz, E., Hile, S. J., House, M. G., Fuechsle, M., Rogge, S., Simmons, M. Y., & Hollen*berg, L. C. L. (2015). A surface code quantum computer in silicon. Science Advances, 1(9), e1500707. doi:10.1126ciadv.1500707 PMID:26601310

Hlali, A., Houaneb, Z., & Zairi, H. (2018). Dual-Band Reconfigurable Graphene- Based Patch Antenna in Terahertz Ba*nd: Design, Analy*sis and Modeling Using WCIP Method. Progress In Electromagnetics Research C, 87, 213–226. doi:10.2528/PIERC18080107

Hlali, A., Houaneb, Z., & Zairi, H. (2019a). Tunable filter based on hybrid metal-graphene structures over an ultrawide terahertz band using an improved Wave Concept Iterative Process metho*d. International Journal for Light and Electron Optics, 181, 423–431. doi:10.1016/j. ijleo.2018.12.091*

Hlali, A., Houaneb, Z., & Zairi, H. (2019b). Effective Modeling of Magnetized Graphene by the Wave Concept Iterative Process Method Using Boundary Conditions. Progress In Electromagnetics Research C, 89, 121–132. doi:10.2528/PIERC18*111514*

Horn, D., & Gottlieb, A. (2001). *Algorithm for data clustering in pattern* recognition problems based on quantum mechanics. Physical Review Letters, 88(1), 018702. doi:10.1103/ PhysRevLett.88.018702 PMID:11800996

*How quantum technolo*gy will change engineering. (n.d.). https://www.sei.cmu.edu

Hrnčič, M. K., Cör, D., & Knez, Ž. (2021). Supercritical Fluids as a Tool for Green Energy and Chemicals. In L. Chen (Ed.), Handbook *of Research on Advancements in Supercritical Fluids Applicat*ions for Sustainable Energy Systems (pp. 761–791). IGI Global. doi:10.4018/978-1-7998-5796-9.ch021

Hu, X. M., Hu, M.-J., Chen, J.-S., Liu, B.-H., Huang, Y.-F., Li, C.-F., Guo, G.-C., & Zhang, Y.-S. (2016). Experimental creation of superposition of un*known photonic quantum states. Physical Review. A, 94(3), 033*844. doi:10.1103/PhysRevA.94.033844

Huang, W., Yang, C. H., Chan, K. W., Tanttu, T., Hensen, B., Leon, R. C. C., Fogarty, M. A., Hwang, J. C. C., Hudson, F. E., Itoh, K. M., Morello, A., Laucht, A., & Dzu*rak, A. S. (2019). Fidelity benchmarks for two-qubit gates* in silicon. Nature, 569(7757), 532–536. doi:10.103841586-019-1197-0 PMID:31086337

Hucul, D., Inlek, I. V., Vittorini, *G., Crocker, C., Debnath,* S., Clark, S. M., & Monroe, C. (2014). Modular entanglement of atomic qubits using photons and phonons. Nature Physics, 11(1), 37–42. doi:10.1038/nphys3150

Huembeli, *P., Dauphin, A., & Wittek, P. (2018). Identifyi*ng Quantum Phase Transitions wi*th* Adversarial Neural Networks. Physical Review. B, 97(13), 134109. doi:10.1103/ PhysRevB.97.134109

Huo, C. (2009). A Bloch Sphere Animation Software using a Three-D*imensional JavaSimulator (Doctoral dissertation). University of Cincinnati.*

Häffner, H., Roos, C. F., & Blatt, R. (2008). Quantum computing with trapped ions. Physics Reports, 469(4), 155–203. doi:10.1016/j.physrep.2008.09.003

Ibrahim, O., Erdem, S., & Gurbuz, E. (2021). Studying Physical and Chemical Proper*ties of Graphene Oxide and Reduced Graphene Oxide and Their Applications in Sustainab*le Building Materials. In R. González-Lezcano (Ed.), Advancements in Sustainable Architecture and Energy Efficiency (pp. 221–238). IGI Global. https://doi.org/10.4018/*978-1-7998-7023-4.ch010*

Ihianle, I. K., Islam, S., Naeem, U., & Ebenuwa, S. H. (2021). Exploiting Patterns of Object Use for Human Activity Recognition. In A. Nwajana & I. Ihianle (Eds.), Handbook of Research on 5G Networks and Advancements in Computing, Ele*ctronics, and Electrical Engineering (pp. 382–401). IGI Global. https://doi.org/10.4018/*978-1-7998-6992-4.ch015

Ijemaru, G. K., Ngharamike, E. T., Oleka, E. U., & Nwajana, A. O. (2021). An Energy-Efficient Model for Opportunistic Data Collection in IoV-Enabled SC Waste Management. In A. Nwajana & I. Ihianle (Eds.), Handbook of Research on *5G Networks and Advancements in Computing, Electronics,* and Electrical Engineering (pp. 1–19). IGI Global. https://doi.org/10.4018/978-1-7998-6992-4.ch001

Ilori, O. O., Adetan, D. A., & Umoru, L. E. (2017). Effect of Cutting *Parameters on the Surf*ace Residual Stress of Face-Milled Pearlitic Ductile Iron. International Journal of Materials Forming and Machining Processes, 4(1), 38–52. *doi:10.4018/IJMFMP.2017010103*

*Imam, M. H., Tasadduq, I. A., Ahmad, A., Aldosari, F., & Kh*an, H. (2017). Automated Generation of Course Improvement Plans Using Expert System. International Journal of Quality Assurance in Engineering and Technology Education, 6(1), 1–12. doi:10.4018/IJQAETE.2017010101

Injeti, S. *K., & Kumar, T. V. (2018).* A WDO Framework for Optimal Deployment of DGs and DSCs in a Radial Distribution System Under Daily Load Pattern to Improve Techno-Economic Benefits. International Journal of Energy Optimization and Engineering, 7(2), 1–38. doi:10.4018/IJEOE.2018040101

*Ishii, N., Anami, K., & Knisely, C. W. (2018). Dynamic Sta*bility of Hydraulic Gates and Engineering for Flood Prevention. Hershey, PA: IGI Global. doi:10.4018/978-1-5225-3079-4

Iwamoto, Y., & Yamaguchi, H. (2021). Application of Supercritical Carbon Dioxide *for Solar Water Heater. In L. Chen (Ed.), Handbook of Research on Advanc*ements in Supercritical Fluids Applications for Sustainable Energy Systems (pp. 370–387). IGI Global. https://doi.org/10.4018/978-1-7998-5796-9.ch010

Jayapalan, S. (2018). A Review of Chemical T*reatments on Natural Fibers-Based Hybrid Composites for Engineering Applic*ations. In K. Kumar & J. Davim (Eds.), Composites and Advanced Materials for Industrial Applications (pp. 16–37). Hershey, PA: IGI Global. doi:10.4018/978-1-5225-5216-1.ch002

Jiang, W., Xiong, J., & Shi, Y. (2021). When M*achine Learning Meets Quantum Computers: A Case Study: (Invited P*aper). In 26th Asia and South Pacific Design Automation Conference (ASPDAC '21). ACM. 10.1145/3394885.3431629

Jiménez-Navajas, L., & Piattini, M. (2020). Reverse engineering of quantum programs toward KDM mode*ls. In Quality of Information and Communications Technology - 13th International Conference, Faro, Portu*gal, September 9-11, 2020, Proceedings. Springer. 10.1007/978-3-030-58793-2_20

Jordan, S. (n.d.). Quantum Algorithm Zoo Archived 2018-04-29 at the Wayback Machine. Academic Press.

Kanamori, Y., & Yoo, S-M. (2020). Quantum *Computing: Principles and Applications. Journal of International* Technology and Information Management, 29(2). Available at: https://scholarworks.lib.csusb.edu/jitim/vol29/iss2/3

Kane, B. E. (1998). A silicon-based nuclear spin quantum computer. Nature, 393(6681), 133–137. doi:10.1038/30156

Kapetanakis, T. N., Vardiambasis, I. O., Ioannidou, M. P., & Konstantaras, A. I. (2021). Modeling Antenna Radiation Using Artificial Intelligence Techniques: The Case of a Circular Loop Antenna. In C. Nikolopoulos (Ed.), Recent Trends on Electromagnetic Environmental Effects for Aeronautics and Space Applications (pp. 186–225). IGI Global. https://doi.org/10.4018/978-1-7998-4879-0.ch007

Karalekas, P. J., Tezak, N. A., Peterson, E. C., Ryan, C. A., Da Silva, M. P., & Smith, R. S. (2020). A quantum-classical cloud platform optimized for variational hybrid algorithms. Quantum Science and Technology, 5(2), 24003. doi:10.1088/2058-9565/ab7559

Karkalos, N. E., Markopoulos, A. P., & Dossis, M. F. (2017). Optimal Model Parameters of Inverse Kinematics Solution of a 3R Robotic Manipulator Using ANN Models. International Journal of Manufacturing, Materials, and Mechanical Engineering, 7(3), 20–40. doi:10.4018/IJMMME.2017070102

Kashefi, E., & Pappa, A. (2017). Multiparty delegated quantum computing. arXiv: 1606.09200.

Kelly, M., Costello, M., Nicholson, G., & O'Connor, J. (2021). The Evolving Integration of BIM Into Built Environment Programmes in a Higher Education Institute. In J. Underwood & M. Shelbourn (Eds.), Handbook of Research on Driving Transformational Change in the Digital Built Environment (pp. 294–326). IGI Global. https://doi.org/10.4018/978-1-7998-6600-8.ch012

Kesimal, A., Karaman, K., Cihangir, F., & Ercikdi, B. (2018). Excavatability Assessment of Rock Masses for Geotechnical Studies. In N. Ceryan (Ed.), Handbook of Research on Trends and Digital Advances in Engineering Geology (pp. 231–256). Hershey, PA: IGI Global. doi:10.4018/978-1-5225-2709-1.ch006

Khammassi, N., Guerreschi, G. G., Ashraf, I., Hogaboam, J. W., Almudever, C. G., & Bertels, K. (2018). cqasm v1. 0: Towards a common quantum assembly language. arXiv preprint arXiv:1805.09607.

Kianinejad, A., Chen, Z. N., & Qiu, Ch. W. (2015). Design and Modeling of Spoof Surface Plasmon Modes-Based Microwave Slow-Wave Transmission Line. IEEE Transactions on Microwave Theory and Techniques, 63(6), 1817–1825. doi:10.1109/TMTT.2015.2422694

Kianinejad, A., Chen, Z. N., & Qiu, Ch. W. (2018). Full Modeling, Loss Reduction, and Mutual Coupling Control of Spoof Surface Plasmon-Based Meander Slow Wave Transmission Lines. IEEE Transactions on Microwave Theory and Techniques, 66(8), 3764–3772. doi:10.1109/TMTT.2018.2841857

Kikkawa, J. M., Smorchkova, I. P., Samarth, N., & Awschalom, D. D. (1997). Room-Temperature Spin Memory in Two-Dimensional Electron Gases. Science, 277(5330), 1284–1287. doi:10.1126cience.277.5330.1284

Kim, D., Shi, Z., *Simmons, C. B., Ward, D. R., Prance, J. R., Koh, T. S., Gamble, J. K., Savage, D. E., Lagally, M. G.,* Friesen, M., Coppersmith, S. N., & Eriksson, M. A. (2014). Quantum control and process tomography of a semiconductor quantum dot hybrid qubit. Nature, 511(7507), 70–74. doi:10.1038/nature13407 PMID:24990747

Kinshuk Sengup*ta, K., & Srivastava, P. R. (2021). Quantum algorithm for quicke*r clinical prognostic analysis: An application and experimental study using CT scan images of COVID-19 patients. BMC Medical Informatics and Decision Making, 21(1), 227. doi:10.118612911-021-01588-6 PMID:*34330278*

*Kiyani, F., & Copuroglu, F. (2018). Quantum Compute*rs *v*s Computers Computing. Int Res J ComputSci, 5, 2014–2018.

Knill, E. (1996). Conventions for quantum pseudocode, Technical Report. Los Alamos National Lab. doi:10.2172/366453

Knoflacher, H. (2017). The Role of Engineers and Their Tools in the Transport Sector after Paradigm Change: From Assumptions and Extra*polations to Science. In H. Knoflacher & E. Ocalir-Akunal (Eds.), Engineering Tools* and Solutions for Sustainable Transportation Planning (pp. 1–29). Hershey, PA: IGI Global. doi:10.4018/978-1-5225-2116-7.ch001

Kopczyk, D. (2018). Quantum machine learning for data scientists. Quantum Physics.

Koppens, F. H. L., Buizert, C., Ti*elrooij, K. J., Vink, I. T.,* Nowack, K. C., Meunier, T., Kouwenhoven, L. P., & Vandersypen, L. M. K. (2006). Driven coherent oscillations of a single electron spin in a quantum dot. Nature, 442(7104), 766–771. doi:10.1038/nature05065 PMID:16915280

Kose, U. (2018). Towards an Intelligent Biomedical *Engineering With Nature-Inspired Artificial Intelligence* Techniques. In U. Kose, G. Guraksin, & O. Deperlioglu (Eds.), Nature-Inspired Intelligent Techniques for Solving Biomedical Engineering Problems (pp. 1–26). Hershey, PA: IGI Global. doi:10.4018/978-1-5225-4769-3.ch001

Kostić, S. *(2018). A Review on Enhanced Stability Analyses of Soil Slopes Using Statistical* Design. In N. Ceryan (Ed.), Handbook of Research on Trends and Digital Advances in Engineering Geology (pp. 446–481). Hershey, PA: IGI Global. doi:10.4018/978-1-5225-2709-1.ch013

Krylov, G., & Lukac, M. (2019, April). Q*uantum encoded quantum evolutionary algorithm for the design of quantum circui*ts. In Proceedings of the 16th ACM International Conference on Computing Frontiers (pp. 220-225). 10.1145/3310273.3322826

Kumar, A., Patil, P. P., & Prajap*ati, Y. K. (2018). Advanced Numerical Simulations in Mechani*cal Engineering. Hershey, PA: IGI Global. doi:10.4018/978-1-5225-3722-9

Kumar, G. R., Rajyalakshmi, G., & Manupati, V. K. (2017). Surface Micro Patterning of Aluminium Reinforced Composite through Laser Peening. International Journal of Manufacturing, Materials, and Mechanical Engineering, 7(4)*, 15–27. doi:10.4018/IJMMME.2017100102*

Kumar, N., Basu, D. N., & Chen, L. (2021). Effect of Flow Acceleration and Buoyancy on Thermalhydraulics of sCO2 in Mini/Micro-Channel. In L. Chen (Ed.), Handbook of Research on Advancements in Supercritical Fluids Applications for Sustainable Energy Systems (pp. 161–182). IGI Global. doi:10.4018/978-1-7998-5796-9.ch005

Kumari, N., & Kumar, K. (2018). Fabrication of Orthotic Calipers With Epoxy-Based Green Composite. In K. Kumar & J. Davim (Eds.), Composites and Advanced Materials for Industrial Applications (pp. 157–176). Hershey, PA: IGI Global. doi:10.4018/978-1-5225-5216-1.ch008

Kuppusamy, R. R. (2018). Development of Aerospace Composite Structures Through Vacuum-Enhanced Resin Transfer Moulding Technology (VERTMTy): Vacuum-Enhanced Resin Transfer Moulding. In K. Kumar & J. Davim (Eds.), Composites and Advanced Materials for Industrial Applications (pp. 99–111). Hershey, PA: IGI Global. doi:10.4018/978-1-5225-5216-1.ch005

Kurganov, V. A., Zeigarnik, Y. A., & Maslakova, I. V. (2021). Normal and Deteriorated Heat Transfer Under Heating Turbulent Supercritical Pressure Coolants Flows in Round Tubes. In L. Chen (Ed.), Handbook of Research on Advancements in Supercritical Fluids Applications for Sustainable Energy Systems (pp. 494–532). IGI Global. https://doi.org/10.4018/978-1-7998-5796-9.ch014

Lamata, L. (2017). Basic protocols in quantum reinforcement learning with superconducting circuits. Scientific Reports, 7(1), 16. doi:10.103841598-017-01711-6 PMID:28487535

Landahl, A. J., Lobser, D. S., Morrison, B. C., Rudinger, K. M., Russo, A. E., Van Der Wall, J. W., & Maunz, P. (2020). Jaqal, the quantum assembly language for QSCOUT. arXiv preprint arXiv:2003.09382. doi:10.2172/1606475

Levy, J. (2002). Oxide – Semiconductor Materials for Quantum Computation. Academic Press.

Leymann, F. (2019). Towards a pattern language for quantum algorithms. International Workshop on Quantum Technology and Optimization Problems, 218–230. 10.1007/978-3-030-14082-3_19

Li, H., & Zhang, Y. (2021). Heat Transfer and Fluid Flow Modeling for Supercritical Fluids in Advanced Energy Systems. In L. Chen (Ed.), Handbook of Research on Advancements in Supercritical Fluids Applications for Sustainable Energy Systems (pp. 388–422). IGI Global. https://doi.org/10.4018/978-1-7998-5796-9.ch011

Li, L., Jiao, L., Zhao, J., Shang, R., & Gong, M. (2017). Quantum-behaved discrete multi-objective particle swarm optimization for complex network clustering. Pattern Recognition, 63, 1–14. doi:10.1016/j.patcog.2016.09.013

Li, S., Okada, T., Chen, X., & Tang, Z. (2006, May). An individual adaptive gain parameter backpropagation algorithm for complex-valued neural networks. In International Symposium on Neural Networks (pp. 551-557). Springer. 10.1007/11759966_82

Lloyd, S., & Weedbrook, C. (2018). Quantum generative adversarial learning. Physical Review Letters, 121(4), 040502. doi:10.1103/PhysRevLett.121.040502 PMID:30095952

Lloyd, S., Garnerone, S., & Zanardi, P. (2016). Quantum algorithms for topological and geometric analysis of data. *Nature Commun., (7). arXiv:140*8.3106

Lloyd, S., Mohseni, M., & Rebentrost, P. (2013). Quantum algorithms for supervised and unsupervised machine learning. arXiv preprint arXiv:1307.0411.

Loss, D., & DiVincenzo, D. P. (1998). Quantum computation wit*h quantum dots. Physical Review A, 57(1), 120–126. doi:10.1103/PhysRevA.57.*120

Lowdin, P. (1998). Linear Algebra for Quantum Theory. John Wiley and Sons, Inc.

Loy, J., Howell, S., & Cooper, R. (20*17). Engineering Teams: Support*ing Diversity in Engineering Education. In M. Gray & K. Thomas (Eds.), Strategies for Increasing Diversity in Engineering Majors and Careers (pp. 106–129). Hershey, PA: IGI Global. do*i:10.4018/978-1-5225-2212-6. ch006*

*Lu, P., & Zhao, A. X. (2010, De*cember). Fuzzy clustering with obstructed distance based on quantum-behaved particle swarm optimization. In 2010 Second WRI Global Congress on Intelligent Systems *(Vol. 1, pp. 302-305). IEEE. 10.1109/GCIS.2010.57*

Lu, S., & Braunstein, S. L. (2014). Quantum decision tree classifier. Quantum Information Processing, 13(3), 757-770.

Macher, G., Armengaud, E., Kreiner, C., *Brenner, E., Schmittne*r, C., Ma, Z., ... Krammer, M. (2018). Integration of Security in the Development Lifecycle of Dependable Automotive CPS. In N. Druml, A. Genser, A. Krieg, M. Menghin, & A. Hoeller (Eds.), Solutions for Cyber-Physical Systems Ubiquity *(pp. 383–423). Hershey, PA: IGI Global. doi:10.4018/978-1-5225-2845-6.*ch015

Madhu, M. N., Singh, J. G., Mohan, V., & Ongsakul, W. (2021). Transmission Risk Optimization in Interconnected Systems: Risk-Adjusted Available Transfer Capability. In P. Vasant, G. Weber, & W. Punurai (Ed.), Research Advancements in Smart Technology, Optimization, *and Renewable Energy (pp. 183-199). IGI Global. https://do*i.org/10.4018/978-1-7998-3970-5.ch010

Mahendramani, G., & Lakshmana Swamy, N. (2018). Effect of Weld Groove Area on Distortion of Butt Welded Joints in Submerged Arc Welding. International Journal of Manufacturi*ng, Materials, and Mechanical Engineering, 8(2), 33–44. doi:10.4018/IJMMME.2018040103*

Makropoulos, G., Koumaras, H., Setaki, F., Filis, K., Lutz, T., Montowtt, P., Tomaszewski, L., Dybiec, P., & Järvet, T. (2021). 5G and Unmanned Aerial Vehicles (UAVs) Use Cases: Analysis of the Ecosystem, Architecture, and Applicatio*ns. In A. Nwajana & I. Ihianle (Eds.), Handbook of Research on 5G Networks* and Advancements in Computing, Electronics, and Electrical Engineering (pp. 36–69). IGI Global. https://doi.org/10.4018/978-1-7998-6992-4.ch003

Marr, B. (n.d.). How Quantum Computers Will Revolutionise Artificial Intelligence, Machine Learning And Big Data. Available at https://*bernardmarr.com/*

*McCulloch, W. S., & Pitts, W. (1943). A logical calculus of*the ideas immanent in nervous activity. The Bulletin of Mathematical Biophysics, 5(4), 115–133. doi:10.1007/BF02478259

Medford, J., Beil, J., Taylor, J. M., Rashba, E. I., Lu, H., Gossard, A. C., & Marcus, C. M. (2013). Quantum-Dot-Based Resonant *Exchange Qubit. Physical Review Letters, 111(5), 050501.* doi:10.1103/PhysRevLett.111.050501 PMID:23952375

Mehta, D., Paharia, A., Singh, S., & Salman, M. (2019). Quantum computing will enhance the power of Artificial Intelligence. A boon for Research endeavors across the globe. Ame*rican Journal of PharmTech Research.*

Meric, E. M., Erdem, S., & Gurbuz, E. (2021). Application of Phase Change Materials in Construction Materials for Thermal Energy Storage Systems in Buildings. In R. González-Lezcano (Ed.), Advancements in Sustainable Architecture and Energy Efficiency *(pp. 1–20). IGI Global. https://doi.org/10.4018/978-1-7998-7023-4.ch0*01

Metwalli, S. (2020). How May Quantum Computing Benefit Machine Learning? Medium. Retrieved 21 December 2020, from https://towardsdatascience.com/how-may-quantum-computing-benefit-machine-learning-c96de0bef0d4

Mihret, E. T., & Yita*yih, K. A. (2021). Operation of VANET Communications: The Convergence* of UAV System With LTE/4G and WAVE Technologies. International Journal of Smart Vehicles and Smart Transportation, 4(1), 29–51. https://doi.org/10.4018/IJSVST.2021010103

Mir, M. A., Bhat, B. A., Sheikh, B. A., Rather, G. A., Mehraj, S., & Mir, W. R. (202*1). Nanomedicine in Human Health Therapeutics and Drug Delivery: Nanobiotechnology* and Nanobiomedicine. In M. Bhat, I. Wani, & S. Ashraf (Eds.), Applications of Nanomaterials in Agriculture, Food Science, and Medicine (pp. 229–251). IGI Global. doi:10.4018/978-1-7998-*5563-7.ch013*

*Miszcza*k, J. A. (2010). Models of quantum computation and quantum programming languages. arXiv preprint arXiv:1012.6035

Mohammadzadeh, S., & Kim, *Y. (2017). Nonlinear* System Identification of Smart Buildings. In P. Samui, S. Chakraborty, & D. Kim (Eds.), Modeling and Simulation Techniques in Structural Engineering (pp. 328–347). Hershey, PA: IGI Global. doi:10.4018/978-1-5225-0588-4.ch011

Molina, G. J., Aktaruzzaman, F., Soloiu, V., & Rahman, M. (2017). Design and Testing of a Jet-Impingement Instrument to Study Surface-Modification Effects by Nanofluids. International Journal of Surface Engineering and Interdisciplinary Materi*als Science, 5(2), 43–61. d*oi:10.4018/IJSEIMS.2017070104

Monroe, C., & Kim, J. (2013). Scaling the Ion Trap Quantum Processor. Science, 339(6124), 1164–1169. doi:10.1126cience.1231298 PMID:23471398

Monz, T., Nigg, D., Martinez, E. A., Brandl, M. F., Schindler, P., Rines, R., Wang, S. X., Chuang, I. L., & Blatt, R. (2016). Realization of a scalable shor algorithm. S*cience, 351(6277), 1068–1070. doi:10.1126cience.aad9480 PMID:26941*315

Moreno-Rangel, A., & Carrillo, G. (2021). Energy-Efficient Homes: A Heaven for Respiratory Illnesses. In R. González-Lezcano (Ed.), Advancements in Sustainable Architectur*e and Energy Efficiency (pp. 49–71). IGI Global. https://doi.org/10.4018/978-1-7998-7023-4.ch003*

Msomi, V., & Jantjies, B. T. (2021). Correlative Analysis Between Tensile Properties and Tool Rotational Speeds of Friction Stir Welded Similar Aluminium Alloy Joints. *International Journal of Surface Engineering and Interdisciplinary Materials Science, 9(2), 58–78.* https://doi.org/10.4018/IJSEIMS.2021070104

Muigai, M. N., Mwema, F. M., Akinlabi, E. T., & Obiko, J. O. (2021). Surface Engineering of Materials Through Weld-Based Technologies: An Overview. In S. Roy & G. Bose (Eds.), Advanced Surface Coating Techniques *for Modern Industrial Applications (pp. 247–260). IGI Global. doi:10.4018/978-1-7998-4870-7.ch011*

Mukherjee, A., Saeed, R. A., Dutta, S., & Naskar, M. K. (2017). Fault Tracking Framework for Software-Defined Networking (SDN). In C. Singhal & S. De (Eds.), Resource Allocation in Next-Generation Broadband Wireless Access Networks (pp. 247–272). Hershey, PA: IG*I Global. doi:10.4018/978-1-5225-2023-8.ch011*

*Mukhopadhyay, A., Barma*n, T. K., & Sahoo, P. (2018). Electroless Nickel Coatings for High Temperature Applications. In K. Kumar & J. Davim (Eds.), Composites and Advanced Materials for Industrial Applications (pp. 297–331). Hershey, PA: *IGI Global. doi:10.4018/978-1-5225-5216-1.ch013*

*Mwema, F. M., & Wamb*ua, J. M. (2022). Machining of Poly Methyl Methacrylate (PMMA) and Other Olymeric Materials: A Review. In K. Kumar, B. Babu, & J. *Davim (Eds.), Handbook of Research on* Advancements in the Processing, Characterization, and Application of Lightweight Materials (pp. 363–379). IGI Global. https://doi.org/10.4018/978-1-7998-7864-3.ch016

Mykhailyshyn, R., Savkiv, V., Boyko, I., Prada, E., & Virgala, I. (2021). Substantiation of Parameters of Friction Elements of Bernoulli Grippers With a Cylindrical Nozzle. International Journal of Manufacturing, Materials, and Mechanical Engineering, 11(2), 17–39. https://doi.org/10.4018/IJMMME.2021040102

Nagayama, S., Fowler, A. G., Horsman, D., Devitt, S. J., & Van Meter, R. (2017). Surface code error correction on a defective lattice. New Journal of Physics, 19(2), 023050. doi:10.1088/1367-2630/aa5918

Nagy, M., & Aki, S. G. (2006). Quantum computation and quantum inf*ormation. International Journal of Parallel Emergent and Distri*buted Systems, 21(1), 1–59. doi:10.1080/17445760500355678

Narayanan, A., & Moore, M. (1996, May). Quantum-inspired genetic algorithms. In Proceedings of IEEE international conference on evolutionary computation (pp. 61-66). IEEE. 10.1109/ICEC.1996.542334

*Nautiyal, L., Shivach, P., & Ram, M. (2018). Optimal Designs by Means of Genetic Algorith*ms. In M. Ram & J. Davim (Eds.), Soft Computing Techniques and Applications in Mechanical Engineering (pp. 151–161). Hershey, PA: IGI Global. doi:10.4018/978-1-5225-3035-0.ch007

Nazir, R. (2017). Advanced Nanomaterials for Water Engineering and Treatment: Nano-Metal Oxides and Their *Nanocomposites. In T. Saleh (Ed.), Advanced Nanomaterials for Water Engineering, Treatment, and Hydraul*ics (pp. 84–126). Hershey, PA: IGI Global. doi:10.4018/978-1-5225-2136-5.ch005

Nielsen, M. A., & Chuang, I. L. (1997). Programmable quantum gate arrays. Physical Review Letters, 79(2), 321–324. doi:10.1103/PhysRevLett.79.321

*Nikolopoulos, C. D. (2021). Recent Advances on Measuring and Mod*eling ELF-Radiated Emissions for Space Applications. In C. Nikolopoulos (Ed.), Recent Trends on Electromagnetic Environmental Effects for Aeronautics and Space Applications (pp. 1–38). IGI G*lobal. https:// doi.org/10.4018/978-1-7998-4879-0.ch001*

Nitta, T. (1993, October). A back-propagation algorithm for complex numbered neural networks. In Proceedings of 1993 International Conference on Neural Networks (IJCNN-93-Nagoya, Japan) (Vol. 2, pp. 1649-1652). IEEE. 10.1109/IJCNN.1993.716968

Nitta, T. (1994, *June). Structure of learning in the complex numbered back*-propagation network. In Proceedings of 1994 IEEE International Conference on Neural Networks *(ICNN'94) (Vol. 1, pp. 269-274). IEEE. 10.1109/ICNN.1994.374173*

*Noguei*ra, A. F., Ribeiro, J. C., Fernández de Vega, F., & Zenha-Rela, M. A. (2018). Evolutionary Approaches to Test Data Generation for Object-Oriented Software: Overview of Techniques and *Tools. In M. Khosrow-Pour, D.B.A. (Ed.), Incorporating Nature-Inspired Paradigms in Computational Appl*ications (pp. 162-194). Hershey, PA: IGI Global. https://doi.org/ doi:10.4018/978-1-5225-5020-4.ch006

Nowack, K. C., Koppens, F. H. L., Nazarov, Y. V., & Vandersypen, L. M. K. (2007). Coherent Control of a Single Electron Spin with E*lectric Fields. Science, 318(5855), 1430–1433. doi:10.1126cie*nce.1148092 PMID:17975030

Nwajana, A. O., Obi, E. R., Ijemaru, G. K., Oleka, E. U., & Anthony, D. C. (2021). Fundamentals of RF/Microwave Bandpass Filter Design. In A. Nwajana & I. Ihianle (Eds.), *Handbook of Research on 5G Networks and Advancements in Computing, E*lectronics, and Electrical Engineering (pp. 149–164*). IGI Global. https://doi.org/10.4018/978-1-7998-6992-4.ch005*

Náprstek, J., & Fischer, C. (2017). Dynamic Stability and Post-Critical Processes of Slender Auto-Par*ametric Systems. In V. Plevris, G. Kremmyda, & Y. Fahjan (Eds.),* Performance-Based Seismic Design of Concrete Structures and Infrastructures (pp. 128–171). Hershey, PA: IGI Global. doi:10.4018/978-1-5225-2089-4.ch006

Ofek, N., Petrenko, A., Heeres, R., Reinhold, P., Leghtas, Z., Vlastakis, B., Liu, Y., Frunzio, L., Girvin, S. M., Jiang, L., Mirrahimi, M., De*voret, M. H., & Schoelkopf, R. J. (2016). Extending the lifetime of a quantum bit with error* correction in superconducting circuits. Nature, 536(7617), 441–445. doi:10.1038/nature18949 PMID:27437573

Ogbodo, E. A. (2021). Comparative Study of Transmission Line Junction vs. Asynchronously Coupled Junction Diplexers. In A. Nwajana & I. Ihianle (Eds.), *Handbook of Research on 5G Networks* and Advancements in Computing, Electronics, and Electrical Engineering (pp. 326–336). IGI Global. https://doi.org/10.4018/978-1-7998-6992-4.ch013

Ono, K., Austing, D. G., Tokura, Y., & Tarucha, S. (2002*). Current Rectification by Pauli Exclusion in a Weakly Coupled Double Quant*um Dot System. Science, 297(5585), 1313–1317. doi:10.1126cience.1070958 PMID:12142438

Orosa, J. A., Vergara, D., Fraguela, F., & Masdías-Bonome, A. (2021). Statistical Understanding and Optimization of Building Energy Consumption and Climate Chan*ge Consequences. In R. González-Lezcano (Ed.), Advancements in Sustainable Architecture* and Energy Efficiency (pp. 195–220). IGI Global. https://doi.org/10.4018/978-1-7998-7023-4.ch009

Orsucci, D., Tiersch, M., & Briegel, H. J. (2016). Estimation of coherent error sources from stabilizer measurements. Phys., 93*(4), 042303. doi:10.1103/PhysRevA.93.042303*

Osho, M. B. (2018). Industrial Enzyme Technology: Potential Applications. In S. Bharati & P. Chaurasia (Eds.), Research Advancements in Pharmaceutical, Nutritional, and Industrial Enzymology (pp. 375–394). Hersh*ey, PA: IGI Global. doi:10.4018/978-1-5225-5237-6.ch017*

Oszmaniec, M., Grudka, A., Horodecki, M., & Wojcik, A. (2016). Creating a superposition of unknown quantum state*s. Physical Review Le*tters, 116(11), 110403. doi:10.1103/PhysRevLett.116.110403 PMID:27035290

Ouadi, A., & Zitouni, A. (2021). Phasor Measurement Improvement Using Digital Filter in a Smart Grid. In A. Recioui & H. Bentarzi (Eds.), Op*timizing and Measuring Smart Grid Operation and Control (pp. 100–117). I*GI Global. https://doi.org/10.4018/978-1-7998-4027-5.ch005

Padmaja, P., & Marutheswar, G. (2017*). Certain Investigation on Secured Data Tr*ansmission in Wireless Sensor Networks. International Journal of Mobile Computing and Multimedia Communications, 8(1), 48–61. doi:10.4018/IJMCMC.2017010104

Palmer, S., & Hall, W. (2017). An *Evaluation of Group Work in First-Year Engineering Design Education. In R. Tucker* (Ed.), Collaboration and Student Engagement in Design Education (pp. 145–168). Hershey, PA: IGI Global. doi:10.4018/978-1-5225-0726-0.ch007

Panchenko, V. (2021). Photovoltaic Thermal Module Wit*h Paraboloid Type Solar Concentrators. International Journal of Energy Op*timization and Engineering, 10(2), 1–23. https://doi.org/10.4018/IJEOE.2021040101

Panchenko, V. (2021). Prospects for Energy Supply *of the Arctic Zone Objects of Russia Using Frost-Resis*tant Solar Modules. In P. Vasant, G. Weber, & W. Punurai (Eds.), Research Advancements in Smart Technology, Optimization, and Renewable Energy (pp. 149-169). IGI Global. https://doi.org/10.4018/*978-1-7998-3970-5.ch008*

Pandey, K., & Datta, S. (2021). Dry Machining of Inconel 825 Superalloys: Performance of Tool Inserts (Carbide, Cermet, and SiAlON). International Journal of Manufacturing, Materials, and Mechanical Engineering, 11(4), 26–39. doi:10.*4018/IJMMME.2021100102*

*Panneer, R. (2017). Effect of Composi*tion of Fibers on Properties of Hybrid Composites. International Journal of Manufacturing, Materials, and Mechanical Engineering, 7(4), 28–43. doi:10.4018/IJMMME.2017100103

Pany, C. (2021). Estimation of Correct Long-Seam Mismatch *Using FEA to Compare the Measured Strain in a Non-Destructive Testing of a Pressurant Tank: A Reverse* Problem. International Journal of Smart Vehicles and Smart Transportation, 4(1), 16–28. doi:10.4018/IJSVST.2021010102

Pasieka, A., Kribs, D. W., Laflamme, R., & Pereira, R. (2009). On the geometric interpretation of single qubit quantum operations on the Bloch sphere. Acta Appl*icandae Mathematicae, 108(3), 697–707. doi:10.100710440-008-9423-z*

Patra, B. (2017). Cryo-CMOS circuits and systems for quantum computing applications. IEEE Journal of Solid-State Circuits, 1–13.

Paul, S., & Roy, P. (2018). Optimal Design of Power System Stabilizer Using a Novel Evolutionary Algorithm. International Journal of Ener*gy Optimization and Engineering, 7(3), 24–46. doi:10.4018/IJEOE.2018070102*

Paul, S., & Roy, P. K. (2021). Oppositional Differential Search Algorithm for the Optimal Tuning of Both Single Input and Dual Input Power System Stabilizer. In P. Vasant, G. Weber, & W. Punurai (Eds.), Research Advancements in Smart Technology, Optimization, and Renewable Energy (pp. 256-282). IGI Global. https://doi.org/10.4018/978-1-7998-3970-5.ch013

Pavaloiu, A. (2018). Artificial Intelligence Ethics in Biomedical-Engineering-Oriented Problems. In U. Kose, *G. Guraksin, & O. Deperlioglu (Eds.), Nature-Inspired Intelligent Techniques for Solving Biomedical En*gineering Problems (pp. 219–231). Hershey, PA: IGI Global. doi:10.4018/978-1-5225-4769-3.ch010

Perdomo-Ortiz, A., Benedetti, *M., Realpe-Gómez, J., & Biswas, R. (2018). Opportunities and challe*nges for quantum-assisted machine learning in near-ter*m quantum computers. Quantum Scie*nce and Technology, 3(3), 030502. doi:10.1088/2058-9565/aab859

Petta, J. R., Johnson, A. C., Taylor, J. M., Laird, E. A., Yacoby, A., Lukin, M. D., Marcus, C. M., Hanso*n, M. P., & Gossard, A. C. (2005). Coherent Manipulation of Coupled* Electron Spins in Semiconductor Quantum Dots. Science, 309(5744), 2180–2184. doi:10.1126cience.1116955 PMID:16141370

Pfeiffer, P., Egusquiza, I. L., *Di Ventra, M., Sanz, M., & Solano*, E. (2016). Quantum memristors. Scientific Reports, 6(6), 29507. doi:10.1038rep29507 PMID:27381511

Piattini & Pérez-Castillo. (2020). Quantum computing: A new software engineering golden age. SIGSOFT Softw. Eng. Notes, 45, 12–14. doi:10.1145/3402127.3402131

Pioro, I., Mahdi, M., & Popov, R. (2017). Application of Supercritical Pressures in Power Engineering. In L. Chen & Y. Iwamoto (Eds.), Advanced Applications of Supercritical Fluids in Energy Systems (pp. 404–457). Hershey, PA: IGI Global. doi:10.4018/978-1-5225-2047-4.ch013

Plaksina, T., & Gildin, E. (2017). Rigorous Integrated Evolutionary Workflow for Optimal Exploitation of Unconventional Gas Assets. International Journal of Energy Optimization and Engineering, 6(1), 101–122. doi:10.4018/IJEOE.2017010106

Popat, J., Kakadiya, H., Tak, L., Singh, N. K., Majeed, M. A., & Mahajan, V. (2021). Reliability of Smart Grid Including Cyber Impact: A Case Study. In R. Singh, A. Singh, A. Dwivedi, & P. Nagabhushan (Eds.), Computational Methodologies for Electrical and Electronics Engineers (pp. 163–174). IGI Global. https://doi.org/10.4018/978-1-7998-3327-7.ch013

Powell, P. (2015). ASCR Report on Quantum Computing for Science. doi:10.13140/RG.2.1.3656.5200

Pozar, D. M. (2011). Microwave Engineering. New York: John Wiley & Sons.

Preskill, J. (2018). Quantum Computing in the NISQ era and beyond. Quantum, 2, 79. arXiv preprint arXiv:1801.00862.

Preskill, J. (2018). Quantum computing in the NISQ era and beyond. Quantum, 2, 79. doi:10.22331/q-2018-08-06-79

Press, G. (2020). Calling on AI and Quantum Computing to Fight the Coronavirus. Forbes.

Pudenz, K. L., & Lidar, D. A. (2013). Quantum adiabatic machine learning. Quantum Information Processing, 12(5), 2027–2070. doi:10.100711128-012-0506-4

Pérez-Delgado, C. A., & Perez-Gonzalez, H. G. (2020). Towards a quantum software modeling language. Proceedings of the IEEE/ACM 42nd International Conference on Software Engineering Workshops, 442–444. 10.1145/3387940.3392183

Qiskit Development team. (2021). Representing Qubit States by Qiskit. Retrieved May 5, 2021, from https://qiskit.org/textbook/ch-states/representing-qubit-states.html

Quantum Computing and AI. (2021). A Transformational Match. Available at https://www.bbvaopenmind.com/

Quantum software engineering challenges. (n.d.). https://www.cutter.co

Quiza, R., La Fé-Perdomo, I., Rivas, M., & Ramtahalsing, V. (2021). Triple Bottom Line-Focused Optimization of Oblique Turning Processes Based on Hybrid Modeling: A Study Case on AISI 1045 Steel Turning. In L. Burstein (Ed.), Handbook of Research on Advancements in Manufacturing, Materials, and Mechanical Engineering (pp. 215–241). IGI Global. https://doi.org/10.4018/978-1-7998-4939-1.ch010

Rahmani, M. K. (2022). B*lockchain Technology: Principles and Algorithms. In S. Khan,* M. Syed, R. Hammad, & A. Bushager (Eds.), Blockchain Technology and Computational Excellence for Society 5.0 (pp. 16–27). IGI Global. https://doi.org/10.4018/978-1-7998-8382-1.ch002

Rai, B. (2019). Advanced Deep Learning with R: Become an Expert *at Designing, Building, and Improving Advanced Neural Network Models Using R. Packt P*ublishing. doi:10.1002/9781119564843.ch5

Ramdani, N., & Azibi, M. (2018). Polymer Composite Materials for Microelectronics Packaging Applications: Composites for Microelectronic*s Packaging. In K. Kumar & J. Davim (Eds.),* Composites and Adv*anced Materials for Industrial Applications (pp. 177–211). Hershey, PA: IGI Global. doi:10.4018/978-1-5225-5216-1.ch009

Ramesh, M., Garg, R., & Subrahmanyam, G. V. (2017). Investigation of Influence of Quenching and Annealing on the Plane Fra*cture Toughness and Brittle to Ductile Transition Temperature of the Zinc Coated Str*uc*tural Steel Materials. International Journal of Surface Engineering and Interdisciplinary Materials Science, 5(2), 33–42. doi:10.4018/IJSEIMS.2017070103

Rebentrost, P., Mohseni, M., & Lloyd, S. (2014). Quantum support vector machine *for big data classification. Physical Review Letters, 113(13), 130503.* doi:10.1103/PhysRevLett.113.130503 PMID:25302877

Rebollo-Monedero, D., & Girod, B. (2009). Lloyd Algorithm. Science Direct. https://www.sciencedirect.com/topics/computer-science/lloyd-algorithm

Riste, D., Poletto, S., H*uang, M.-Z., Bruno, A., Vesterinen, V., Saira, O.-P., & DiCarlo, L. (2015).* Detecting bit-flip errors in a logical qubit using stabilizer measurements. Nature Communications, 6(6), 6983. doi:10.1038/ncomms7983 PMID:25923318

Robinson, J., & Beneroso, D. (2022). Project-Based Learning in Chemical E*ngineering: Curriculum and Assessment, Culture and Learning S*paces. In A. Alves & N. van Hattum-Janssen (Eds.), Training Engineering Students for Modern Technological Advancement (pp. 1–19). IGI Global. https://doi.org/10.4018/978-1-7998-8816-1.ch001

Rondon, B. (2021). Experimental Characterization of *Admittance Meter With Crude Oil Emulsions. International Journal of Electronics, Communications, and Measurement* Engineering, 10(2), 51–59. https://doi.org/10.4018/IJECME.2021070104

Rosenblatt, F. (1958). The perceptron: A probabilistic model for information storage and organization in the brain. Psychological Review, 65(6), 386–408. doi:10.1037/h0042519 PMID:*13602029*

*Rudolf, S., Biryuk, V. V., & Volov, V. (2018). Vortex Effect, Vortex Pow*er: Technology of Vortex Power Engineering. In V. Kharchenko & P. Vasant (Eds.), Handbook of Research on Renewable Energy and El*ectric Resources for Sustainable Rural Development (pp. 500–533). He*rshey, PA: IGI Global. doi:10.4018/978-1-5225-3867-7.ch021

Sah, A., Bhadula, S. J., Dumka, A., & Rawat, S. (2018). A Software Engineering Perspective for Development of Enterprise Applications. In A. Elçi (Ed.), *Handbook of Research on Contemporary Perspectives on Web-Based Systems (pp.* 1–23). Hershey, PA: IGI Global. doi:10.4018/978-1-5225-5384-7.ch001

Sahni, V., & Srivastava, D. P. (2015). Quantum Information and Com*putation Systems. CSI Communications.*

Sahoo, P., & Roy, S. (2017). *Tri*bological Behavior of Electroless Ni-P, Ni-P-W and Ni-P-Cu Coatings: A Comparison. International Journal of Surface Engineering and Interdisciplinary Materials Science, 5(1), 1–15. doi:10.4018/IJSEIMS.2017010101

Sahoo, S. (2018). *Laminated Composite Hypar Shells as Roofing Units: Static and Dynamic Behavior. In* K. Kumar & J. Davim (Eds.), Composites and Advanced Materials for Industrial Applications (pp. 249–269). Hershey, PA: IGI Global. doi:10.4018/978-1-5225-5216-1.ch011

Sahu, H., & Hungyo, M. (2018). Introduction to SDN and NFV. In A. Dumka (Ed.), Innovations in Software-Defined Networking and Network Functions Virtualization (pp. 1–25). Hershey, PA: IGI Global. doi:10.4018/978-1-5225-3640-6.ch001

Salem, A. M., & Shmelova, T. (2018). Intelligent Expert Decision Support Systems: Methodologies, Applications, and Challenges. In T. Shmelova, Y. Sikirda, N. Rizun, A. Salem, & Y. Kovalyov (Eds.), Socio-Technical Decision Support in Air N*avigation Systems: Emerging Research and Opportunities (pp. 215–242). Hershey, PA: IGI Global. doi:10.4018/*978-1-5225-3108-1.ch007

Salmilehto, J., Deppe, F., Ventra, M., & Di. (2017). Quantum memristors with superconducting circuits. Scientific Reports, 7(1), 42044. doi:10.1038rep42044 PMID:28195193

Samal, M. (2017). FE Analysis an*d Experimental Investigation of Cracked and Un-Cracked Thin-Walled Tubular Components to Evaluate Mechanic*al and Fracture Properties. In P. Samui, S. Chakraborty, & D. Kim (Eds.), Modeling and Simulation Techniques in Structural Engineering (pp. 266–293). Hershey, PA: IGI Global. doi:10.4018/978-1-5225-0588-4.ch009

Samal, M., & Balakrishnan, K. (2017). Experiments on a Ring Tension Setu*p and FE Analysis to Evaluate Transverse Mechanical Properties* of Tubular Components. In P. Samui, S. Chakraborty, & D. Kim (Eds.), Modeling and Simulation Techniques in Structural Engineering (pp. 91–115). Hershey, PA: IGI Global. doi:10.4018/978-1-*5225-0588-4.ch004*

Samarasinghe, D. A., & Wood, E. (2021). *Innovative Digital Te*chnologies. In J. Underwood & M. Shelbourn (Eds.), Handbook of Research on Driving Transformational Change in the Digital Built Environment (pp. 142–163). IGI Global. https://doi.org/10.4018/978-1-7998-6600-8.ch006

Samkharadze, N., Zheng, G., Kalhor, N., Brousse, D., Sam*mak, A., Mendes, U. C., Blais, A., Scappucci, G., & Vandersypen, L. M. K. (2018). Strong spin-photon coupling in silicon. Science, 359(6380), 1123–1127. doi:10.1126cience.aar4054 PMID:29371427

Sarma, S. D., Freedman, M., & Nayak, C. (2015). Majorana zero modes and to*pological quantum computation. NPJ Quantum Information, 1(1), 15001. doi:10.1038/npjqi.2015.1

Sawant, S. (2018). Deep Learning and Biomedical Engineering. In U. Kose, *G. Guraksin, & O. Deperlioglu (Eds.), Nature-Inspired In*telligent Techniques for Solving Biomedical Engineering Problems (pp. 283–296). Hershey, PA: IGI Global. doi:10.4018/978-1-5225-4769-3.ch014

Schuld, M., & Sinayskiy, I. (2014, October 15). An introduction to quantum machine learning. Taylor Franc*is Online. https://www.tandfonline.com/doi/abs/10.1080/00107514.2014.964942*

Schuld, M., Sinayskiy, I., & Petruccione, F. (2014). An introduction to quantum machine learning. Contemporary Physics, 56(2), 172–185. doi:10.1080/00107514.2014.964942

*Schulenberg, T. (2021). Energy Conversion Using the Superc*ritical Steam Cycle. In L. Chen (Ed.), Handbook of Research on Advancements in Supercritical Fluids Applications for Sustainable Energy Systems (pp. 659–681). IGI Global. doi:*10.4018/978-1-7998-5796-9.ch018*

*Sengupta, S., Basak, S., & Peters, R. A. (2018, January). Da*ta *c*lustering using a hybrid of fuzzy c-means and quantum-behaved particle swarm optimization. In 2018 IEEE 8th Annual Computing and Co*mmunication Workshop and Conference (CCWC) (pp. 137-142). IEEE. 10.1109/CCWC.20*18.8301693

Sentis, G., Calsamiglia, J., Munoz-Tapia, R., & Bagan, E. (2012). Quantum learning without quantum memory. Scientific Reports, 2(708), 1–8. PMID:23050092

Sezgin, H., & Berkalp, O. B. (2018). Textile-R*einforced Composites for the Automotive Industry. In K. Kumar & J.* Davim (Eds.), Composites and Advanced Materials for Industrial Applications (pp. 129–156). Hershey, PA: IGI Global. doi:10.4018/*978-1-5225-5216-1.ch007*

Shaaban, A. A., & Shehata, O. M. (2021). Combining Response Surface Method and Metaheuristic Algorithms for Optimizing SPIF Process. International Journal of Manufacturing, Materials, and Mechanical Engineering, 11(4), 1–25. *https://doi.org/10.4018/IJMMME.2021100101*

Shafaati Shemami, M., & Sefid, M. (2022). Implementation and Demonstration of Electric Vehicle-to-Home (V2H) Application: A Case Study. In M. Alam, R. Pillai, & N. Murugesan (Eds.), Developing Charging Infrastructure *and Technologies for Electric Vehicles (pp. 268–293). IGI Gl*obal. https://doi.org/10.4018/978-1-7998-6858-3.ch015

Shah, M. Z., Gazder, U., Bhatti, M. S., & Hussain, M. (2018). Comparative Performance Evaluation of Effects of Modifier in Asphaltic Conc*rete Mix. International Journal of Strategic Engineering, 1(2), 13–25. doi:10.4018/*IJoSE.2018070102

Shalf, J. (2020). The future of computing beyond Moore's Law. Philosophical Transactions - Royal Society. Mathematical, Physical, and Engineering Sciences, 378(2166), 20190061. doi:10.1098/rsta.2019.0061 PMID:31955683

Sharma, N., *& Kumar, K. (2018). Fabricatio*n of Porous NiTi Alloy Using Organic Binders. In K. Kumar & J. Davim (Eds.), Composites and Advanced Materials for Industrial Applications (pp. 38–62). Hershey, PA: IGI Global. doi:*10.4018/978-1-5225-5216-1.ch003*

*Shary, S. (2011). Java Simulat*or of Qubits and Quantum-Mechanical Gates Using the Bloch Sphere Representation (Doctoral dissertation). University of Cincinnati.

Shivach, P., Nautiyal, L., & Ram, M. (2018). Applying Multi-Objective Optimization *Algorithms to Mechanical Engineering. In M. Ram & J. Davim* (Eds.), Soft Computing Techniques and Applications in Mechanical Engineering (pp. 287–301). Hershey, PA: IGI Global. doi:10.4018/978-1-5225-3035-0.ch014

Shmelova, T. (2018). Stochastic Methods for Estimation and Problem Solving in Engineering: Stochas*tic Methods of Decision Making in Aviation. In S. Kadry (Ed.), Stocha*stic Methods for Estimation and Problem Solving in Engineering (pp. 139–160). Hershey, PA: IGI *Global. doi:10.4018/978-1-5225-5045-7.ch006*

Shor, P. W. (1994). Article. In Proc. 1st Internat. Symp., Algorithmic Number Theory. Springer-Verl*ag.*

*Sh*or, P. W. (1994, November). Algorithms for quantum computation: discrete logarithms and factoring. In Proceedings *35th annual symposium on foun*dations of computer science (pp. 124-134). IEEE. 10.1109/SFCS.1994.365700

Shor, P. W. (1996). Article. In Proc. 37th Conf. Foundations of Computer Science. IEEE Comput. Soc. Press.

Shulman, M. D., Dial, O. E., Harvey, S. P., Bluhm, H., Umansky, V., & Yacoby, A. (2012). Dem*onstration of Entanglement of Electrostatically Coupled Singlet-Triplet Qubits. Science, 336*(6078), 202–205. doi:10.1126cience.1217692 PMID:22499942

Siero González, L. R., & Romo Vázquez, A. (2017). Didactic Sequences Teaching Mathematics for Engineers With Focus on Differential Equations. In M. *Ramírez-Montoya (Ed.), Handbook of Research on Driving STEM Lear*ning With Educational Technologies (pp. 129–151). Hershey, PA: IGI Global. doi:10.4018/978-1-5225-2026-9.ch007

Sim, M. S., You, K. Y., Esa, F., & Chan, Y. L. (2021). Nanostructured Electromagnetic Metamaterials for Sensing Applications. In M. Bhat, I. Wa*ni, & S. Ashraf (Eds.), Applications of Nanomaterials in Agri*culture, Food Science, and Medicine (pp. 141–164). IGI Global. https://doi.org/10.4018/978-1-7998-5563-7.ch009

Simmons, C. B., Thalakulam, M., Shaji, N., Klein, L. J., Qin, H., Blick, R. H., Savage, D. E., Lagally, M. G., Coppersmith, S. N., & Eriksson, M. A. (2007). Single-electron quantum dot in Si/SiGe *with integrated charge sensing. Applied Physics Letters, 91(21), 213103. doi:10.1063/1.28*16331

Singh, R., & Dutta, S. (2018). Visible Light Active Nanocomposites for Photocatalytic Applications. In K. Kumar & J. Davim (Eds.), Composites and *Advanced Materials for Indu*strial Applications (pp. 270–296). Hershey, PA: IGI Global. doi:10.4018/978-1-5225-5216-1.ch012

Skripov, *P. V., Yampol'sk*iy, A. D., & Rutin, S. B. (2021). High-Power Heat Transfer in Supercritical Fluids: Microscale Times and Sizes. In L. Chen (Ed.), Handbook of Research on Advancements in Supercritical Fluids Applications for Sustainable Energy Systems (pp. 424–450). IGI Global. https://doi.*org/10.4018/978-1-7998-5796-9.ch012*

Sofge, D. A. (2008), A survey of quantum programming languages: History, methods, and tools. Second International Conference on Quantum, Nano and Micro Technologies (ICQNM 2008), 66–71. 10.1109/ICQNM.2008.15

Solenov, D., Brieler, J., & Scherrer, J. F. (2018). The Potential of Quantum Computing and Machine Learning to Advance Clinical Research and Change the Practice of Medicine. Missouri Medicine, 115(5), 463–467. PMID:30385997

Somaschiet, N. (2016). Near-optimal single-photon source*s in the solid state. Nature Photon., 10(5), 340–345.*

Spector, L., Barnum, H., & Bernstein, H. J. (1999). Quantum Computing Applications of Genetic Programming. In L. Spector, U.-M. O'Reilly, W. Langdon, & P. Angeline (Eds.), Advances in Genetic Programming (Vol. 3, pp. 135–160). MIT Press. doi:10.7551/mitpress/1110.003.0010

*Srinivasan, K., Satyajit, S., & Behera, B. K. (2018). Efficient quant*um algorithm for solving travelling salesman problem: An IBM quantum experience. https://arxiv.org/abs/1805.10928

Stanciu, I. (2018). Stochastic Methods in Microsystems Engineering. In S. Kadry (Ed.), Stochastic Methods for Estimation and Problem Solving in Engineering (pp. 161–176). Hersh*ey, PA: IGI Global. doi:10.4018/978-1-5225-5045-7.ch007*

Strebkov, D., Nekrasov, A., Trubnikov, V., & Nekrasov, A. (2018). Single-Wire Resonant Electric Power Systems for Renewable-Based Electric Grid. In V. Kharchenko & P. Vasant (Eds.), Handbook *of Research on Renewable Energy and Electric Resources for Sustainable Rural Developme*nt (pp. 449–474). Hershey, PA: IGI Global. doi:10.4018/978-1-5225-3867-7.ch019

Sukhyy, K., Belyanovskaya, E., & Sukhyy, M. (2021). Basic Principles for Substantiation of Wor*king Pair Choice. IGI Global. doi:10.4018/978-1-7998-4432-7.ch*002

Sun, J., & Hao, S. N. (2009, January). Research of fuzzy neural network model based on quantum clustering. In 2009 Second International Workshop on K*nowledge Discovery and Data Mining (pp. 133-136). IEEE. 10.1109/WKDD.2009.193*

Su*ri, M. S., & Kaliyaperumal, D. (2022). Extension of Aspiration Level Model for Optimal Planning of Fast Charging Stations. In A. Fekik & N. Benamrouche (Eds.), Modeling and Control of Static Converters for Hybrid Storage Systems (pp. 91–106). IGI Global. https://doi. org/10.4018/978-1-7998-7447-8.ch004*

*Sözbilir, H., Özkaymak, Ç., Uzel, B., & Sümer, Ö. (2018). Crite*ria for Surface Rupture Microzonation of Active Faults for Earthquake Hazards in Urban Areas. In N. Ceryan (Ed.), Handbook of Research on Trends and Digital Advances in Engineering Geology (pp. 187–230). Hershey, PA: IGI Global. doi:10.4018/978-1-5225-2709-1.ch005

Takahashi, Kurokawa, & H*ashimoto. (2014). Multi-layer Quantum Neural Network Control*ler Trained by Real-Coded Genetic Algorithm. Elsevier.

Tallet, E., Gledson, B., Rogage, K., Thompson, A., & Wiggett, D. (2021). Digitally-Enabled Design Management. In J. Underwood & M. Shelbourn (Eds.), Handbook of Research on Driving Transformational Change in the Digital Built *Environment (pp. 63–89). IGI Global. https://doi. org/10.4018/*978-1-7998-6600-8.ch003

Tang, W. L., Zhang, H. Ch., Ma, H. F., Jiang, W. X., & Cui, T. J. (2019). Concept, Theory, Design, and Applications of Spoof Surface Plasmon Polaritons at Microwav*e Frequencies. Advanced Optical Materials, 7, 1–22.*

*Taulli, T. (2020). Quantum Computi*ng: What Does It Mean For AI (Artificial Intelligence)? Available at https://www.forbes.com

Teng-Fei, Y., & Xue-Ping, Z. (2010, September). Spatial clustering algorithm with obstacles con*straints by quantum particle swarm optimization and K-Medoids. In 2010 Second Inte*rnational Conference on Computational Intelligence and Natural Computing (Vol. 2, pp. 105-108). IEEE. 10.1109/CINC.2010.5643776

*Terki, A., & Boubertakh, H. (2021). A Ne*w Hybrid Binary-Real Coded Cuckoo Search and Tabu Search Algorithm for Solving the Unit-Commitment Problem. International Journal of Energy Optimization and Engineering, 10(2), 104–119. htt*ps://doi.org/10.4018/*IJEOE.2021040105

The Economist. (2020). Wall Street's latest shiny new thing: quantum computing. The Economist. https://www.economist.com/finance-an*d-economics/2020/12/19/wall-streets-latest-shiny-new-thing-quantum-computing*

*Torgler, B. (2020). Big D*ata, Artificial Intelligence, and Quantum Computing in Sports. Academic Press.

Tüdeş, Ş., Kumlu, K. B., & Ceryan, S. (2018). Integration Between Urban Planning and Natural *Hazards For Resili*ent City. In N. Ceryan (Ed.), Handbook of Research on Trends and Digital Advances in Engineering Geology (pp. 591–630). Hershey, PA: IGI Global. doi:10.4018*/978-1-5225-2709-1.ch017*

*Ulamis, K. (2018). Soil Liquefactio*n Assessment by Anisotropic Cyclic Triaxial Test. In N. Ceryan (Ed.), Handbook of Research on Trends and Digital Advances in Engineering Geology (pp. 631–664). Hershey, PA: IGI Global. doi:10.4018/978-1-5225-2709-*1.ch018*

*Valente, M., & Milani, G. (2017). Seismic Assessment and Retrofitt*ing of an Under-Designed RC Frame Through a Displacement-Based Approach. In V. Plevris, G. Kremmyda, & Y. Fahjan (Eds.), Performance-Based Seismic Design of Concrete Structures and Infrastructures (pp. 36–58). Hershey, PA: IGI Global. doi:1*0.4018/978-1-5225-2089-4.ch002*

Vandersypen, L.M.K., & Chuang, I.L. (2005). NMR techniques for quantum control and computation. Rev. Mod. Phys., 76, 1037-69.

Vandersypen, L. M. K., Bluhm, H., Clarke, J. S., Dzurak, A. S., Ishihara, R., Morello, A., Reilly, D. J., Schreiber, L. R., & Veldhorst, M. *(2017). Interfacing spin qubits in quantum d*ots and donors— Hot, dense, and coherent. NPJ Quantum Information, 3(1), 34. doi:10.103841534-017-0038-y

Van Meter, R., & Devitt, S. J. (2016). Local and distributed quantum computation. IEEE Comput., 49(9), 31–42. arXiv:1605.06951v1.

Vargas-Bernal, R. (2021). Advances in Electromagnetic Environmental Shielding for Aeronautics and Space Applications. In C. Nikolopoulos (Ed.), Recent Trends on Electromagnetic Environmental Effects for Aeronautics and Space Applications (pp. 80–96). IGI Global. https://doi.org/10.4018/978-1-7998-4879-0.ch003

Vasant, P. (2018). A General Medical Diagnosis System Formed by Artificial Neural Networks and Swarm Intelligence Techniques. In U. Kose, G. Guraksin, & O. Deperlioglu (Eds.), Nature-Inspired Intelligent Techniques for Solving Biomedical Engineering Problems (pp. 130–145). Hershey, PA: IGI Global. doi:10.4018/978-1-5225-4769-3.ch006

Veldhorst, M., Hwang, J. C. C., Yang, C. H., Leenstra, A. W., de Ronde, B., Dehollain, J. P., Muhonen, J. T., Hudson, F. E., Itoh, K. M., Morello, A., & Dzurak, A. S. (2014). An addressable quantum dot qubit with fault-tolerant control fidelity. Nature Nanotechnology, 9(9), 981–985. doi:10.1038/nnano.2014.216 PMID:25305743

Veldhorst, M., Yang, C. H., Hwang, J. C. C., Huang, W., Dehollain, J. P., Muhonen, J. T., Simmons, S., Laucht, A., Hudson, F. E., Itoh, K. M., Morello, A., & Dzurak, A. S. (2015). A two-qubit logic gate in silicon. Nature, 526(7573), 410–414. doi:10.1038/nature15263 PMID:26436453

Vermersch, B., Guimond, P. O., Pichler, H., & Zoller, P. (2016). Quantum state transfer via noisy photonic and phononic waveguides. arXiv:1611.10240.

Verner, C. M., & Sarwar, D. (2021). Avoiding Project Failure and Achieving Project Success in NHS IT System Projects in the United Kingdom. International Journal of Strategic Engineering, 4(1), 33–54. https://doi.org/10.4018/IJoSE.2021010103

Verrollot, J., Tolonen, A., Harkonen, J., & Haapasalo, H. J. (2018). Challenges and Enablers for Rapid Product Development. International Journal of Applied Industrial Engineering, 5(1), 25–49. doi:10.4018/IJAIE.2018010102

Vizzotto, J. K. (2013). Quantum computing: state-of-art and challenges. Proceedings of the 2nd Workshop-School of Theoretical Computer Science, 9-13.

Wan, A. C., Zulu, S. L., & Khosrow-Shahi, F. (2021). Industry Views on BIM for Site Safety in Hong Kong. In J. Underwood & M. Shelbourn (Eds.), Handbook of Research on Driving Transformational Change in the Digital Built Environment (pp. 120–140). IGI Global. https://doi.org/10.4018/978-1-7998-6600-8.ch005

Wang, Y., Feng, X. Y., Huang, Y. X., Pu, D. B., Zhou, W. G., Liang, Y. C., & Zhou, C. G. (2007). A novel quantum swarm evolutionary algorithm and its applications. Neurocomputing, 70(4-6), 633–640. doi:10.1016/j.neucom.2006.10.001

Weber, J. R., Koehl, W. F., Varley, J. B., Janotti, A., Buckley, B. B., Van de Walle, C. G., & Awschalom, D. D. (2010). Quantum computing with defects. Proceedings of the National Academy of Sciences of the United States of *America, 107(19), 8513–8518. doi:10.1073/pnas.1003052107* PMID:20404195

Wendin, G. (2017). Quantum information processing with superconducting circuits: A review. Rep. Prog. Phys., 80(24).

What is Quantum Machine Learning? (2021). Retrieved 7 October 2021, from https://pennylane. ai/qml/whatisqml.html

Wiebe, N., Kapoor, A., & Svore, K. (2014). Quantum Algorithms for Nearest-Neighbor Methods for Supervised and Unsupervised Learning. Quantum Information & Computation, 15(3), 318–358.

Wigley, P. B., Everitt, P. J., van den Hengel, A., Bastian, J. W., Sooriyabandara, M. A., McDonald, G. D., Hardman, K. S., Quinlivan, C. D., Manju, P., Kuhn, C. C. N., Petersen, I. R., Luiten, A. N., Hope, J. J., Robins, N. P., & Hush, M. R. (2016). Fast machine-learning online optimization of ultra-cold atom experiments. Scientific Reports, 6(6), 258. doi:10.1038rep25890 PMID:27180805

Wittek, P. (2014). Quantum Machine Learning: What Quantum Computing Means to Data Mining. Academic Press.

Xie, X. L., & Beni, G. (1991). A validity measure for fuzzy clustering. IEEE Transactions on Pattern Analysis and Machine Intelligence, 13(8), 841–847. doi:10.1109/34.85677

Xin, Z., Hai-Ou, L., & Ke, W. (2018). Qubits based on semiconductor quantum dots. Chinese Physics B, 27(2), 020305. doi:10.1088/1674-1056/27/2/020305

Xu, R., & Wunsch, D. II. (2005). Survey of clustering algorithms. IEEE Transactions on Neural Networks, 16(3), 645–678. doi:10.1109/TNN.2005.845141 PMID:15940994

Yardimci, A. G., & Karpuz, C. (2018). Fuzzy Rock Mass Rating: Soft-Computing-Aided Preliminary Stability Analysis of Weak Rock Slopes. In N. Ceryan (Ed.), Handbook of Research on Trends and Digital Advances in Engineering Geology (pp. 97–131). Hershey, PA: IGI Global. doi:10.4018/978-1-5225-2709-1.ch003

Yilmaz, T., DePriest, C. M., & Delfyett, P. J. Jr. (2001). Complete noise characterisation of external cavity semiconductor laser hybridly modelocked at 10 GHz. Electronics Letters, 37(22), 1338. doi:10.1049/el:20010919

Ying, M. (2010). Quantum computation, quantum theory and AI. Artificial Intelligence, 174(2), 162–176. doi:10.1016/j.artint.2009.11.009

Ying, M., & Feng, Y. (2010). Quantum loop programs. Acta Informatica, 47(4), 221–250. doi:10.100700236-010-0117-4

Yoneda, J., Takeda, K., Otsuka, T., Nakajima, T., Delbecq, M. R., Allison, G., Honda, T., Kodera, T., Oda, S., Hoshi, Y., *Usami, N., Itoh, K. M., & Tarucha, S. (2018). A quantum-dot spin qubit* with coherence limited by charge noise and fidelity higher than 99.9%. Nature Nanotechnology, 13(2), 102–106. doi:10.103841565-017-0014-x PMID:29255292

You, K. Y. (2021). Development Electronic Design Automation for RF/Microwave Antenna Using MATLAB GUI. In A. Nwaj*ana & I. Ihianle (Eds.), Handbook of Research on 5G Networks and Advancement*s in Computing, Electronics, and Electrical Engineering (pp. 70–148). IGI Global. https://doi.org/10.4018/978-1-7998-6992-4.ch004

Yousefi, Y., Gratton, P., & Sarwar, D. (2021). Investigating the Opportunities to Improve *the Thermal Performance of a Case Study Building in London. International Journal of Strate*gic Engineering, 4(1), 1–18. https://doi.org/10.4018/IJoSE.2021010101

Zhang, A. Q., Liu, Z. G., Lu, W. B., & Chen, H. (2019a). Dynamically Tunable Attenuator on a Graphene-Based Microstrip Line. IEEE Transactions on Microwave Theory and Techniques, *67(2), 746–753. doi:10.1109/TMTT.2018.2885761*

*Zhang, A. Q., Liu, Z. G., Lu, W. B., & Chen, H. (2019b). Graphene-Based Dynamically Tunable Attenuator on a Coplanar Waveguide or a Slotline. IEEE Transactions on Microwave Theory and Techniques, 67(1), 70–77. doi:10.1109/TMTT.2018.2875078

Zhang, A. Q., *Lu, W. B., Liu, Z. G., Chen, H., & Huang, B*. H. (2018). Dynamically Tunable Substrate Integrated Waveguide Attenuator Using Graphene. IEEE Transactions on Microwave Theory and Techniques, 66(6), 3081–3089. doi:10.1109/TMTT.2018.*2809577*

*Zhang, A. Q., Lu, W. B., Liu, Z. G., Wu, B., & Chen, H. (2019). Flexible and Dynamically Tunable Attenuator Based on Spoof Surface Plasmon Polaritons Waveguide L*oaded With Graphene. IEEE *Transactions on Antennas and Propagation, 67(8), 5582–5589. doi:10.1109/TAP.2019.2911590*

Zhang, G. (2011). Quantum-inspired evolutionary algorithms: A survey and empirical study. Journal of Heuris*tics, 17(3), 303–351. doi:10.100710732-010-9136-0*

*Zhang, L., Lu, Y., & Liu, J. (2010, A*ugust). Deep web interfaces classification using QCGBP network. In 2010 5th International Conference on Computer Science & Education (pp. 457-461). IEEE. 10.1109/ICCSE.2010.5593580

Zhang, L., Zhang, L., Yang, G. Z., & Zhang, M. (2012). A quantum particle swarm optimization clustering algorithm using variable dimensions se*arching. Journal of Chinese Computer* Systems, 33(4), 804–808.

Zhang, Q., *Lai, X., & Liu, G. (2016, August). Emotion recognition of GSR based* on an improved quantum neural network. In 2016 8th International Conference on Intelligent Human-Machine Systems and Cybernetics (IHMSC) (Vol. 1, pp. 488-492). IEEE. 10.1109/*IHMSC.2016.66*

*Zhang, X., Zhang, H. Ch., Tang, W. X., Liu, J. F., Fang, Z., Wu, J. W., & Cui, J. W. (2017). Loss Analysis and Engineering of Spoof Surface Plasmons Based on Circuit Topology. IEEE Antennas and Wi*reless Propagation Lett*ers, 16, 3204–3207. doi:10.1109/LAWP.2017.2768551*

Zhao, J. (2020). Quantum software engineering: Landscapes and horizons. arXiv preprint arXiv:2007.07047

Zhong, Q., Yao, M., & Jiang, W. (20*10, April). Quantum fuzzy particle swarm optimization algorithm for image clustering. In 2010 Internationa*l Conference on Image Analysis and Signal Processing (pp. 276-279). IEEE. 10.1109/IASP.2010.5476115

Zindani, D., & Kumar, K. (2018). Industrial Applications of Polymer Composite Materials. In K. Kumar & J. Davim (Eds.), Compo*sites and Advanced Materials for Industrial Ap*plications (pp. 1–15). Hershey, PA: IGI Global. doi:10.4018/978-1-5225-5216-1.ch001

Zindani, D., Maity, S. R., & Bhowmik, S. (2018). A Decision-Making Approach for Material S*election of Polymeric Composite Bumper Beam. In K. Kumar & J.* Davim (Eds.), Composites and Advanced Materials for Industrial Applications (pp. 112–128). Hershey, PA: IGI Global. doi:10.4018/978-1-5225-5216-1.ch006

da Cruz, A. A., Vellasco, M. M. B. R., & Pacheco, M. A. C. (2007). Quantum-inspired evol*utionary algorithm for numerical optimization. In Hybrid evol*utionary algorithms (pp. 19–37). Springer. doi:10.1007/978-3-540-73297-6_2

Related References

To continue our tradition of advancing academic research, we have compiled a list of recommended IGI Global readings. These references will provide additional information and guidance to further enrich your knowledge and assist you with your own research and future publications.

Abbasnejad, B., Moeinzadeh, S., Ahankoob, A., & Wong, P. S. (2021). The Role of Collaboration in the Implementation of BIM-Enabled Projects. In J. Underwood & M. Shelbourn (Eds.), *Handbook of Research on Driving Transformational Change in the Digital Built Environment* (pp. 27–62). IGI Global. https://doi.org/10.4018/978-1-7998-6600-8.ch002

Abdulrahman, K. O., Mahamood, R. M., & Akinlabi, E. T. (2022). Additive Manufacturing (AM): Processing Technique for Lightweight Alloys and Composite Material. In K. Kumar, B. Babu, & J. Davim (Ed.), *Handbook of Research on Advancements in the Processing, Characterization, and Application of Lightweight Materials* (pp. 27-48). IGI Global. https://doi.org/10.4018/978-1-7998-7864-3.ch002

Agrawal, R., Sharma, P., & Saxena, A. (2021). A Diamond Cut Leather Substrate Antenna for BAN (Body Area Network) Application. In V. Singh, V. Dubey, A. Saxena, R. Tiwari, & H. Sharma (Eds.), *Emerging Materials and Advanced Designs for Wearable Antennas* (pp. 54–59). IGI Global. https://doi.org/10.4018/978-1-7998-7611-3.ch004

Ahmad, F., Al-Ammar, E. A., & Alsaidan, I. (2022). Battery Swapping Station: A Potential Solution to Address the Limitations of EV Charging Infrastructure. In M. Alam, R. Pillai, & N. Murugesan (Eds.), *Developing Charging Infrastructure and Technologies for Electric Vehicles* (pp. 195–207). IGI Global. doi:10.4018/978-1-7998-6858-3.ch010

Aikhuele, D. (2018). A Study of Product Development Engineering and Design Reliability Concerns. *International Journal of Applied Industrial Engineering*, *5*(1), 79–89. doi:10.4018/IJAIE.2018010105

Al-Khatri, H., & Al-Atrash, F. (2021). Occupants' Habits and Natural Ventilation in a Hot Arid Climate. In R. González-Lezcano (Ed.), *Advancements in Sustainable Architecture and Energy Efficiency* (pp. 146–168). IGI Global. https://doi.org/10.4018/978-1-7998-7023-4.ch007

Al-Shebeeb, O. A., Rangaswamy, S., Gopalakrishan, B., & Devaru, D. G. (2017). Evaluation and Indexing of Process Plans Based on Electrical Demand and Energy Consumption. *International Journal of Manufacturing, Materials, and Mechanical Engineering*, *7*(3), 1–19. doi:10.4018/IJMMME.2017070101

Amuda, M. O., Lawal, T. F., & Akinlabi, E. T. (2017). Research Progress on Rheological Behavior of AA7075 Aluminum Alloy During Hot Deformation. *International Journal of Materials Forming and Machining Processes*, *4*(1), 53–96. doi:10.4018/IJMFMP.2017010104

Amuda, M. O., Lawal, T. F., & Mridha, S. (2021). Microstructure and Mechanical Properties of Silicon Carbide-Treated Ferritic Stainless Steel Welds. In L. Burstein (Ed.), *Handbook of Research on Advancements in Manufacturing, Materials, and Mechanical Engineering* (pp. 395–411). IGI Global. https://doi.org/10.4018/978-1-7998-4939-1.ch019

Anikeev, V., Gasem, K. A., & Fan, M. (2021). Application of Supercritical Technologies in Clean Energy Production: A Review. In L. Chen (Ed.), *Handbook of Research on Advancements in Supercritical Fluids Applications for Sustainable Energy Systems* (pp. 792–821). IGI Global. https://doi.org/10.4018/978-1-7998-5796-9.ch022

Arafat, M. Y., Saleem, I., & Devi, T. P. (2022). Drivers of EV Charging Infrastructure Entrepreneurship in India. In M. Alam, R. Pillai, & N. Murugesan (Eds.), *Developing Charging Infrastructure and Technologies for Electric Vehicles* (pp. 208–219). IGI Global. https://doi.org/10.4018/978-1-7998-6858-3.ch011

Araujo, A., & Manninen, H. (2022). Contribution of Project-Based Learning on Social Skills Development: An Industrial Engineer Perspective. In A. Alves & N. van Hattum-Janssen (Eds.), *Training Engineering Students for Modern Technological Advancement* (pp. 119–145). IGI Global. https://doi.org/10.4018/978-1-7998-8816-1.ch006

Armutlu, H. (2018). Intelligent Biomedical Engineering Operations by Cloud Computing Technologies. In U. Kose, G. Guraksin, & O. Deperlioglu (Eds.), *Nature-Inspired Intelligent Techniques for Solving Biomedical Engineering Problems* (pp. 297–317). Hershey, PA: IGI Global. doi:10.4018/978-1-5225-4769-3.ch015

Atik, M., Sadek, M., & Shahrour, I. (2017). Single-Run Adaptive Pushover Procedure for Shear Wall Structures. In V. Plevris, G. Kremmyda, & Y. Fahjan (Eds.), *Performance-Based Seismic Design of Concrete Structures and Infrastructures* (pp. 59–83). Hershey, PA: IGI Global. doi:10.4018/978-1-5225-2089-4.ch003

Attia, H. (2021). Smart Power Microgrid Impact on Sustainable Building. In R. González-Lezcano (Ed.), *Advancements in Sustainable Architecture and Energy Efficiency* (pp. 169–194). IGI Global. https://doi.org/10.4018/978-1-7998-7023-4.ch008

Aydin, A., Akyol, E., Gungor, M., Kaya, A., & Tasdelen, S. (2018). Geophysical Surveys in Engineering Geology Investigations With Field Examples. In N. Ceryan (Ed.), *Handbook of Research on Trends and Digital Advances in Engineering Geology* (pp. 257–280). Hershey, PA: IGI Global. doi:10.4018/978-1-5225-2709-1.ch007

Ayoobkhan, M. U. D., Y., A., J., Easwaran, B., & R., T. (2021). Smart Connected Digital Products and IoT Platform With the Digital Twin. In P. Vasant, G. Weber, & W. Punurai (Ed.), Research Advancements in Smart Technology, Optimization, and Renewable Energy (pp. 330-350). IGI Global. https://doi.org/ doi:10.4018/978-1-7998-3970-5.ch016

Baeza Moyano, D., & González Lezcano, R. A. (2021). The Importance of Light in Our Lives: Towards New Lighting in Schools. In R. González-Lezcano (Ed.), *Advancements in Sustainable Architecture and Energy Efficiency* (pp. 239–256). IGI Global. https://doi.org/10.4018/978-1-7998-7023-4.ch011

Bagdadee, A. H. (2021). A Brief Assessment of the Energy Sector of Bangladesh. *International Journal of Energy Optimization and Engineering*, *10*(1), 36–55. doi:10.4018/IJEOE.2021010103

Baklezos, A. T., & Hadjigeorgiou, N. G. (2021). Magnetic Sensors for Space Applications and Magnetic Cleanliness Considerations. In C. Nikolopoulos (Ed.), *Recent Trends on Electromagnetic Environmental Effects for Aeronautics and Space Applications* (pp. 147–185). IGI Global. https://doi.org/10.4018/978-1-7998-4879-0.ch006

Related References

Bas, T. G. (2017). Nutraceutical Industry with the Collaboration of Biotechnology and Nutrigenomics Engineering: The Significance of Intellectual Property in the Entrepreneurship and Scientific Research Ecosystems. In T. Bas & J. Zhao (Eds.), *Comparative Approaches to Biotechnology Development and Use in Developed and Emerging Nations* (pp. 1–17). Hershey, PA: IGI Global. doi:10.4018/978-1-5225-1040-6.ch001

Bazeer Ahamed, B., & Periakaruppan, S. (2021). Taxonomy of Influence Maximization Techniques in Unknown Social Networks. In P. Vasant, G. Weber, & W. Punurai (Eds.), *Research Advancements in Smart Technology, Optimization, and Renewable Energy* (pp. 351-363). IGI Global. https://doi.org/10.4018/978-1-7998-3970-5.ch017

Beale, R., & André, J. (2017). *Design Solutions and Innovations in Temporary Structures*. Hershey, PA: IGI Global. doi:10.4018/978-1-5225-2199-0

Behnam, B. (2017). Simulating Post-Earthquake Fire Loading in Conventional RC Structures. In P. Samui, S. Chakraborty, & D. Kim (Eds.), *Modeling and Simulation Techniques in Structural Engineering* (pp. 425–444). Hershey, PA: IGI Global. doi:10.4018/978-1-5225-0588-4.ch015

Ben Hamida, I., Salah, S. B., Msahli, F., & Mimouni, M. F. (2018). Distribution Network Reconfiguration Using SPEA2 for Power Loss Minimization and Reliability Improvement. *International Journal of Energy Optimization and Engineering*, 7(1), 50–65. doi:10.4018/IJEOE.2018010103

Bentarzi, H. (2021). Fault Tree-Based Root Cause Analysis Used to Study Mal-Operation of a Protective Relay in a Smart Grid. In A. Recioui & H. Bentarzi (Eds.), *Optimizing and Measuring Smart Grid Operation and Control* (pp. 289–308). IGI Global. https://doi.org/10.4018/978-1-7998-4027-5.ch012

Beysens, D. A., Garrabos, Y., & Zappoli, B. (2021). Thermal Effects in Near-Critical Fluids: Piston Effect and Related Phenomena. In L. Chen (Ed.), *Handbook of Research on Advancements in Supercritical Fluids Applications for Sustainable Energy Systems* (pp. 1–31). IGI Global. https://doi.org/10.4018/978-1-7998-5796-9.ch001

Bhaskar, S. V., & Kudal, H. N. (2017). Effect of TiCN and AlCrN Coating on Tribological Behaviour of Plasma-nitrided AISI 4140 Steel. *International Journal of Surface Engineering and Interdisciplinary Materials Science*, 5(2), 1–17. doi:10.4018/IJSEIMS.2017070101

Bhuyan, D. (2018). Designing of a Twin Tube Shock Absorber: A Study in Reverse Engineering. In K. Kumar & J. Davim (Eds.), *Design and Optimization of Mechanical Engineering Products* (pp. 83–104). Hershey, PA: IGI Global. doi:10.4018/978-1-5225-3401-3.ch005

Blumberg, G. (2021). Blockchains for Use in Construction and Engineering Projects. In J. Underwood & M. Shelbourn (Eds.), *Handbook of Research on Driving Transformational Change in the Digital Built Environment* (pp. 179–208). IGI Global. https://doi.org/10.4018/978-1-7998-6600-8.ch008

Bolboaca, A. M. (2021). Considerations Regarding the Use of Fuel Cells in Combined Heat and Power for Stationary Applications. In G. Badea, R. Felseghi, & I. Aşchilean (Eds.), *Hydrogen Fuel Cell Technology for Stationary Applications* (pp. 239–275). IGI Global. https://doi.org/10.4018/978-1-7998-4945-2.ch010

Burstein, L. (2021). Simulation Tool for Cable Design. In L. Burstein (Ed.), *Handbook of Research on Advancements in Manufacturing, Materials, and Mechanical Engineering* (pp. 54–74). IGI Global. https://doi.org/10.4018/978-1-7998-4939-1.ch003

Calderon, F. A., Giolo, E. G., Frau, C. D., Rengel, M. G., Rodriguez, H., Tornello, M., ... Gallucci, R. (2018). Seismic Microzonation and Site Effects Detection Through Microtremors Measures: A Review. In N. Ceryan (Ed.), *Handbook of Research on Trends and Digital Advances in Engineering Geology* (pp. 326–349). Hershey, PA: IGI Global. doi:10.4018/978-1-5225-2709-1.ch009

Ceryan, N., & Can, N. K. (2018). Prediction of The Uniaxial Compressive Strength of Rocks Materials. In N. Ceryan (Ed.), *Handbook of Research on Trends and Digital Advances in Engineering Geology* (pp. 31–96). Hershey, PA: IGI Global. doi:10.4018/978-1-5225-2709-1.ch002

Ceryan, S. (2018). Weathering Indices Used in Evaluation of the Weathering State of Rock Material. In N. Ceryan (Ed.), *Handbook of Research on Trends and Digital Advances in Engineering Geology* (pp. 132–186). Hershey, PA: IGI Global. doi:10.4018/978-1-5225-2709-1.ch004

Chen, H., Padilla, R. V., & Besarati, S. (2017). Supercritical Fluids and Their Applications in Power Generation. In L. Chen & Y. Iwamoto (Eds.), *Advanced Applications of Supercritical Fluids in Energy Systems* (pp. 369–402). Hershey, PA: IGI Global. doi:10.4018/978-1-5225-2047-4.ch012

Related References

Chen, H., Padilla, R. V., & Besarati, S. (2021). Supercritical Fluids and Their Applications in Power Generation. In L. Chen (Ed.), *Handbook of Research on Advancements in Supercritical Fluids Applications for Sustainable Energy Systems* (pp. 566–599). IGI Global. https://doi.org/10.4018/978-1-7998-5796-9.ch016

Chen, L. (2017). Principles, Experiments, and Numerical Studies of Supercritical Fluid Natural Circulation System. In L. Chen & Y. Iwamoto (Eds.), *Advanced Applications of Supercritical Fluids in Energy Systems* (pp. 136–187). Hershey, PA: IGI Global. doi:10.4018/978-1-5225-2047-4.ch005

Chen, L. (2021). Principles, Experiments, and Numerical Studies of Supercritical Fluid Natural Circulation System. In L. Chen (Ed.), *Handbook of Research on Advancements in Supercritical Fluids Applications for Sustainable Energy Systems* (pp. 219–269). IGI Global. https://doi.org/10.4018/978-1-7998-5796-9.ch007

Chiba, Y., Marif, Y., Henini, N., & Tlemcani, A. (2021). Modeling of Magnetic Refrigeration Device by Using Artificial Neural Networks Approach. *International Journal of Energy Optimization and Engineering*, *10*(4), 68–76. https://doi.org/10.4018/IJEOE.2021100105

Clementi, F., Di Sciascio, G., Di Sciascio, S., & Lenci, S. (2017). Influence of the Shear-Bending Interaction on the Global Capacity of Reinforced Concrete Frames: A Brief Overview of the New Perspectives. In V. Plevris, G. Kremmyda, & Y. Fahjan (Eds.), *Performance-Based Seismic Design of Concrete Structures and Infrastructures* (pp. 84–111). Hershey, PA: IGI Global. doi:10.4018/978-1-5225-2089-4.ch004

Codinhoto, R., Fialho, B. C., Pinti, L., & Fabricio, M. M. (2021). BIM and IoT for Facilities Management: Understanding Key Maintenance Issues. In J. Underwood & M. Shelbourn (Eds.), *Handbook of Research on Driving Transformational Change in the Digital Built Environment* (pp. 209–231). IGI Global. doi:10.4018/978-1-7998-6600-8.ch009

Cortés-Polo, D., Calle-Cancho, J., Carmona-Murillo, J., & González-Sánchez, J. (2017). Future Trends in Mobile-Fixed Integration for Next Generation Networks: Classification and Analysis. *International Journal of Vehicular Telematics and Infotainment Systems*, *1*(1), 33–53. doi:10.4018/IJVTIS.2017010103

Costa, H. G., Sheremetieff, F. H., & Araújo, E. A. (2022). Influence of Game-Based Methods in Developing Engineering Competences. In A. Alves & N. van Hattum-Janssen (Eds.), *Training Engineering Students for Modern Technological Advancement* (pp. 69–88). IGI Global. https://doi.org/10.4018/978-1-7998-8816-1.ch004

Cui, X., Zeng, S., Li, Z., Zheng, Q., Yu, X., & Han, B. (2018). Advanced Composites for Civil Engineering Infrastructures. In K. Kumar & J. Davim (Eds.), *Composites and Advanced Materials for Industrial Applications* (pp. 212–248). Hershey, PA: IGI Global. doi:10.4018/978-1-5225-5216-1.ch010

Dalgıç, S., & Kuşku, İ. (2018). Geological and Geotechnical Investigations in Tunneling. In N. Ceryan (Ed.), *Handbook of Research on Trends and Digital Advances in Engineering Geology* (pp. 482–529). Hershey, PA: IGI Global. doi:10.4018/978-1-5225-2709-1.ch014

Dang, C., & Hihara, E. (2021). Study on Cooling Heat Transfer of Supercritical Carbon Dioxide Applied to Transcritical Carbon Dioxide Heat Pump. In L. Chen (Ed.), *Handbook of Research on Advancements in Supercritical Fluids Applications for Sustainable Energy Systems* (pp. 451–493). IGI Global. https://doi.org/10.4018/978-1-7998-5796-9.ch013

Daus, Y., Kharchenko, V., & Yudaev, I. (2021). Research of Solar Energy Potential of Photovoltaic Installations on Enclosing Structures of Buildings. *International Journal of Energy Optimization and Engineering*, *10*(4), 18–34. https://doi.org/10.4018/IJEOE.2021100102

Daus, Y., Kharchenko, V., & Yudaev, I. (2021). Optimizing Layout of Distributed Generation Sources of Power Supply System of Agricultural Object. *International Journal of Energy Optimization and Engineering*, *10*(3), 70–84. https://doi.org/10.4018/IJEOE.2021070104

de la Varga, D., Soto, M., Arias, C. A., van Oirschot, D., Kilian, R., Pascual, A., & Álvarez, J. A. (2017). Constructed Wetlands for Industrial Wastewater Treatment and Removal of Nutrients. In Á. Val del Río, J. Campos Gómez, & A. Mosquera Corral (Eds.), *Technologies for the Treatment and Recovery of Nutrients from Industrial Wastewater* (pp. 202–230). Hershey, PA: IGI Global. doi:10.4018/978-1-5225-1037-6.ch008

Deb, S., Ammar, E. A., AlRajhi, H., Alsaidan, I., & Shariff, S. M. (2022). V2G Pilot Projects: Review and Lessons Learnt. In M. Alam, R. Pillai, & N. Murugesan (Eds.), *Developing Charging Infrastructure and Technologies for Electric Vehicles* (pp. 252–267). IGI Global. https://doi.org/10.4018/978-1-7998-6858-3.ch014

Dekhandji, F. Z., & Rais, M. C. (2021). A Comparative Study of Power Quality Monitoring Using Various Techniques. In A. Recioui & H. Bentarzi (Eds.), *Optimizing and Measuring Smart Grid Operation and Control* (pp. 259–288). IGI Global. https://doi.org/10.4018/978-1-7998-4027-5.ch011

Related References

Deperlioglu, O. (2018). Intelligent Techniques Inspired by Nature and Used in Biomedical Engineering. In U. Kose, G. Guraksin, & O. Deperlioglu (Eds.), *Nature-Inspired Intelligent Techniques for Solving Biomedical Engineering Problems* (pp. 51–77). Hershey, PA: IGI Global. doi:10.4018/978-1-5225-4769-3.ch003

Dhurpate, P. R., & Tang, H. (2021). Quantitative Analysis of the Impact of Inter-Line Conveyor Capacity for Throughput of Manufacturing Systems. *International Journal of Manufacturing, Materials, and Mechanical Engineering*, *11*(1), 1–17. https://doi.org/10.4018/IJMMME.2021010101

Dinkar, S., & Deep, K. (2021). A Survey of Recent Variants and Applications of Antlion Optimizer. *International Journal of Energy Optimization and Engineering*, *10*(2), 48–73. doi:10.4018/IJEOE.2021040103

Dixit, A. (2018). Application of Silica-Gel-Reinforced Aluminium Composite on the Piston of Internal Combustion Engine: Comparative Study of Silica-Gel-Reinforced Aluminium Composite Piston With Aluminium Alloy Piston. In K. Kumar & J. Davim (Eds.), *Composites and Advanced Materials for Industrial Applications* (pp. 63–98). Hershey, PA: IGI Global. doi:10.4018/978-1-5225-5216-1.ch004

Drabecki, M. P., & Kułak, K. B. (2021). Global Pandemics on European Electrical Energy Markets: Lessons Learned From the COVID-19 Outbreak. *International Journal of Energy Optimization and Engineering*, *10*(3), 24–46. https://doi.org/10.4018/IJEOE.2021070102

Dutta, M. M. (2021). Nanomaterials for Food and Agriculture. In M. Bhat, I. Wani, & S. Ashraf (Eds.), *Applications of Nanomaterials in Agriculture, Food Science, and Medicine* (pp. 75–97). IGI Global. doi:10.4018/978-1-7998-5563-7.ch004

Dutta, M. M., & Goswami, M. (2021). Coating Materials: Nano-Materials. In S. Roy & G. Bose (Eds.), *Advanced Surface Coating Techniques for Modern Industrial Applications* (pp. 1–30). IGI Global. doi:10.4018/978-1-7998-4870-7.ch001

Elsayed, A. M., Dakkama, H. J., Mahmoud, S., Al-Dadah, R., & Kaialy, W. (2017). Sustainable Cooling Research Using Activated Carbon Adsorbents and Their Environmental Impact. In T. Kobayashi (Ed.), *Applied Environmental Materials Science for Sustainability* (pp. 186–221). Hershey, PA: IGI Global. doi:10.4018/978-1-5225-1971-3.ch009

Ercanoglu, M., & Sonmez, H. (2018). General Trends and New Perspectives on Landslide Mapping and Assessment Methods. In N. Ceryan (Ed.), *Handbook of Research on Trends and Digital Advances in Engineering Geology* (pp. 350–379). Hershey, PA: IGI Global. doi:10.4018/978-1-5225-2709-1.ch010

Faroz, S. A., Pujari, N. N., Rastogi, R., & Ghosh, S. (2017). Risk Analysis of Structural Engineering Systems Using Bayesian Inference. In P. Samui, S. Chakraborty, & D. Kim (Eds.), *Modeling and Simulation Techniques in Structural Engineering* (pp. 390–424). Hershey, PA: IGI Global. doi:10.4018/978-1-5225-0588-4.ch014

Fekik, A., Hamida, M. L., Denoun, H., Azar, A. T., Kamal, N. A., Vaidyanathan, S., Bousbaine, A., & Benamrouche, N. (2022). Multilevel Inverter for Hybrid Fuel Cell/PV Energy Conversion System. In A. Fekik & N. Benamrouche (Eds.), *Modeling and Control of Static Converters for Hybrid Storage Systems* (pp. 233–270). IGI Global. https://doi.org/10.4018/978-1-7998-7447-8.ch009

Fekik, A., Hamida, M. L., Houassine, H., Azar, A. T., Kamal, N. A., Denoun, H., Vaidyanathan, S., & Sambas, A. (2022). Power Quality Improvement for Grid-Connected Photovoltaic Panels Using Direct Power Control. In A. Fekik & N. Benamrouche (Eds.), *Modeling and Control of Static Converters for Hybrid Storage Systems* (pp. 107–142). IGI Global. https://doi.org/10.4018/978-1-7998-7447-8.ch005

Fernando, P. R., Hamigah, T., Disne, S., Wickramasingha, G. G., & Sutharshan, A. (2018). The Evaluation of Engineering Properties of Low Cost Concrete Blocks by Partial Doping of Sand with Sawdust: Low Cost Sawdust Concrete Block. *International Journal of Strategic Engineering*, *1*(2), 26–42. doi:10.4018/IJoSE.2018070103

Ferro, G., Minciardi, R., Parodi, L., & Robba, M. (2022). Optimal Charging Management of Microgrid-Integrated Electric Vehicles. In M. Alam, R. Pillai, & N. Murugesan (Eds.), *Developing Charging Infrastructure and Technologies for Electric Vehicles* (pp. 133–155). IGI Global. https://doi.org/10.4018/978-1-7998-6858-3.ch007

Flumerfelt, S., & Green, C. (2022). Graduate Lean Leadership Education: A Case Study of a Program. In A. Alves & N. van Hattum-Janssen (Eds.), *Training Engineering Students for Modern Technological Advancement* (pp. 202–224). IGI Global. https://doi.org/10.4018/978-1-7998-8816-1.ch010

Galli, B. J. (2021). Implications of Economic Decision Making to the Project Manager. *International Journal of Strategic Engineering*, *4*(1), 19–32. https://doi.org/10.4018/IJoSE.2021010102

Gento, A. M., Pimentel, C., & Pascual, J. A. (2022). Teaching Circular Economy and Lean Management in a Learning Factory. In A. Alves & N. van Hattum-Janssen (Eds.), *Training Engineering Students for Modern Technological Advancement* (pp. 183–201). IGI Global. https://doi.org/10.4018/978-1-7998-8816-1.ch009

Ghosh, S., Mitra, S., Ghosh, S., & Chakraborty, S. (2017). Seismic Reliability Analysis in the Framework of Metamodelling Based Monte Carlo Simulation. In P. Samui, S. Chakraborty, & D. Kim (Eds.), *Modeling and Simulation Techniques in Structural Engineering* (pp. 192–208). Hershey, PA: IGI Global. doi:10.4018/978-1-5225-0588-4.ch006

Gil, M., & Otero, B. (2017). Learning Engineering Skills through Creativity and Collaboration: A Game-Based Proposal. In R. Alexandre Peixoto de Queirós & M. Pinto (Eds.), *Gamification-Based E-Learning Strategies for Computer Programming Education* (pp. 14–29). Hershey, PA: IGI Global. doi:10.4018/978-1-5225-1034-5.ch002

Gill, J., Ayre, M., & Mills, J. (2017). Revisioning the Engineering Profession: How to Make It Happen! In M. Gray & K. Thomas (Eds.), *Strategies for Increasing Diversity in Engineering Majors and Careers* (pp. 156–175). Hershey, PA: IGI Global. doi:10.4018/978-1-5225-2212-6.ch008

Godzhaev, Z., Senkevich, S., Kuzmin, V., & Melikov, I. (2021). Use of the Neural Network Controller of Sprung Mass to Reduce Vibrations From Road Irregularities. In P. Vasant, G. Weber, & W. Punurai (Ed.), *Research Advancements in Smart Technology, Optimization, and Renewable Energy* (pp. 69-87). IGI Global. https://doi.org/10.4018/978-1-7998-3970-5.ch005

Gomes de Gusmão, C. M. (2022). Digital Competencies and Transformation in Higher Education: Upskilling With Extension Actions. In A. Alves & N. van Hattum-Janssen (Eds.), *Training Engineering Students for Modern Technological Advancement* (pp. 313–328). IGI Global. https://doi.org/10.4018/978-1-7998-8816-1.ch015A

Goyal, N., Ram, M., & Kumar, P. (2017). Welding Process under Fault Coverage Approach for Reliability and MTTF. In M. Ram & J. Davim (Eds.), *Mathematical Concepts and Applications in Mechanical Engineering and Mechatronics* (pp. 222–245). Hershey, PA: IGI Global. doi:10.4018/978-1-5225-1639-2.ch011

Gray, M., & Lundy, C. (2017). Engineering Study Abroad: High Impact Strategy for Increasing Access. In M. Gray & K. Thomas (Eds.), *Strategies for Increasing Diversity in Engineering Majors and Careers* (pp. 42–59). Hershey, PA: IGI Global. doi:10.4018/978-1-5225-2212-6.ch003

Güler, O., & Varol, T. (2021). Fabrication of Functionally Graded Metal and Ceramic Powders Synthesized by Electroless Deposition. In S. Roy & G. Bose (Eds.), *Advanced Surface Coating Techniques for Modern Industrial Applications* (pp. 150–187). IGI Global. https://doi.org/10.4018/978-1-7998-4870-7.ch007

Guraksin, G. E. (2018). Internet of Things and Nature-Inspired Intelligent Techniques for the Future of Biomedical Engineering. In U. Kose, G. Guraksin, & O. Deperlioglu (Eds.), *Nature-Inspired Intelligent Techniques for Solving Biomedical Engineering Problems* (pp. 263–282). Hershey, PA: IGI Global. doi:10.4018/978-1-5225-4769-3.ch013

Hamida, M. L., Fekik, A., Denoun, H., Ardjal, A., & Bokhtache, A. A. (2022). Flying Capacitor Inverter Integration in a Renewable Energy System. In A. Fekik & N. Benamrouche (Eds.), *Modeling and Control of Static Converters for Hybrid Storage Systems* (pp. 287–306). IGI Global. https://doi.org/10.4018/978-1-7998-7447-8.ch011

Hasegawa, N., & Takahashi, Y. (2021). Control of Soap Bubble Ejection Robot Using Facial Expressions. *International Journal of Manufacturing, Materials, and Mechanical Engineering, 11*(2), 1–16. https://doi.org/10.4018/IJMMME.2021040101

Hejazi, T., & Akbari, L. (2017). A Multiresponse Optimization Model for Statistical Design of Processes with Discrete Variables. In M. Ram & J. Davim (Eds.), *Mathematical Concepts and Applications in Mechanical Engineering and Mechatronics* (pp. 17–37). Hershey, PA: IGI Global. doi:10.4018/978-1-5225-1639-2.ch002

Hejazi, T., & Hejazi, A. (2017). Monte Carlo Simulation for Reliability-Based Design of Automotive Complex Subsystems. In M. Ram & J. Davim (Eds.), *Mathematical Concepts and Applications in Mechanical Engineering and Mechatronics* (pp. 177–200). Hershey, PA: IGI Global. doi:10.4018/978-1-5225-1639-2.ch009

Hejazi, T., & Poursabbagh, H. (2017). Reliability Analysis of Engineering Systems: An Accelerated Life Testing for Boiler Tubes. In M. Ram & J. Davim (Eds.), *Mathematical Concepts and Applications in Mechanical Engineering and Mechatronics* (pp. 154–176). Hershey, PA: IGI Global. doi:10.4018/978-1-5225-1639-2.ch008

Henao, J., Poblano-Salas, C. A., Vargas, F., Giraldo-Betancur, A. L., Corona-Castuera, J., & Sotelo-Mazón, O. (2021). Principles and Applications of Thermal Spray Coatings. In S. Roy & G. Bose (Eds.), *Advanced Surface Coating Techniques for Modern Industrial Applications* (pp. 31–70). IGI Global. https://doi.org/10.4018/978-1-7998-4870-7.ch002

Henao, J., & Sotelo, O. (2018). Surface Engineering at High Temperature: Thermal Cycling and Corrosion Resistance. In A. Pakseresht (Ed.), *Production, Properties, and Applications of High Temperature Coatings* (pp. 131–159). Hershey, PA: IGI Global. doi:10.4018/978-1-5225-4194-3.ch006

Related References

Hrnčič, M. K., Cör, D., & Knez, Ž. (2021). Supercritical Fluids as a Tool for Green Energy and Chemicals. In L. Chen (Ed.), *Handbook of Research on Advancements in Supercritical Fluids Applications for Sustainable Energy Systems* (pp. 761–791). IGI Global. doi:10.4018/978-1-7998-5796-9.ch021

Ibrahim, O., Erdem, S., & Gurbuz, E. (2021). Studying Physical and Chemical Properties of Graphene Oxide and Reduced Graphene Oxide and Their Applications in Sustainable Building Materials. In R. González-Lezcano (Ed.), *Advancements in Sustainable Architecture and Energy Efficiency* (pp. 221–238). IGI Global. https://doi.org/10.4018/978-1-7998-7023-4.ch010

Ihianle, I. K., Islam, S., Naeem, U., & Ebenuwa, S. H. (2021). Exploiting Patterns of Object Use for Human Activity Recognition. In A. Nwajana & I. Ihianle (Eds.), *Handbook of Research on 5G Networks and Advancements in Computing, Electronics, and Electrical Engineering* (pp. 382–401). IGI Global. https://doi.org/10.4018/978-1-7998-6992-4.ch015

Ijemaru, G. K., Ngharamike, E. T., Oleka, E. U., & Nwajana, A. O. (2021). An Energy-Efficient Model for Opportunistic Data Collection in IoV-Enabled SC Waste Management. In A. Nwajana & I. Ihianle (Eds.), *Handbook of Research on 5G Networks and Advancements in Computing, Electronics, and Electrical Engineering* (pp. 1–19). IGI Global. https://doi.org/10.4018/978-1-7998-6992-4.ch001

Ilori, O. O., Adetan, D. A., & Umoru, L. E. (2017). Effect of Cutting Parameters on the Surface Residual Stress of Face-Milled Pearlitic Ductile Iron. *International Journal of Materials Forming and Machining Processes*, 4(1), 38–52. doi:10.4018/IJMFMP.2017010103

Imam, M. H., Tasadduq, I. A., Ahmad, A., Aldosari, F., & Khan, H. (2017). Automated Generation of Course Improvement Plans Using Expert System. *International Journal of Quality Assurance in Engineering and Technology Education*, 6(1), 1–12. doi:10.4018/IJQAETE.2017010101

Injeti, S. K., & Kumar, T. V. (2018). A WDO Framework for Optimal Deployment of DGs and DSCs in a Radial Distribution System Under Daily Load Pattern to Improve Techno-Economic Benefits. *International Journal of Energy Optimization and Engineering*, 7(2), 1–38. doi:10.4018/IJEOE.2018040101

Ishii, N., Anami, K., & Knisely, C. W. (2018). *Dynamic Stability of Hydraulic Gates and Engineering for Flood Prevention*. Hershey, PA: IGI Global. doi:10.4018/978-1-5225-3079-4

Iwamoto, Y., & Yamaguchi, H. (2021). Application of Supercritical Carbon Dioxide for Solar Water Heater. In L. Chen (Ed.), *Handbook of Research on Advancements in Supercritical Fluids Applications for Sustainable Energy Systems* (pp. 370–387). IGI Global. https://doi.org/10.4018/978-1-7998-5796-9.ch010

Jayapalan, S. (2018). A Review of Chemical Treatments on Natural Fibers-Based Hybrid Composites for Engineering Applications. In K. Kumar & J. Davim (Eds.), *Composites and Advanced Materials for Industrial Applications* (pp. 16–37). Hershey, PA: IGI Global. doi:10.4018/978-1-5225-5216-1.ch002

Kapetanakis, T. N., Vardiambasis, I. O., Ioannidou, M. P., & Konstantaras, A. I. (2021). Modeling Antenna Radiation Using Artificial Intelligence Techniques: The Case of a Circular Loop Antenna. In C. Nikolopoulos (Ed.), *Recent Trends on Electromagnetic Environmental Effects for Aeronautics and Space Applications* (pp. 186–225). IGI Global. https://doi.org/10.4018/978-1-7998-4879-0.ch007

Karkalos, N. E., Markopoulos, A. P., & Dossis, M. F. (2017). Optimal Model Parameters of Inverse Kinematics Solution of a 3R Robotic Manipulator Using ANN Models. *International Journal of Manufacturing, Materials, and Mechanical Engineering*, 7(3), 20–40. doi:10.4018/IJMMME.2017070102

Kelly, M., Costello, M., Nicholson, G., & O'Connor, J. (2021). The Evolving Integration of BIM Into Built Environment Programmes in a Higher Education Institute. In J. Underwood & M. Shelbourn (Eds.), *Handbook of Research on Driving Transformational Change in the Digital Built Environment* (pp. 294–326). IGI Global. https://doi.org/10.4018/978-1-7998-6600-8.ch012

Kesimal, A., Karaman, K., Cihangir, F., & Ercikdi, B. (2018). Excavatability Assessment of Rock Masses for Geotechnical Studies. In N. Ceryan (Ed.), *Handbook of Research on Trends and Digital Advances in Engineering Geology* (pp. 231–256). Hershey, PA: IGI Global. doi:10.4018/978-1-5225-2709-1.ch006

Knoflacher, H. (2017). The Role of Engineers and Their Tools in the Transport Sector after Paradigm Change: From Assumptions and Extrapolations to Science. In H. Knoflacher & E. Ocalir-Akunal (Eds.), *Engineering Tools and Solutions for Sustainable Transportation Planning* (pp. 1–29). Hershey, PA: IGI Global. doi:10.4018/978-1-5225-2116-7.ch001

Kose, U. (2018). Towards an Intelligent Biomedical Engineering With Nature-Inspired Artificial Intelligence Techniques. In U. Kose, G. Guraksin, & O. Deperlioglu (Eds.), *Nature-Inspired Intelligent Techniques for Solving Biomedical Engineering Problems* (pp. 1–26). Hershey, PA: IGI Global. doi:10.4018/978-1-5225-4769-3.ch001

Kostić, S. (2018). A Review on Enhanced Stability Analyses of Soil Slopes Using Statistical Design. In N. Ceryan (Ed.), *Handbook of Research on Trends and Digital Advances in Engineering Geology* (pp. 446–481). Hershey, PA: IGI Global. doi:10.4018/978-1-5225-2709-1.ch013

Kumar, A., Patil, P. P., & Prajapati, Y. K. (2018). *Advanced Numerical Simulations in Mechanical Engineering*. Hershey, PA: IGI Global. doi:10.4018/978-1-5225-3722-9

Kumar, G. R., Rajyalakshmi, G., & Manupati, V. K. (2017). Surface Micro Patterning of Aluminium Reinforced Composite through Laser Peening. *International Journal of Manufacturing, Materials, and Mechanical Engineering, 7*(4), 15–27. doi:10.4018/IJMMME.2017100102

Kumar, N., Basu, D. N., & Chen, L. (2021). Effect of Flow Acceleration and Buoyancy on Thermalhydraulics of sCO2 in Mini/Micro-Channel. In L. Chen (Ed.), *Handbook of Research on Advancements in Supercritical Fluids Applications for Sustainable Energy Systems* (pp. 161–182). IGI Global. doi:10.4018/978-1-7998-5796-9.ch005

Kumari, N., & Kumar, K. (2018). Fabrication of Orthotic Calipers With Epoxy-Based Green Composite. In K. Kumar & J. Davim (Eds.), *Composites and Advanced Materials for Industrial Applications* (pp. 157–176). Hershey, PA: IGI Global. doi:10.4018/978-1-5225-5216-1.ch008

Kuppusamy, R. R. (2018). Development of Aerospace Composite Structures Through Vacuum-Enhanced Resin Transfer Moulding Technology (VERTMTy): Vacuum-Enhanced Resin Transfer Moulding. In K. Kumar & J. Davim (Eds.), *Composites and Advanced Materials for Industrial Applications* (pp. 99–111). Hershey, PA: IGI Global. doi:10.4018/978-1-5225-5216-1.ch005

Kurganov, V. A., Zeigarnik, Y. A., & Maslakova, I. V. (2021). Normal and Deteriorated Heat Transfer Under Heating Turbulent Supercritical Pressure Coolants Flows in Round Tubes. In L. Chen (Ed.), *Handbook of Research on Advancements in Supercritical Fluids Applications for Sustainable Energy Systems* (pp. 494–532). IGI Global. https://doi.org/10.4018/978-1-7998-5796-9.ch014

Li, H., & Zhang, Y. (2021). Heat Transfer and Fluid Flow Modeling for Supercritical Fluids in Advanced Energy Systems. In L. Chen (Ed.), *Handbook of Research on Advancements in Supercritical Fluids Applications for Sustainable Energy Systems* (pp. 388–422). IGI Global. https://doi.org/10.4018/978-1-7998-5796-9.ch011

Loy, J., Howell, S., & Cooper, R. (2017). Engineering Teams: Supporting Diversity in Engineering Education. In M. Gray & K. Thomas (Eds.), *Strategies for Increasing Diversity in Engineering Majors and Careers* (pp. 106–129). Hershey, PA: IGI Global. doi:10.4018/978-1-5225-2212-6.ch006

Macher, G., Armengaud, E., Kreiner, C., Brenner, E., Schmittner, C., Ma, Z., ... Krammer, M. (2018). Integration of Security in the Development Lifecycle of Dependable Automotive CPS. In N. Druml, A. Genser, A. Krieg, M. Menghin, & A. Hoeller (Eds.), *Solutions for Cyber-Physical Systems Ubiquity* (pp. 383–423). Hershey, PA: IGI Global. doi:10.4018/978-1-5225-2845-6.ch015

Madhu, M. N., Singh, J. G., Mohan, V., & Ongsakul, W. (2021). Transmission Risk Optimization in Interconnected Systems: Risk-Adjusted Available Transfer Capability. In P. Vasant, G. Weber, & W. Punurai (Ed.), *Research Advancements in Smart Technology, Optimization, and Renewable Energy* (pp. 183-199). IGI Global. https://doi.org/10.4018/978-1-7998-3970-5.ch010

Mahendramani, G., & Lakshmana Swamy, N. (2018). Effect of Weld Groove Area on Distortion of Butt Welded Joints in Submerged Arc Welding. *International Journal of Manufacturing, Materials, and Mechanical Engineering*, 8(2), 33–44. doi:10.4018/IJMMME.2018040103

Makropoulos, G., Koumaras, H., Setaki, F., Filis, K., Lutz, T., Montowtt, P., Tomaszewski, L., Dybiec, P., & Järvet, T. (2021). 5G and Unmanned Aerial Vehicles (UAVs) Use Cases: Analysis of the Ecosystem, Architecture, and Applications. In A. Nwajana & I. Ihianle (Eds.), *Handbook of Research on 5G Networks and Advancements in Computing, Electronics, and Electrical Engineering* (pp. 36–69). IGI Global. https://doi.org/10.4018/978-1-7998-6992-4.ch003

Meric, E. M., Erdem, S., & Gurbuz, E. (2021). Application of Phase Change Materials in Construction Materials for Thermal Energy Storage Systems in Buildings. In R. González-Lezcano (Ed.), *Advancements in Sustainable Architecture and Energy Efficiency* (pp. 1–20). IGI Global. https://doi.org/10.4018/978-1-7998-7023-4.ch001

Mihret, E. T., & Yitayih, K. A. (2021). Operation of VANET Communications: The Convergence of UAV System With LTE/4G and WAVE Technologies. *International Journal of Smart Vehicles and Smart Transportation*, 4(1), 29–51. https://doi.org/10.4018/IJSVST.2021010103

Mir, M. A., Bhat, B. A., Sheikh, B. A., Rather, G. A., Mehraj, S., & Mir, W. R. (2021). Nanomedicine in Human Health Therapeutics and Drug Delivery: Nanobiotechnology and Nanobiomedicine. In M. Bhat, I. Wani, & S. Ashraf (Eds.), *Applications of Nanomaterials in Agriculture, Food Science, and Medicine* (pp. 229–251). IGI Global. doi:10.4018/978-1-7998-5563-7.ch013

Related References

Mohammadzadeh, S., & Kim, Y. (2017). Nonlinear System Identification of Smart Buildings. In P. Samui, S. Chakraborty, & D. Kim (Eds.), *Modeling and Simulation Techniques in Structural Engineering* (pp. 328–347). Hershey, PA: IGI Global. doi:10.4018/978-1-5225-0588-4.ch011

Molina, G. J., Aktaruzzaman, F., Soloiu, V., & Rahman, M. (2017). Design and Testing of a Jet-Impingement Instrument to Study Surface-Modification Effects by Nanofluids. *International Journal of Surface Engineering and Interdisciplinary Materials Science*, 5(2), 43–61. doi:10.4018/IJSEIMS.2017070104

Moreno-Rangel, A., & Carrillo, G. (2021). Energy-Efficient Homes: A Heaven for Respiratory Illnesses. In R. González-Lezcano (Ed.), *Advancements in Sustainable Architecture and Energy Efficiency* (pp. 49–71). IGI Global. https://doi.org/10.4018/978-1-7998-7023-4.ch003

Msomi, V., & Jantjies, B. T. (2021). Correlative Analysis Between Tensile Properties and Tool Rotational Speeds of Friction Stir Welded Similar Aluminium Alloy Joints. *International Journal of Surface Engineering and Interdisciplinary Materials Science*, 9(2), 58–78. https://doi.org/10.4018/IJSEIMS.2021070104

Muigai, M. N., Mwema, F. M., Akinlabi, E. T., & Obiko, J. O. (2021). Surface Engineering of Materials Through Weld-Based Technologies: An Overview. In S. Roy & G. Bose (Eds.), *Advanced Surface Coating Techniques for Modern Industrial Applications* (pp. 247–260). IGI Global. doi:10.4018/978-1-7998-4870-7.ch011

Mukherjee, A., Saeed, R. A., Dutta, S., & Naskar, M. K. (2017). Fault Tracking Framework for Software-Defined Networking (SDN). In C. Singhal & S. De (Eds.), *Resource Allocation in Next-Generation Broadband Wireless Access Networks* (pp. 247–272). Hershey, PA: IGI Global. doi:10.4018/978-1-5225-2023-8.ch011

Mukhopadhyay, A., Barman, T. K., & Sahoo, P. (2018). Electroless Nickel Coatings for High Temperature Applications. In K. Kumar & J. Davim (Eds.), *Composites and Advanced Materials for Industrial Applications* (pp. 297–331). Hershey, PA: IGI Global. doi:10.4018/978-1-5225-5216-1.ch013

Mwema, F. M., & Wambua, J. M. (2022). Machining of Poly Methyl Methacrylate (PMMA) and Other Olymeric Materials: A Review. In K. Kumar, B. Babu, & J. Davim (Eds.), *Handbook of Research on Advancements in the Processing, Characterization, and Application of Lightweight Materials* (pp. 363–379). IGI Global. https://doi.org/10.4018/978-1-7998-7864-3.ch016

Mykhailyshyn, R., Savkiv, V., Boyko, I., Prada, E., & Virgala, I. (2021). Substantiation of Parameters of Friction Elements of Bernoulli Grippers With a Cylindrical Nozzle. *International Journal of Manufacturing, Materials, and Mechanical Engineering*, *11*(2), 17–39. https://doi.org/10.4018/IJMMME.2021040102

Náprstek, J., & Fischer, C. (2017). Dynamic Stability and Post-Critical Processes of Slender Auto-Parametric Systems. In V. Plevris, G. Kremmyda, & Y. Fahjan (Eds.), *Performance-Based Seismic Design of Concrete Structures and Infrastructures* (pp. 128–171). Hershey, PA: IGI Global. doi:10.4018/978-1-5225-2089-4.ch006

Nautiyal, L., Shivach, P., & Ram, M. (2018). Optimal Designs by Means of Genetic Algorithms. In M. Ram & J. Davim (Eds.), *Soft Computing Techniques and Applications in Mechanical Engineering* (pp. 151–161). Hershey, PA: IGI Global. doi:10.4018/978-1-5225-3035-0.ch007

Nazir, R. (2017). Advanced Nanomaterials for Water Engineering and Treatment: Nano-Metal Oxides and Their Nanocomposites. In T. Saleh (Ed.), *Advanced Nanomaterials for Water Engineering, Treatment, and Hydraulics* (pp. 84–126). Hershey, PA: IGI Global. doi:10.4018/978-1-5225-2136-5.ch005

Nikolopoulos, C. D. (2021). Recent Advances on Measuring and Modeling ELF-Radiated Emissions for Space Applications. In C. Nikolopoulos (Ed.), *Recent Trends on Electromagnetic Environmental Effects for Aeronautics and Space Applications* (pp. 1–38). IGI Global. https://doi.org/10.4018/978-1-7998-4879-0.ch001

Nogueira, A. F., Ribeiro, J. C., Fernández de Vega, F., & Zenha-Rela, M. A. (2018). Evolutionary Approaches to Test Data Generation for Object-Oriented Software: Overview of Techniques and Tools. In M. Khosrow-Pour, D.B.A. (Ed.), Incorporating Nature-Inspired Paradigms in Computational Applications (pp. 162-194). Hershey, PA: IGI Global. https://doi.org/ doi:10.4018/978-1-5225-5020-4.ch006

Nwajana, A. O., Obi, E. R., Ijemaru, G. K., Oleka, E. U., & Anthony, D. C. (2021). Fundamentals of RF/Microwave Bandpass Filter Design. In A. Nwajana & I. Ihianle (Eds.), *Handbook of Research on 5G Networks and Advancements in Computing, Electronics, and Electrical Engineering* (pp. 149–164). IGI Global. https://doi. org/10.4018/978-1-7998-6992-4.ch005

Ogbodo, E. A. (2021). Comparative Study of Transmission Line Junction vs. Asynchronously Coupled Junction Diplexers. In A. Nwajana & I. Ihianle (Eds.), *Handbook of Research on 5G Networks and Advancements in Computing, Electronics, and Electrical Engineering* (pp. 326–336). IGI Global. https://doi.org/10.4018/978-1-7998-6992-4.ch013

Orosa, J. A., Vergara, D., Fraguela, F., & Masdías-Bonome, A. (2021). Statistical Understanding and Optimization of Building Energy Consumption and Climate Change Consequences. In R. González-Lezcano (Ed.), *Advancements in Sustainable Architecture and Energy Efficiency* (pp. 195–220). IGI Global. https://doi.org/10.4018/978-1-7998-7023-4.ch009

Osho, M. B. (2018). Industrial Enzyme Technology: Potential Applications. In S. Bharati & P. Chaurasia (Eds.), *Research Advancements in Pharmaceutical, Nutritional, and Industrial Enzymology* (pp. 375–394). Hershey, PA: IGI Global. doi:10.4018/978-1-5225-5237-6.ch017

Ouadi, A., & Zitouni, A. (2021). Phasor Measurement Improvement Using Digital Filter in a Smart Grid. In A. Recioui & H. Bentarzi (Eds.), *Optimizing and Measuring Smart Grid Operation and Control* (pp. 100–117). IGI Global. https://doi.org/10.4018/978-1-7998-4027-5.ch005

Padmaja, P., & Marutheswar, G. (2017). Certain Investigation on Secured Data Transmission in Wireless Sensor Networks. *International Journal of Mobile Computing and Multimedia Communications*, 8(1), 48–61. doi:10.4018/IJMCMC.2017010104

Palmer, S., & Hall, W. (2017). An Evaluation of Group Work in First-Year Engineering Design Education. In R. Tucker (Ed.), *Collaboration and Student Engagement in Design Education* (pp. 145–168). Hershey, PA: IGI Global. doi:10.4018/978-1-5225-0726-0.ch007

Panchenko, V. (2021). Prospects for Energy Supply of the Arctic Zone Objects of Russia Using Frost-Resistant Solar Modules. In P. Vasant, G. Weber, & W. Punurai (Eds.), *Research Advancements in Smart Technology, Optimization, and Renewable Energy* (pp. 149-169). IGI Global. https://doi.org/10.4018/978-1-7998-3970-5.ch008

Panchenko, V. (2021). Photovoltaic Thermal Module With Paraboloid Type Solar Concentrators. *International Journal of Energy Optimization and Engineering*, 10(2), 1–23. https://doi.org/10.4018/IJEOE.2021040101

Pandey, K., & Datta, S. (2021). Dry Machining of Inconel 825 Superalloys: Performance of Tool Inserts (Carbide, Cermet, and SiAlON). *International Journal of Manufacturing, Materials, and Mechanical Engineering*, 11(4), 26–39. doi:10.4018/IJMMME.2021100102

Panneer, R. (2017). Effect of Composition of Fibers on Properties of Hybrid Composites. *International Journal of Manufacturing, Materials, and Mechanical Engineering*, 7(4), 28–43. doi:10.4018/IJMMME.2017100103

Pany, C. (2021). Estimation of Correct Long-Seam Mismatch Using FEA to Compare the Measured Strain in a Non-Destructive Testing of a Pressurant Tank: A Reverse Problem. *International Journal of Smart Vehicles and Smart Transportation*, 4(1), 16–28. doi:10.4018/IJSVST.2021010102

Paul, S., & Roy, P. (2018). Optimal Design of Power System Stabilizer Using a Novel Evolutionary Algorithm. *International Journal of Energy Optimization and Engineering*, 7(3), 24–46. doi:10.4018/IJEOE.2018070102

Paul, S., & Roy, P. K. (2021). Oppositional Differential Search Algorithm for the Optimal Tuning of Both Single Input and Dual Input Power System Stabilizer. In P. Vasant, G. Weber, & W. Punurai (Eds.), *Research Advancements in Smart Technology, Optimization, and Renewable Energy* (pp. 256-282). IGI Global. https://doi.org/10.4018/978-1-7998-3970-5.ch013

Pavaloiu, A. (2018). Artificial Intelligence Ethics in Biomedical-Engineering-Oriented Problems. In U. Kose, G. Guraksin, & O. Deperlioglu (Eds.), *Nature-Inspired Intelligent Techniques for Solving Biomedical Engineering Problems* (pp. 219–231). Hershey, PA: IGI Global. doi:10.4018/978-1-5225-4769-3.ch010

Pioro, I., Mahdi, M., & Popov, R. (2017). Application of Supercritical Pressures in Power Engineering. In L. Chen & Y. Iwamoto (Eds.), *Advanced Applications of Supercritical Fluids in Energy Systems* (pp. 404–457). Hershey, PA: IGI Global. doi:10.4018/978-1-5225-2047-4.ch013

Plaksina, T., & Gildin, E. (2017). Rigorous Integrated Evolutionary Workflow for Optimal Exploitation of Unconventional Gas Assets. *International Journal of Energy Optimization and Engineering*, 6(1), 101–122. doi:10.4018/IJEOE.2017010106

Popat, J., Kakadiya, H., Tak, L., Singh, N. K., Majeed, M. A., & Mahajan, V. (2021). Reliability of Smart Grid Including Cyber Impact: A Case Study. In R. Singh, A. Singh, A. Dwivedi, & P. Nagabhushan (Eds.), *Computational Methodologies for Electrical and Electronics Engineers* (pp. 163–174). IGI Global. https://doi.org/10.4018/978-1-7998-3327-7.ch013

Quiza, R., La Fé-Perdomo, I., Rivas, M., & Ramtahalsing, V. (2021). Triple Bottom Line-Focused Optimization of Oblique Turning Processes Based on Hybrid Modeling: A Study Case on AISI 1045 Steel Turning. In L. Burstein (Ed.), *Handbook of Research on Advancements in Manufacturing, Materials, and Mechanical Engineering* (pp. 215–241). IGI Global. https://doi.org/10.4018/978-1-7998-4939-1.ch010

Rahmani, M. K. (2022). Blockchain Technology: Principles and Algorithms. In S. Khan, M. Syed, R. Hammad, & A. Bushager (Eds.), *Blockchain Technology and Computational Excellence for Society 5.0* (pp. 16–27). IGI Global. https://doi. org/10.4018/978-1-7998-8382-1.ch002

Ramdani, N., & Azibi, M. (2018). Polymer Composite Materials for Microelectronics Packaging Applications: Composites for Microelectronics Packaging. In K. Kumar & J. Davim (Eds.), *Composites and Advanced Materials for Industrial Applications* (pp. 177–211). Hershey, PA: IGI Global. doi:10.4018/978-1-5225-5216-1.ch009

Ramesh, M., Garg, R., & Subrahmanyam, G. V. (2017). Investigation of Influence of Quenching and Annealing on the Plane Fracture Toughness and Brittle to Ductile Transition Temperature of the Zinc Coated Structural Steel Materials. *International Journal of Surface Engineering and Interdisciplinary Materials Science, 5*(2), 33–42. doi:10.4018/IJSEIMS.2017070103

Robinson, J., & Beneroso, D. (2022). Project-Based Learning in Chemical Engineering: Curriculum and Assessment, Culture and Learning Spaces. In A. Alves & N. van Hattum-Janssen (Eds.), *Training Engineering Students for Modern Technological Advancement* (pp. 1–19). IGI Global. https://doi.org/10.4018/978-1-7998-8816-1.ch001

Rondon, B. (2021). Experimental Characterization of Admittance Meter With Crude Oil Emulsions. *International Journal of Electronics, Communications, and Measurement Engineering, 10*(2), 51–59. https://doi.org/10.4018/IJECME.2021070104

Rudolf, S., Biryuk, V. V., & Volov, V. (2018). Vortex Effect, Vortex Power: Technology of Vortex Power Engineering. In V. Kharchenko & P. Vasant (Eds.), *Handbook of Research on Renewable Energy and Electric Resources for Sustainable Rural Development* (pp. 500–533). Hershey, PA: IGI Global. doi:10.4018/978-1-5225-3867-7.ch021

Sah, A., Bhadula, S. J., Dumka, A., & Rawat, S. (2018). A Software Engineering Perspective for Development of Enterprise Applications. In A. Elçi (Ed.), *Handbook of Research on Contemporary Perspectives on Web-Based Systems* (pp. 1–23). Hershey, PA: IGI Global. doi:10.4018/978-1-5225-5384-7.ch001

Sahli, Y., Zitouni, B., & Hocine, B. M. (2021). Three-Dimensional Numerical Study of Overheating of Two Intermediate Temperature P-AS-SOFC Geometrical Configurations. In G. Badea, R. Felseghi, & I. Aşchilean (Eds.), *Hydrogen Fuel Cell Technology for Stationary Applications* (pp. 186–222). IGI Global. https://doi. org/10.4018/978-1-7998-4945-2.ch008

Sahoo, P., & Roy, S. (2017). Tribological Behavior of Electroless Ni-P, Ni-P-W and Ni-P-Cu Coatings: A Comparison. *International Journal of Surface Engineering and Interdisciplinary Materials Science, 5*(1), 1–15. doi:10.4018/IJSEIMS.2017010101

Sahoo, S. (2018). Laminated Composite Hypar Shells as Roofing Units: Static and Dynamic Behavior. In K. Kumar & J. Davim (Eds.), *Composites and Advanced Materials for Industrial Applications* (pp. 249–269). Hershey, PA: IGI Global. doi:10.4018/978-1-5225-5216-1.ch011

Sahu, H., & Hungyo, M. (2018). Introduction to SDN and NFV. In A. Dumka (Ed.), *Innovations in Software-Defined Networking and Network Functions Virtualization* (pp. 1–25). Hershey, PA: IGI Global. doi:10.4018/978-1-5225-3640-6.ch001

Salem, A. M., & Shmelova, T. (2018). Intelligent Expert Decision Support Systems: Methodologies, Applications, and Challenges. In T. Shmelova, Y. Sikirda, N. Rizun, A. Salem, & Y. Kovalyov (Eds.), *Socio-Technical Decision Support in Air Navigation Systems: Emerging Research and Opportunities* (pp. 215–242). Hershey, PA: IGI Global. doi:10.4018/978-1-5225-3108-1.ch007

Samal, M. (2017). FE Analysis and Experimental Investigation of Cracked and Un-Cracked Thin-Walled Tubular Components to Evaluate Mechanical and Fracture Properties. In P. Samui, S. Chakraborty, & D. Kim (Eds.), *Modeling and Simulation Techniques in Structural Engineering* (pp. 266–293). Hershey, PA: IGI Global. doi:10.4018/978-1-5225-0588-4.ch009

Samal, M., & Balakrishnan, K. (2017). Experiments on a Ring Tension Setup and FE Analysis to Evaluate Transverse Mechanical Properties of Tubular Components. In P. Samui, S. Chakraborty, & D. Kim (Eds.), *Modeling and Simulation Techniques in Structural Engineering* (pp. 91–115). Hershey, PA: IGI Global. doi:10.4018/978-1-5225-0588-4.ch004

Samarasinghe, D. A., & Wood, E. (2021). Innovative Digital Technologies. In J. Underwood & M. Shelbourn (Eds.), *Handbook of Research on Driving Transformational Change in the Digital Built Environment* (pp. 142–163). IGI Global. https://doi.org/10.4018/978-1-7998-6600-8.ch006

Sawant, S. (2018). Deep Learning and Biomedical Engineering. In U. Kose, G. Guraksin, & O. Deperlioglu (Eds.), *Nature-Inspired Intelligent Techniques for Solving Biomedical Engineering Problems* (pp. 283–296). Hershey, PA: IGI Global. doi:10.4018/978-1-5225-4769-3.ch014

Schulenberg, T. (2021). Energy Conversion Using the Supercritical Steam Cycle. In L. Chen (Ed.), *Handbook of Research on Advancements in Supercritical Fluids Applications for Sustainable Energy Systems* (pp. 659–681). IGI Global. doi:10.4018/978-1-7998-5796-9.ch018

Sezgin, H., & Berkalp, O. B. (2018). Textile-Reinforced Composites for the Automotive Industry. In K. Kumar & J. Davim (Eds.), *Composites and Advanced Materials for Industrial Applications* (pp. 129–156). Hershey, PA: IGI Global. doi:10.4018/978-1-5225-5216-1.ch007

Shaaban, A. A., & Shehata, O. M. (2021). Combining Response Surface Method and Metaheuristic Algorithms for Optimizing SPIF Process. *International Journal of Manufacturing, Materials, and Mechanical Engineering, 11*(4), 1–25. https://doi.org/10.4018/IJMMME.2021100101

Shafaati Shemami, M., & Sefid, M. (2022). Implementation and Demonstration of Electric Vehicle-to-Home (V2H) Application: A Case Study. In M. Alam, R. Pillai, & N. Murugesan (Eds.), *Developing Charging Infrastructure and Technologies for Electric Vehicles* (pp. 268–293). IGI Global. https://doi.org/10.4018/978-1-7998-6858-3.ch015

Shah, M. Z., Gazder, U., Bhatti, M. S., & Hussain, M. (2018). Comparative Performance Evaluation of Effects of Modifier in Asphaltic Concrete Mix. *International Journal of Strategic Engineering, 1*(2), 13–25. doi:10.4018/IJoSE.2018070102

Sharma, N., & Kumar, K. (2018). Fabrication of Porous NiTi Alloy Using Organic Binders. In K. Kumar & J. Davim (Eds.), *Composites and Advanced Materials for Industrial Applications* (pp. 38–62). Hershey, PA: IGI Global. doi:10.4018/978-1-5225-5216-1.ch003

Shivach, P., Nautiyal, L., & Ram, M. (2018). Applying Multi-Objective Optimization Algorithms to Mechanical Engineering. In M. Ram & J. Davim (Eds.), *Soft Computing Techniques and Applications in Mechanical Engineering* (pp. 287–301). Hershey, PA: IGI Global. doi:10.4018/978-1-5225-3035-0.ch014

Shmelova, T. (2018). Stochastic Methods for Estimation and Problem Solving in Engineering: Stochastic Methods of Decision Making in Aviation. In S. Kadry (Ed.), *Stochastic Methods for Estimation and Problem Solving in Engineering* (pp. 139–160). Hershey, PA: IGI Global. doi:10.4018/978-1-5225-5045-7.ch006

Siero González, L. R., & Romo Vázquez, A. (2017). Didactic Sequences Teaching Mathematics for Engineers With Focus on Differential Equations. In M. Ramírez-Montoya (Ed.), *Handbook of Research on Driving STEM Learning With Educational Technologies* (pp. 129–151). Hershey, PA: IGI Global. doi:10.4018/978-1-5225-2026-9.ch007

Sim, M. S., You, K. Y., Esa, F., & Chan, Y. L. (2021). Nanostructured Electromagnetic Metamaterials for Sensing Applications. In M. Bhat, I. Wani, & S. Ashraf (Eds.), *Applications of Nanomaterials in Agriculture, Food Science, and Medicine* (pp. 141–164). IGI Global. https://doi.org/10.4018/978-1-7998-5563-7.ch009

Singh, R., & Dutta, S. (2018). Visible Light Active Nanocomposites for Photocatalytic Applications. In K. Kumar & J. Davim (Eds.), *Composites and Advanced Materials for Industrial Applications* (pp. 270–296). Hershey, PA: IGI Global. doi:10.4018/978-1-5225-5216-1.ch012

Skripov, P. V., Yampol'skiy, A. D., & Rutin, S. B. (2021). High-Power Heat Transfer in Supercritical Fluids: Microscale Times and Sizes. In L. Chen (Ed.), *Handbook of Research on Advancements in Supercritical Fluids Applications for Sustainable Energy Systems* (pp. 424–450). IGI Global. https://doi.org/10.4018/978-1-7998-5796-9.ch012

Sözbilir, H., Özkaymak, Ç., Uzel, B., & Sümer, Ö. (2018). Criteria for Surface Rupture Microzonation of Active Faults for Earthquake Hazards in Urban Areas. In N. Ceryan (Ed.), *Handbook of Research on Trends and Digital Advances in Engineering Geology* (pp. 187–230). Hershey, PA: IGI Global. doi:10.4018/978-1-5225-2709-1.ch005

Stanciu, I. (2018). Stochastic Methods in Microsystems Engineering. In S. Kadry (Ed.), *Stochastic Methods for Estimation and Problem Solving in Engineering* (pp. 161–176). Hershey, PA: IGI Global. doi:10.4018/978-1-5225-5045-7.ch007

Strebkov, D., Nekrasov, A., Trubnikov, V., & Nekrasov, A. (2018). Single-Wire Resonant Electric Power Systems for Renewable-Based Electric Grid. In V. Kharchenko & P. Vasant (Eds.), *Handbook of Research on Renewable Energy and Electric Resources for Sustainable Rural Development* (pp. 449–474). Hershey, PA: IGI Global. doi:10.4018/978-1-5225-3867-7.ch019

Sukhyy, K., Belyanovskaya, E., & Sukhyy, M. (2021). *Basic Principles for Substantiation of Working Pair Choice*. IGI Global. doi:10.4018/978-1-7998-4432-7.ch002

Related References

Suri, M. S., & Kaliyaperumal, D. (2022). Extension of Aspiration Level Model for Optimal Planning of Fast Charging Stations. In A. Fekik & N. Benamrouche (Eds.), *Modeling and Control of Static Converters for Hybrid Storage Systems* (pp. 91–106). IGI Global. https://doi.org/10.4018/978-1-7998-7447-8.ch004

Tallet, E., Gledson, B., Rogage, K., Thompson, A., & Wiggett, D. (2021). Digitally-Enabled Design Management. In J. Underwood & M. Shelbourn (Eds.), *Handbook of Research on Driving Transformational Change in the Digital Built Environment* (pp. 63–89). IGI Global. https://doi.org/10.4018/978-1-7998-6600-8.ch003

Terki, A., & Boubertakh, H. (2021). A New Hybrid Binary-Real Coded Cuckoo Search and Tabu Search Algorithm for Solving the Unit-Commitment Problem. *International Journal of Energy Optimization and Engineering*, *10*(2), 104–119. https://doi.org/10.4018/IJEOE.2021040105

Tüdeş, Ş., Kumlu, K. B., & Ceryan, S. (2018). Integration Between Urban Planning and Natural Hazards For Resilient City. In N. Ceryan (Ed.), *Handbook of Research on Trends and Digital Advances in Engineering Geology* (pp. 591–630). Hershey, PA: IGI Global. doi:10.4018/978-1-5225-2709-1.ch017

Ulamis, K. (2018). Soil Liquefaction Assessment by Anisotropic Cyclic Triaxial Test. In N. Ceryan (Ed.), *Handbook of Research on Trends and Digital Advances in Engineering Geology* (pp. 631–664). Hershey, PA: IGI Global. doi:10.4018/978-1-5225-2709-1.ch018

Valente, M., & Milani, G. (2017). Seismic Assessment and Retrofitting of an Under-Designed RC Frame Through a Displacement-Based Approach. In V. Plevris, G. Kremmyda, & Y. Fahjan (Eds.), *Performance-Based Seismic Design of Concrete Structures and Infrastructures* (pp. 36–58). Hershey, PA: IGI Global. doi:10.4018/978-1-5225-2089-4.ch002

Vargas-Bernal, R. (2021). Advances in Electromagnetic Environmental Shielding for Aeronautics and Space Applications. In C. Nikolopoulos (Ed.), *Recent Trends on Electromagnetic Environmental Effects for Aeronautics and Space Applications* (pp. 80–96). IGI Global. https://doi.org/10.4018/978-1-7998-4879-0.ch003

Vasant, P. (2018). A General Medical Diagnosis System Formed by Artificial Neural Networks and Swarm Intelligence Techniques. In U. Kose, G. Guraksin, & O. Deperlioglu (Eds.), *Nature-Inspired Intelligent Techniques for Solving Biomedical Engineering Problems* (pp. 130–145). Hershey, PA: IGI Global. doi:10.4018/978-1-5225-4769-3.ch006

Verner, C. M., & Sarwar, D. (2021). Avoiding Project Failure and Achieving Project Success in NHS IT System Projects in the United Kingdom. *International Journal of Strategic Engineering*, 4(1), 33–54. https://doi.org/10.4018/IJoSE.2021010103

Verrollot, J., Tolonen, A., Harkonen, J., & Haapasalo, H. J. (2018). Challenges and Enablers for Rapid Product Development. *International Journal of Applied Industrial Engineering*, 5(1), 25–49. doi:10.4018/IJAIE.2018010102

Wan, A. C., Zulu, S. L., & Khosrow-Shahi, F. (2021). Industry Views on BIM for Site Safety in Hong Kong. In J. Underwood & M. Shelbourn (Eds.), *Handbook of Research on Driving Transformational Change in the Digital Built Environment* (pp. 120–140). IGI Global. https://doi.org/10.4018/978-1-7998-6600-8.ch005

Yardimci, A. G., & Karpuz, C. (2018). Fuzzy Rock Mass Rating: Soft-Computing-Aided Preliminary Stability Analysis of Weak Rock Slopes. In N. Ceryan (Ed.), *Handbook of Research on Trends and Digital Advances in Engineering Geology* (pp. 97–131). Hershey, PA: IGI Global. doi:10.4018/978-1-5225-2709-1.ch003

You, K. Y. (2021). Development Electronic Design Automation for RF/Microwave Antenna Using MATLAB GUI. In A. Nwajana & I. Ihianle (Eds.), *Handbook of Research on 5G Networks and Advancements in Computing, Electronics, and Electrical Engineering* (pp. 70–148). IGI Global. https://doi.org/10.4018/978-1-7998-6992-4.ch004

Yousefi, Y., Gratton, P., & Sarwar, D. (2021). Investigating the Opportunities to Improve the Thermal Performance of a Case Study Building in London. *International Journal of Strategic Engineering*, 4(1), 1–18. https://doi.org/10.4018/IJoSE.2021010101

Zindani, D., & Kumar, K. (2018). Industrial Applications of Polymer Composite Materials. In K. Kumar & J. Davim (Eds.), *Composites and Advanced Materials for Industrial Applications* (pp. 1–15). Hershey, PA: IGI Global. doi:10.4018/978-1-5225-5216-1.ch001

Zindani, D., Maity, S. R., & Bhowmik, S. (2018). A Decision-Making Approach for Material Selection of Polymeric Composite Bumper Beam. In K. Kumar & J. Davim (Eds.), *Composites and Advanced Materials for Industrial Applications* (pp. 112–128). Hershey, PA: IGI Global. doi:10.4018/978-1-5225-5216-1.ch006

About the Contributors

Brojo Kishore Mishra awarded Ph.D. in Computer Science from Berhampur University in the year 2012 for his excellent work in the field of Web Mining. He worked in several reputed private Engineering Colleges and state University at a different level for more than last 15 years. Presently, he is a Professor with the Department of Computer Science & Engineering and Associate Dean - International Affairs at GIET University, Gunupur, India and also working as Joint Secretary of IEEE Bhubaneswar subsection. He has published more than 80 publications in reputed international conferences, journals and online book chapter contributions (Indexed By: SCI, SCIE, SSCI, Scopus, DBLP) and 13 edited books, 02 authored books, 02 patents, 01 copyright and 03 book series. He has successfully guided 01 Ph.D. research scholar and currently 06 research scholars are continuing. He served in the capacity of keynote speaker, program chair, proceeding chair, publicity chair, and as advisory board members of many International conferences also. He is also a life member of ISTE, CSI, and senior member of IEEE.

* * *

Anubhav Agrawal comes from a family of educationists, his father is Professor in mathematics and mother is educated in English Literature. He completed his PhD in Electrical Engineering from IIT Roorkee with a fellowship from MHRD. He is actively involved in the research front.

Ankur Biswas is currently serving as an Assistant Professor in the Department of Computer Applications at the University of Engineering & Management (UEM), Kolkata, India. He did his M.E. in Software Engineering from Jadavpur University and MBA in Operations Management from IGNOU. He did his B.E. in Information technology from Rashtrasant Tukadoji Maharaj Nagpur University and he has more than 12 years of education and industry experience. His areas of interest are Blockchain, Quantum Blockchain, Semantic Web, Green Computing.

Amartya Chakraborty is currently serving as an Assistant Professor in the department of Computer Science and Engineering, University of Engineering and Management (UEM), Kolkata, India. With a Master of Technology (M.Tech.) in Computer Science and Engineering from Jadavpur University in 2020, he has also qualified UGC National Eligibility Test (NET) for Assistant Professor in the same year. He is an enthusiastic researcher with keen interest in the domains of Sensor Networks, IoT enabled systems, Social Network Analysis, etc. He has published in several peer-reviewed journals, conferences and book chapters and reviews for 2 SCI indexed journals.

Prasant Kumar Dash has received his MCA degree from Veer Surendra Sai University of Technology, Burla in the year 2009. Also, he has obtained M.Tech degree in Computer Science & Engineering from Biju Patanaik University of Technology, Rourkela in the year 2014. Currently, he is a PhD scholar in the Department of Computer Science and Engineering at SUIIT, Sambalpur, Odisha. His research areas involve ad-hoc, cable and sensor networks, congestion control in WSN and USN. He has published more than 10 research papers in various reputed international journal, conferences and book chapter. Currently, working as a Programmer in the department of CSE, C.V.Raman Global University, Bhubaneswar, Odisha, India.

Lopamudra Hota has received her MTech degree in Computer Science and Engineering from Veer Surendra Sai University of Technology, Burla, Odisha, India, in 2017. She is pursuing Ph.D degree in Computer Science and Engineering from National Institute of Technology, Rourkela, Odisha, India. Her research involves Wireless Sensor Networks, Underwater Sensor Networks, Vehicular Ad-hoc Networks, Internet of Things, and Machine Learning.

Muralikrishna Iyyanki, PhD from the Premier Institute-Indian Institute of Science (IISc), Bangalore, was Dr Raja Ramanna Distinguished Fellow at Defense Research and Development Organization (DRDO), India, and the National Coordinator for Geospatial Public Health, which is National Networking Government of India Project. He was the Editor and Member of the Editorial board of several S&T Journals. His Present research focuses are on Open innovation, Artificial intelligence and geospatial data analytics and geospatial population and public health management. He was the Professor and Founder Head of the Centre for Spatial Information Technology (CSIT) at Jawaharlal Nehru Technological University (1990 - 2005), and Director of Research and development Centre (2005 -2008). He has served as a guest scientist at German Space Research Institute (DLR) and GKSS Research Centre.

Subramaniam Meenakshi Sundaram is currently working as Professor and Head in the Department of Computer Science and Engineering at GSSS Institute of Engineering and Technology for Women, Mysuru. He obtained Bachelor Degree in Computer Science & Engineering from Bharathidasan University, Tiruchirappalli in 1989, M.Tech from National Institute of Technology, Tiruchirappalli in 2006 and Ph.D.in Computer Science & Engineering from Anna University Chennai in 2014. He has also completed M.B.A. from Madurai Kamaraj University in 2000, Master of Human Resource Management from Pondicherry University in 2003 and Master of Foreign Trade from Pondicherry University in 2005. His area of research is Wireless Communication Networks. He was awarded Ph.D. for his research work entitled "Certain investigations of Multimedia Traffic and Optimization of OLSR Protocol for enhancement of Quality of Service (QoS) in Mobile Ad Hoc Networks". He has published 60 papers in refereed International Journals, presented 10 papers in International Conferences and has delivered more than 50 seminars. He has reviewed more than 110 papers for refereed journals like Springer – Soft Computing Journal, Journal of Computer Science, USA, International Journal of Ah Hoc Network Systems, Journal of Engineering Science and Technology, Taylor's University, Malaysia, International Journal of Computational Science & Engineering, Inder Science Publishers, UK, ICTACT Journal on Communication Technology and for IEEE Conferences. Eight Research Scholars are pursuing Ph.D. at VTU, Belagavi under his guidance in the areas of Computer Networks, Distributed Computing and Cloud Computing. He has organized more than 50 seminars / Workshops / FDPs. He has attended more than 40 Workshops / Seminars / FDPs . He has acted as Chairperson for Conferences and Judge for Technical Symposia in various Engineering Colleges for more than 25 occasions. He has authored 2 books in Fundamentals of Computers and Programming in C in the year 2001. His area of interest includes Computer Networks, Wireless Communication, Software Engineering, Optical Networks and Data Mining. He is a Life Member of Indian Society for Technical Education (ISTE) and a member of Computer Society of India (CSI). He is a member of Advisory Committee for ISRASE eXPLORE Digital Library and Reviewer for International Journal of Recent Advances in Science & Engineering. He is a Fellow of Universal Association of Computers and Electronics Engineers, a Fellow of the International Association of Computer Science & Information Technology, a member of Institute of Doctors, Engineers and Scientists, a member of International Association of Engineers, a member of Computer Science Teachers Association, USA. He has officiated as the Management Committee member of the CSI Chapter, Tiruchirappalli Region, Tamil Nadu State, during the year 2013-2014. He was the Secretary of ISTE Staff and Student's Chapter during the period 2008 – 2014. He acted as Chairman of the CSE Board during the Central Valuation of Anna University, Chennai during the academic year 2012-2013 and is also a Question Paper setter for Madras University, Bharathidasan University, SASTRA University and VTU, Belagavi. He has been a member of the Staff Selection Committee for more than 15 Engineering Colleges for the past 30 years. He has officiated as the Management Representative for obtaining ISO 9001:2008 for a period of 4 years during 2010-2014 and is also a Certified Auditor for ISO 9001:2008 Quality Management Systems. Also he has acted as NBA Co-ordinator for five Engineering Colleges since 2008. He has received a grant of Rupees Thirty Lakhs from VGST, Government of Karnataka for establishing a Smart Systems and IoT Laboratory at GSSS Institute of Engineering and Technology for Women, Mysuru during the period 2016 - 2019, He has 32 Years of rich experience in teaching since 1989 and more than 30 years of experience as HoD of CSE Department.

Anirban Mitra, Ph.D. in Science & Technology - Computer Science, is working as an Associate Professor of Computer Science and Engineering in the School of Engineering and Technology at Amity University, Kolkata, India. He is a senior member of IEEE and ACM.

Tejaswini R. Murgod received B.E. Degree in Computer Science and Engineering from Visvesvarya Technological University, Belagavi, India in June 2008. She acquired her Master's Degree in from Visvesvarya Technological University, Belagavi, India in Jan 2015. At present she is working as Assistant Professor at GSSS Institute of Technology for Women, Mysuru. Currently she is pursuing Ph. D at Visvesvaraya Technological University, Belagavi and completed comprehensive viva. Her research focus includes underwater communication, optical networks, and wireless networks.

R. Nagarajan received his B.E. in Electrical and Electronics Engineering from Madurai Kamarajar University, Madurai, India, in 1997. He received his M.E. in Power Electronics and Drives from Anna University, Chennai, India, in 2008. He received his Ph.D in Electrical Engineering from Anna University, Chennai, India, in 2014. He has worked in the industry as an Electrical Engineer. He is currently working as Professor of Electrical and Electronics Engineering at Gnanamani College of Technology, Namakkal, Tamilnadu, India. He has published more than 70 papers in International Journals and Conferences. His research interest includes Power Electronics, Power System, Communication Engineering, Network Security, Soft Computing Techniques, Cloud Computing, Big Data Analysis and Renewable Energy Sources.

Poornima Nedunchezhian is pursuing Ph.D. under the faculty of Information and Communication Engineering. She acquired her M. E. Network Engineering from Anna University of Technology and completed B. E. Computer Science and Engineering. she is currently working as an Assistant Professor at SRM Valliammai Engineering College. She is a , Life Member of ISTE and CSI. She has more than 20 publications to her credit in reputed International / National journals and conferences. In particular, her recent interests include social network analysis, data mining, and security.

Subrata Paul is currently a PhD scholar under MAKAUT and working as State Coordinator for NSQF Project at SPB Technical INstitute. He is currently pursuing PhD and had completed his B.E(CSE) from VTU – Belgaum, Karnataka in 2010 and M.Tech(CS) from Berhampur University in the year 2013. His research area includes Social Network Analysis, Computational Intelligence and Cloud Computing. He had several publications at national and international levels, both in journals and conferences including papers in IEEE and Elsevier conference. He had an experience of nearly 4.5 years in teaching undergraduate courses and 1 year in handling post graduate classes. He usually teaches papers like Compiler Design, Formal Languages and Automata Theory, Software Engineering, Computer Network, Artificial Intelligence and Programming in C Language.

Bharatendra Rai is Professor of Business Analytics in the Charlton College of Business at UMass Dartmouth. He teaches courses on topics such as Applied Deep Learning, Analyzing Big Data, Business Analytics & Data Mining, Applied Decision Techniques, & Operations Mgt. His current research interests include machine learning & deep learning applications. His YouTube channel that includes lecture videos on deep learning are watched in over 225 countries. For deep learning videos using Keras & TesnsorFlow (see this link: https://goo.gl/PsScA1). Deep learning is a branch of machine learning based on a set of algorithms that attempt to model high-level abstractions in data. Since it performs quite well in a number of diverse problems, Deep Learning is quickly becoming the algorithm of choice for the highest predictive accuracy. He received Ph.D. in Industrial Engineering from Wayne State University, Detroit. His two master's degrees include specializations in quality, reliability, and OR from Indian Statistical Institute, India. He has over 20 years of consulting/training experience that includes industries such as automotive, cutting tool, electronics, food, software, chemical, defense, etc., in the areas of Data Science, Machine Learning, Supply Chain, design of experiments, and Six-Sigma using technologies such as R/RStudio software. His work experience includes over five years at Ford in the area of data analytics, quality, reliability, & 6-sigma. His research publications include journals such as IEEE Transactions on Reliability, Reliability Engineering & System Safety, Quality Engineering, International Journal of Product Development, and International Journal of Business Excellence. He has been keynote speaker at conferences and presented his research work at international conferences. He received an Employee Recognition Award by FAIA for Ph.D. dissertation in support of Ford Motor Co. He is certified as ISO 9000 & ISO 14000 lead assessor, & 6-Sigma Black Belt from ASQ.

Rajkumar Rajasekaran graduated in Electrical and Electronics Engineering and received Master's degree in Computer Science & Engineering. He has completed his Ph.D. from Vellore Institute of Technology University, Vellore in Computer Science and Engineering. His research area includes Data Analytics, Data Mining, Big Data, Machine learning and Data Visualization. He is a Life time member of Computer Society of India and American Association for Advancement Science (AAAS). He has published and communicated more than 60 research papers in SCI, SCIE, and Scopus indexed Journals and Conducted many workshops, Faculty Development Programmes and Seminars at various universities and Colleges. He has filed a 6 Indian Patents. Presently, working at Vellore Institute of Technology Vellore and supervising Ph.D. candidates from VIT University Vellore and from Anna University Chennai. He is Main Editor of the Book entitled "Contemporary Applications on Mobile Computing in Healthcare Settings", "Artificial Intelligence for Social good in Healthcare" published by IGI Global. "Smart Healthcare" by Bentham Science. He is the Deputy Editor Asia for Public Health in Africa (Springer). Editorial Board Member for International Journal of IOT and Cyber Assurance, Associate Editor for International Journal of Social Computing and Cyber Physical Systems (Inderscience). Special Issue Editor for International of Pharma and Bio Science (Scopus) on Smart Healthcare, Scalable Computing Practices and Challenges (Scopus SCI) on Mobile Cloud Computing. He is working on various projects assigned from American Association of Advancement of Sciences (AAAS).He was the Head of Department for Data Analytics, University Coordinator for Apple University Development Program.

Kannadhasan S. is working as an Assistant Professor in the department of Electronics and Communication Engineering in Cheran College of Engineering, karur, Tamilnadu, India. He is currently doing research in the field of Smart Antenna for Anna University. He is ten years of teaching and research experience. He obtained his B.E in ECE from Sethu Institute of Technology, Kariapatti in 2009 and M.E in Communication Systems from Velammal College of Engineering and Technology, Madurai in 2013. He obtained his M.B.A in Human Resources Management from Tamilnadu Open University, Chennai. He obtained his PGVLSI in Post Graduate diploma in VLSI design from Annamalai University, Chidambaram in 2011 and PGDCA in Post Graduate diploma in Computer Applications from Tamil University in 2014. He obtained his PGDRD in Post Graduate diploma in Rural Development from Indira Gandhi National Open University in 2016. He has published around 18 papers in the reputed indexed international journals and more than 125 papers presented/published in national, international journal and conferences. Besides he has contributed a book chapter also. He also serves as a board member, reviewer, speaker, session chair, advisory and technical committee of various colleges and conferences. He is also to attend the various workshop, seminar, conferences, faculty development programme, STTP and Online courses. His areas of interest are Smart Antennas, Digital Signal Processing, Wireless Communication, Wireless Networks, Embedded System, Network Security, Optical Communication, Microwave Antennas, Electromagnetic Compatibility and Interference, Wireless Sensor Networks, Digital Image Processing, Satellite Communication, Cognitive Radio Design and Soft Computing techniques. He is Member of IEEE, ISTE, IEI, IETE, CSI, IAENG, SEEE, IEAE, INSC, IARDO, ISRPM, IACSIT, ICSES, SPG, SDIWC, IJSPR and EAI Community.

Kanagaraj Venusamy obtained his MBA degree in Production Management from Manonmanium Sundaranar University, Tamilnadu, India in 2011 and B.E (Electronics and Communication Engineering) in 2005 from Anna University, M.E in Mechatronics Engineering, India in 2019 from Anna university affiliated college. Presently pursuing Doctorate in Management studies at Bharathidasan University, Tamilnadu, India. His main interests of research are Control systems, Industrial automation, Artificial Intelligence, Robotics, Drone, IoT, Entrepreneurship and Human Resource management. He had 12 years of teaching experience in reputed institution in India and Oman and two year of industrial experience at Saudi Arabia. He has technically assisted various short term course for students, faculty development program and International Robotics Competition. He has acted as co principle investigator in sultanate of Oman government funded research projects. Currently working as a Control Systems Instructor in University of Technology and Applied Sciences - Al Mussanah.

Hassen Zairi is a Professor at Ecole Nationale d'ingénieurs de Carthage (ENI-Carthage), University of Carthage, Tunisia. His research interests include microwave antennas and circuits modeling, numerical methods for the analysis of microwave and millimeter-wave circuits, metamaterials, biosensors.

Index

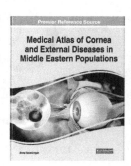

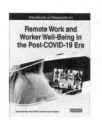

Among Titles Included in the IGI Global e-Book Collection

Printed in the United States
by Baker & Taylor Publisher Services